# AMONG RIGHTEOUS MEN

# AMONG RIGHTEOUS MEN

## A Tale of Vigilantes and Vindication in Hasidic Crown Heights

Matthew Shaer

WILEY

John Wiley & Sons, Inc.

*Library of Congress Cataloging-in-Publication Data*

Shaer, Matthew, date,
  Among righteous men : a tale of vigilantes and vindication in Hasidic Crown Heights /
Matthew Shaer.
     p.   cm.
  Includes bibliographical references and index.
  ISBN 978-0-470-60827-2 (hardback); ISBN 978-1-118-09519-5 (ebk);
  ISBN 978-1-118-09520-1 (ebk); ISBN 978-1-118-09521-8 (ebk)
  1. Jews–New York (State)–New York–Social conditions–21st century. 2. Hershkop,
Aron–Trials, litigation, etc. 3. Vigilantes–New York (State)–New York. 4. Habad–
Social aspects–New York (State)–New York. 5. Crown Heights (New York, N. Y.)–Social
conditions–21st century. I. Title.
  F129.B7S53  2012
  974.70492'4–dc23

                                                                        2011028934

Printed in the United States of America

10 9 8 7 6 5 4 3 2 1

*For my mom, the
first writer I ever knew*

"... and who would venture to come between two righteous men?"

—Martin Buber, *Tales of the Hasidim*

# Contents

# *Author's Note*

This account is based on a range of police and court documentation, hundreds of hours of interviews with dozens of sources, and months of firsthand reporting. Still, the events described herein are extremely controversial, and although I have sought at every juncture to corroborate the often conflicting memories of the participants, I was sometimes forced to fall back on my own best judgment in assembling the narrative. Most of the dialogue comes directly from trial testimony; elsewhere, it was recreated from the recollections of the involved parties. Some proper names have been changed.

# Introduction

# Introduction

In the winter of 2009, I spent several weeks in a harshly lit Brooklyn courtroom, watching the trial of six Lubavitcher Jews, who had been charged by the district attorney with felony gang assault, along with a string of lesser charges, some of them weapons-related. All six defendants were members of a vigilante group called the Crown Heights Shomrim Rescue Patrol; if convicted, each man faced a long spell in federal prison.

The Hasidic community has a storied history of civilian anticrime efforts. There are Shomrim almost everywhere there are large concentrations of Hasidim: in the Williamsburg section of Brooklyn, in Stamford Hill in London, and in Melbourne, Australia. The Shomrim, which means "guards" in Hebrew, function a little like an auxiliary police force. The members, all volunteers, fix tires, help direct traffic, and escort elderly residents to and from the bus stop. They are also regularly involved in more athletic endeavors, such as chasing down purse-snatchers or breaking up street fights.

I was fascinated by the kind of Jew the Shomrim represented: the Jew who fights back. I thought of the fabled Jewish gangsters of the Lower East Side—"Johnny" Levinsky, "Dopey Benny" Fein. These were brash and cunning men who found equality and respect in strength and

1

insisted on their place in the world. I thought, too, of the Odessa stories of Isaak Babel, where an assortment of underbosses schemed their way through the district of Moldavanka. Babel, who was killed in 1940 by the Soviet secret police, took an obvious pride in his characters. He was proud of Benya Krik and Froim Grach, and their refusal to be complacent. He was proud that even at their lowliest, they still sought to shape the world to their liking. To bend fate to their will.

The Crown Heights Shomrim, of course, were not criminals. In fact, their stated role was to protect *against* criminality, to erect a human barrier between the Jewish settlement and the bustle of the world outside city limits. The organization—originally known as the Crown Heights Maccabees—was first pressed into service in the 1960s, when a growing ultra-Orthodox settlement was brought into direct conflict with a much larger black population. (That conflict peaked with the bloody race riots of 1991; Jews in Crown Heights continue to refer to the riots as a "pogrom.") For the most part, the Shomrim were viewed by the city as a helpful community presence. Shomrim volunteers tracked down petty criminals and using a fleet of police vehicles—most of them purchased at city auctions—aided law enforcement in missing person searches.

Yet in fighting back—in their deliberate shows of strength—the Crown Heights Shomrim often came into direct conflict with the NYPD and the very community they were sworn to protect.

Almost two years earlier, the Crown Heights Shomrim had responded to a call about a disturbance at the yeshiva dormitory at 749 Eastern Parkway, in the middle of Crown Heights. Witnesses later reported seeing six members punch, strangle, and kick their way through a crowd of rabbinical students. For their part, the Shomrim claimed to have been ambushed. A video taken by one of the students seemed to back up their account: on the tape, the Shomrim are trapped, hemmed in on all sides by a seething mass of black hats and coats. Still, the Brooklyn district attorney had spent months assembling a case against the Crown Heights Shomrim; meanwhile, the alleged victims had filed a civil suit against the members, seeking millions of dollars in damages.

For the Shomrim themselves, the trial was a particularly painful—and infuriating—experience. Lubavitchers, like all Hasidim, are often loath to sully themselves in a secular court, which they view as less than perfectly attuned to their interests. Under halacha, or Jewish law, any religious Jew should first attempt to settle his dispute through rabbinical arbitration. Yet the alleged victims had not filed first in a rabbinical court and had instead gone directly to the secular authorities. In the formulation of the Shomrim, the yeshiva students were *mosers*, or "rats," who had intentionally flouted religious law—a crime once punishable by death.

As I would soon come to understand, the trial of the six Shomrim members reflected a deep and abiding turmoil on the streets of Crown Heights. Not only was a Jewish security patrol charged with gang assault—a historical rarity—but two groups of Lubavitchers were trading public accusations, in the process allowing outsiders a peek inside a normally closeted world. Although they had friends and supporters across Crown Heights, the members of the Shomrim felt that they had been hung out to dry—and they were angry that more people had not risen up to champion them.

A few decades earlier, the entire imbroglio might have been solved by a wave of the hand of the local rebbe, or Grand Rabbi—a man considered closer to God than other mortals.

In 1994, however, Mendel Menachem Schneerson, the Seventh Rebbe of the Lubavitch dynasty, suffered a stroke and died in his Brooklyn home, surrounded by family and aides. Because the rebbe is such a centrifugal force for a Hasidic community, a successor is usually appointed quickly, to avoid infighting or even the disintegration of an entire movement. Yet an eighth Lubavitcher rebbe has never been named. The reason is primarily eschatological: even before Schneerson's death, a segment of the Lubavitch community had come to believe that their rebbe was the Messiah.

Technically, all Lubavitchers are messianists, in that they believe that a messianic age is imminent. After Schneerson's death, though, the Lubavitch community quickly broke open along messianist lines. The *mischistizn*, as they are known in Crown Heights, announced that it was their duty to spread the word of the Messiah's arrival. Moderate Lubavitchers, on the other hand, worried that if the *mischistizn* came to dominate the Lubavitch movement, it might scare away prospective converts. This religious schism extended through the heart of Lubavitch society and all the way to the level of the criminal trial of the six Shomrim members.

The Crown Heights Shomrim consisted mostly of moderates, or non-messianists. The yeshiva dormitory where the brawl took place, on the other hand, was a stronghold of the *mischistizn*. Clearly, more than a verdict from a secular jury hung in the balance.

The Shomrim were led by two brothers, Gedalia Hershkop and Aron Hershkop. Gedalia, the older of the pair, had been implicated in the dormitory incident and featured prominently in the video captured by the yeshiva students. Aron, who owned a car repair service on East New York Avenue, was not among the six defendants, but as a coordinator of the Shomrim, he was named by proxy in the civil lawsuit; some speculated that he was the real target of the petition.

Aron was prickly, profane, and smart. He had joined the Shomrim as a teenager and had served as a leader of the patrol for more than a decade; he rightly saw the trial as a referendum on the very existence of the organization. Beyond that, however, he believed fervently in the righteousness of his cause and in the essential underhandedness of his enemies.

During the long year that preceded the trial, he lobbied ceaselessly on behalf of the Shomrim, pointing out to whomever would listen that the group did important, brave work. When his entreaties went unanswered, he ramped up the scale of his rhetoric, assailing the local leaders who had failed to put a stop to this "blood libel." In the process, he became an outsider in an inward-facing world; he was the Shakespearean hero who had allowed his search for justice to consume him.

Perched in the back row of a Brooklyn Supreme Courtroom, I thought I understood the parameters of the conflict, because in many ways, there was nothing new about this story. It was a very human struggle, a very ancient struggle. It was the oldest story on earth. That the Lubavitchers fundamentally saw the world very differently from, say, the secular Jews of Park Slope, did nothing to soften the hard edges of human nature. In fact, in the case of the Shomrim, the constrictive bounds of the community seemed to have made the feud worse.

Several decades ago, a Lubavitch rabbi in Crown Heights had proudly proclaimed that "eight blocks away was the end of the world." This tenet holds true even for many young Lubavitchers today, who browse the Web and watch TV and bicker with alacrity about the latest headlines. The only world that matters begins on Eastern Parkway and ends on Empire Boulevard and is bounded by New York Avenue to the west and Troy Avenue to the east.

The Jewish settlement in Crown Heights is not only a neighbor-hood but a latter-day Sparta—a city-state with its own democratically appointed political apparatus and foreign policy. Where many of us see "subtle, shifting variations in racial demography and social class," the anthropologist Henry Goldschmidt has written, the Lubavitchers see "unambiguous lines of distinction: 'It's a different world over there.'"

Thus, the "militarized border" between the densely Jewish settle-ment and the rest of Crown Heights. Thus, the need for a self-sufficient criminal justice system and ambulance service. Thus, the need for a volunteer security force, which dutifully patrols the bounds of the Lubavitch nation-state.

All this I understood. And yet there was much I did not understand—peculiar exigencies; extenuating circumstances; a slice of Brooklyn real estate that seems to operate by the codes and customs of a bygone era. This book in many ways is an attempt to come to grips with that world, and each chapter, I hope, represents a step closer to comprehension.

• • •

In *Cities on a Hill*, the journalist Frances FitzGerald noted that American enclaves often function as "single organisms or personalities," with unified "kinships systems, customs, and rituals." The Jews of Crown Heights had for many years benefited from such a biological construction. Between 1970 and the early 1990s, Lubavitch leadership worked diligently to control the sixteen-square-block area directly surrounding Kingston Avenue, the High Street of the Hasidic settlement.

Mendel Menachem Schneerson commanded his Hasidim to fight for their foothold in Crown Heights. "Do what is right and good in the sight of the Lord," he ordered, quoting from Deuteronomy, "so that all may go well with you and that you may be able to possess the good land that the Lord your God promised on oath to your fathers, and that all your enemies may be driven out before you." It was under Schneerson's guidance that the Lubavitchers adopted a policy of demographic consolidation. The consolidation, unsurprisingly, did not go unnoticed by the local black community; one woman complained to the *Times* in 1987 that blacks in Crown Heights were "living in an apartheid state where a tiny minority is controlling our state."

Nor did consolidation offer a perfect dam against the same kind of troubles—crime, jealousy, anger—so common in the secular world. In some ways, quite the opposite occurred. As the walls grew higher and higher, so, too, did the magnitude of the struggles inside Jewish Crown Heights.

"You're dealing with island people," a Hasidic Jew once told the scholar Jerome Mintz, "who are somehow geographically separated from the outside world, and still going to work, passing a newsstand, passing a movie, watching the street, no matter how much you close your eyes you're exposed to the secular, what you would call, the real orgiastic, materialistic world from which one would like to insulate oneself as much as possible."

What made the case of the Shomrim Six so interesting—and what brought me to the Brooklyn Supreme Court in the first place—was that it seemed to represent one logical apotheosis of an "island" community: build the walls high enough, succeed in warding off the external threats, and, after a while, the only person left to fight with is your neighbor.

Indeed, during my time reporting this book, the Shomrim and their supporters often complained of the shtetl mentality of their peers—they mentioned the old line about sunlight being the best disinfectant. They hoped that I might help wrest open the window.

# 1

The oldest yeshiva dormitory in Crown Heights sits on a quarter-acre slab of rumpled concrete at 749 Eastern Parkway, not far from the corner of Kingston Avenue. It is an unlovely building, four stories high and chapped gray-white by the sun. Most of the window panes facing the street are cracked or blacked out or missing altogether; pillows and mattresses and dirty newspapers fill the empty frames. Years ago, some enterprising soul clambered up onto the roof of 749, as the dormitory is known locally, and dropped over the top of the building a long white-and-blue banner heralding the arrival of the Messiah.

The residents of 749 are members of the Chabad Lubavitch sect of Hasidic Judaism. They come to Crown Heights, Brooklyn—the seat of the Lubavitch empire—to earn their rabbinical ordination, during which time they maintain a self-imposed exile, shuttling back and forth between the dormitory and the basement shul on the other side of Eastern Parkway. To old-school Lubavitchers, who have lived in the neighborhood for decades, the *bochurim*—literally, "boys," in Hebrew—of 749 are zealots and fodder for derision. They are often addressed by a range of names: terrorists, the Taliban. The fervor of the *bochurim* is considered somehow disgraceful, even here, among the ritually fervent.

On December 29, 2007, one of these *bochurim*, a stout, tousle-headed rabbinical student named Joshua Gur, was sitting in his bedroom on the first floor of 749, surrounded by several friends. The time was 9 p.m. A couple of hours earlier, Gur had attended shul, and walked back across Eastern Parkway under a hushed and heavy sky. Now, his black fedora hanging on the edge of his bed, his black suit jacket draped over a nearby chair, he listened to what sounded like the beginnings of a major league brawl in the room at the end of the hall.

The walls of the dormitory were notoriously thin—essentially, sheets of yellowed paper with only air and roaches and rats in between—and every thump, threat, and body slam was amplified sevenfold, as if the dorm itself were the interior of a giant hand drum. Gur stirred restlessly and pushed his black velvet yarmulke back across his head.

He was twenty-three then. He had fragile brown eyes, always wet to the point of brimming over, and a thick brown beard, which he wore long and unkempt, in accordance with the dictates of the Torah. He had lived in the dormitory for three years, longer than almost anyone else. He knew its rituals. He knew how to kill the rats (sticky pads or poison, preferably both), stave off those slippery, silvery million-legged bugs (Raid, rubbing alcohol, or an open flame), and fix the leaks in the shower room (with chewing gum). Best of all, he spoke English fluently, something his peers couldn't claim to do.

American cities have always played host to ethnic enclaves—the Chinatowns and the Koreatowns, the Russian villages and the Puerto Rican neighborhoods, where locals can go for weeks without speaking a word of English. Jewish Crown Heights was this, and it was more. It was a kind of modern shtetl, recreated within the bustling sprawl of central Brooklyn. The short distances between the west, east, north, and south borders made it easy for Lubavitchers to get around, even on the Sabbath, when driving and work were prohibited. And the sheer density of the settlement—the majority of Jews in Crown Heights lived within a sixteen-square-block area—fostered a sense of community, solidarity, and intimacy.

Still, the outside world often stuck its nose into the affairs of the boys at 749. Once, for instance, the fire department responded to an alarm at the dormitory and found about ten buck-naked Lubavitchers frolicking and swaying in a giant tub in the basement. Gur was there to help explain to the befuddled firemen that this was no sex party but a *mikvah*—a ritual bath intended to help slough away the month's transgressions. "*Relax*, gentlemen. This kind of thing is *normal* in our culture." Welcome to Crown Heights. Welcome to life in the Lubavitch kingdom.


Gur heard the voices in the hallway grow louder. Ten to one, he knew exactly what the racket was about. The feud had been building for days. The two roommates down the hall had never gotten along, but had recently settled into a kind of brooding mutual antipathy, awful to behold.

Outside, the hallway swelled with bodies. Depending on the time of year, there were at least 100 yeshiva students living at 749—during the high holidays the number was closer to 150, not counting the squatters in the basement, who arrived in November, content to crash on the floor in tattered Coleman sleeping bags. Tonight most of them seemed to have trotted down to the first floor, drawn by the promise of a fight. Some held point-and-shoot digital cameras over their heads. Others chattered excitedly. Gur dug into the crowd with his elbows and his right shoulder, twisting and thrashing forward, ignoring the protestations of the onlookers, until he burst across the threshold of Room 107.

According to Gur, a few *bochurim* stood under a single yellow bulb. "Hey, Shuki," one of the boys said, using Gur's nickname. Gur pulled the door shut behind him to get some privacy. Two years later, sitting in a Brooklyn courtroom, Gur would swear to a jury of his peers that the the fight appeared to have been resolved. He chatted briefly with his classmates, received their assurances they were okay. He turned to go, and ran right into two men wearing dark-blue police uniforms.

Gur recognized both of them. The thinner of the pair was a twenty-one-year-old man named Binyomin Lifshitz. Lifshitz's full-time gig was running CrownHeights.info, a website that purported to cover all aspects of Hasidic life in the neighborhood. Yet he was best known as a member of the Shomrim Rescue Patrol, a Lubavitch security patrol operating out of a car repair shop in south Brooklyn.

The way Gur understood it, the all-volunteer Shomrim, or "guards" in Hebrew, had been founded to do the things that the police wouldn't or couldn't do: chase down purse snatchers, fix flat tires, and direct traffic. Which was all fine with him.

The real police couldn't be in all places all of the time, and sometimes it fell to his fellow Jews to stand up for themselves. In practice, a disciplined Shomrim patrol could help shield the community from the crimes of outsiders. The group could also help mediate internal conflicts before the secular justice system—a system often ignorant of Jewish tradition and law—got involved. But as far as Gur was concerned, the arrival of these Shomrim—the Crown Heights Shomrim—often meant that the shit was about to hit the fan.

"Out," he said now to Lifshitz.

"Kiss my ass," Lifshitz said.

"Please—"

"Kiss my ass."

Lifshitz pulled a Motorola shortwave radio from his belt. The radio spluttered; Lifshitz shouted back some instructions in a mixture of Yiddish and English. He was calling in reinforcements, Gur knew.

Gur had seconds to set this thing right before the rest of the squad arrived. He crab-walked over to Yossi Frankel, the second of the two Shomrim boys, and held his hand toward the ceiling to show that he meant no harm. "Yossi," he said in English. "This is not your problem."

"We're just trying to get things under control."

"There's nothing to get under control. It's over."

Frankel dropped his chin a little, and for a moment, Gur thought he'd finally gotten through to Frankel—that maybe the Shomrim would turn their backs and leave. But then the door opened again, and everything went white.

Modern Hasidism, which has its roots in eighteenth-century Europe, comprises a very loosely confederated group of courts, each led by a rebbe, or grand rabbi. Generally speaking, a court takes its name from its village of origin: the Satmar Hasidim come from Szatmár, in modern-day Hungary, the Lubavitchers from Lyubavichi, in Russia. All Hasidim—the "pious ones" in Hebrew—share a strict allegiance to the dictates of traditional Jewish law. Their lives are circumscribed by prayer, study, familial obligation, and a deep commitment to their rebbe. Every court maintains a central shul—a large and accessible synagogue where the rebbe can speak to his Hasidim. Ground Zero for the Lubavitch movement has long been the shul at 770 Eastern Parkway, a stately brick building divided into offices and prayer rooms on the first and second floors and a partitioned synagogue—with a smaller area reserved for women and the larger for the men—in the basement.

On the evening of December 27, 2007, the *bochur* Noach Beliniski was slumped at a table in the basement shul, his eyelids lowering, his hands heavy and inert at his sides. Like Gur, Beliniski had spent most of the day in prayer, but when the rest of the *bochurim* headed back to the dormitory, he'd begged off and returned to shul. The way Beliniski saw it, there was no time for rest. Not when the age of *Moshiach* was at hand. In two years, Beliniski, tall and blond and shaped like an understuffed scarecrow, would find a wife from a well-connected Lubavitch family, perhaps with the help of a professional matchmaker. He would follow the familiar and furrowed path of the thousands of Lubavitch men who had come before him: the outreach work in the field, the rapidly growing family, the regular visits back to Brooklyn, to pay homage to the memory of Menachem Mendel Schneerson, the late rebbe of Lubavitch.

Beliniski had heard from other *bochurim* that the shul had once belonged to a prominent secular Jewish doctor, who had performed illegal abortions in the same chambers that now belonged to the Lubavitch rabbinical leadership. Who knew what the basement—the room in which he now sat—had been used for. The chamber was long, not particularly wide, and harshly lit. It reminded Beliniski of an operating theater. The light turned your skin translucent; if you looked closely enough, you could see the slow pulse of blue blood through your veins. Above Beliniski was the mezzanine floor, where women could daven, separated from the men by a wall of Plexiglas. Outsiders frequently complained that women were second-class citizens in Lubavitch life, but as far as most Lubavitchers were concerned, the barrier was a boon to both genders: women were out of view of the men, and the men, free from distraction, could concentrate on the holy work at hand.

On Friday nights, the shul might hold a thousand men or more—a writhing, gesticulating, davening ocean of black suits and black hats and upraised hands. But by 9 p.m. on a Saturday, the crowd had begun to thin. Four boys gathered around the chair—now covered by a throw—where the rebbe had once sat for hours on end, discussing philosophy with his Hasidim. Beliniski stood up and shook the life back into his knees, his long shins, his feet. He was halfway to the other *bochurim*, his hand outstretched in greeting, when he heard someone call his name.

Maybe the voice belonged to someone Beliniski knew well. Maybe it didn't. At any rate, in his testimony before the Brooklyn Supreme Court, in the fall of 2009, Beliniski never gave the name of the messenger who had been sent from 749 to fetch him. Only the nature of the message: the Shomrim were coming. The kid might as well have been Paul Revere. *The Shomrim are coming!*

Beliniski, who normally had all the grace of an adolescent giraffe, nevertheless could move when he needed to, and now he was moving fast, past the benches, past the rebbe's chair, the tails of his coat flapping behind him, his hand clasping his black fedora—and the yarmulke underneath—to his hand. First stop: the locker. Because the *bochurim* spent so much of their day in the shul—twelve-hour shifts were not unheard of—many of the boys kept their belongings and changes of clothes in lockers on the north side of the shul. Beliniski's was full of the normal clutter: pads of paper and prayer books, moldy sandwiches and flat soda and pictures of home.

And a video camera. Beliniski was no fool. He, too, had been present at the riot of 2006, when the Shomrim and the *bochurim* had first faced off. He'd seen a friend throttled, had seen some *meshugeh* idiot pick up a heavy wooden bench over his head and contemplate an act that might have resulted in decapitation. Beliniski was there when the ambulance arrived, when the goy cops paraded—bareheaded—through the holy shul as if it were their living room.

Since then, Beliniski had the distinct sense that he and his friends were being hunted. He saw the three-wheeled Shomrim carts on every corner, watched the Shomrim boys roll by in their cars, the windows down, with their middle fingers extended. It was considered a grave sin to rat out a fellow Jew—an act, Beliniski had been told, once punishable by death—but at some point, you had to look out for yourself.

Beliniski shouldered the camera and stepped out of the shul, shivering in the sharp cold. The rumpled ribbon of Eastern Parkway opened before him, sliding west toward Park Slope and east into Brownsville. The stars in Brooklyn are infinitesimally small, a fact noted regularly by out-of-towners and almost never by native Crown Heights kids, who didn't know any better—who had in some cases had never been beyond Queens. By comparison, Beliniski was positively worldly. He knew that the glow of the row houses was no substitute for the natural light of the desert at sunset. He understood that the pools of milky yellow light cast by the streetlights were nothing compared to a big fat country moon.

He ran across the access road and the six lanes of traffic, ignoring the car horns that rose and fell in his wake. He ran as if he were on stilts. As if the world depended on it. Pausing for a moment at the front door of the dormitory, Beliniski double-checked the tape, cued up the camera, filled his lungs with grimy city air, and dashed up the stairwell toward Room 107.


Q: Describe the people you saw inside Room 107.
A: Outside I saw people, then I went inside.
Q: When you went inside.
A: I went through the door and I saw the policemen, people in
    uniform and my friends, my colleagues.


If you believed the testimony he gave two years later—and neither the jury nor Judge Albert Tomei found any immediate reason not to— Gavriel Braunstein was unfamiliar with the Shomrim Rescue Patrol before the evening of December 29, 2007. He couldn't have identified any of the members if his life depended on it. On entering Room 107, Braunstein, a stocky twenty-five-year-old, saw seven men in navy blue uniforms and thought, *Police*.

He saw Shuki Gur, his old friend from Israel, knotted up in the center of the room, his hands outstretched, his face impossibly red, his throat muscles stretched like old rope. He saw tall, skeletal Noach Beliniski, swaying with the movement of the crowd, a camera slung over his shoulder. He saw faces illuminated by the sharp and frightening white light of the camera. He saw thirty bodies, sixty elbows, sixty knee bones. He saw two men who appeared to be paralyzed with fright.

Q: And when you got to Room 107, what did you see?
A: I saw many people, chaos, confusion.
Q: Chaos?
A: Tumult.

Gavriel Braunstein—former rabbinical student, current rabbi, alleged victim, exceptionally useful witness. For most of the night, Braunstein had been buried in his books. But unfortunately for Braunstein, his window looked over the same air shaft as Room 107. By 9 p.m., study had become all but impossible. So he found a shirt in the closet, adjusted his thick, tangled brown hair in front of the mirror, edged his glasses up his nose with one finger, and pulled on his suit jacket. Just as each Hasidic court has its own cultural and religious customs, which have been passed down from generation to generation, so, too, do many Hasidic courts maintain an informal—and unmandated—sartorial tradition.

The members of the Ger court, for example, wear tall fur hats called *spodiks*, while Satmar Hasids favor rounded bowler-type hats. In dress situations—work, prayer, the shabbos—Lubavitch men sport black fedoras and simple business suits, an homage to their Seventh Rebbe, who wore the same thing. Braunstein, being a *bochur* and required at all times to represent his yeshiva and his religion, never left his room without his suit jacket. It was a matter of dignity. Now he buttoned the jacket tightly around his midsection—right over left, always, as the Kabbalah proscribes—and checked the tack of his *tzitzis*, the white fringes of his ritual undergarment. *Speak to the children of Israel, and bid them that they make them fringes on the borders of their garments throughout their generations.* He knew the commandment by heart.

Braunstein got to the first floor around 9:15 p.m. He pushed through the crowd in the hallway and tumbled into Room 107 maybe a minute later. A minute and a half, maximum. Just in time.

A: What I saw, when I entered, they were shaking the lads, the boys, the young boys.
Q: When you say shaking these boys, who were these boys?
A: They were my friends.

And thus did Braunstein enter a fight that should never have been his. He waded forward, intent on playing hero. Room 107 had one window and two beds, on which groups of men stood like scared little chickens, peering over the fray. As Braunstein watched, a man he would eventually identify as Binyomin Lifshitz pointed in his direction and shouted, "I want him."

*Me?* Allegedly, Braunstein didn't know Lifshitz from a hole in the wall, but it didn't matter anyway, because he couldn't move backward—the door had slammed shut behind him. He was propelled forward. A boat on autopilot, heading for the waterfall. Things moved quickly; time went slippery, limp. Braunstein ducked, and felt the impact of a fist, which rocketed from somewhere out of his field of vision and collided with Braunstein's exposed forehead, sending him reeling toward the floor.

A: He had black gloves.
Q: And describe how those gloves looked, please.
A: They were very large. They were very large. And while the blow was given, it was very hard.
Q: How did you feel after the punch to your head?
A: I felt like my head is exploding and my eyes are moving out of the sockets.

Once the brawl had subsided, a rumor began to circulate among the *bochurim*: Gedalia Hershkop, the owner of the fist in question, had been wearing gloves stuffed with shot. Black leather sap gloves—the kind worn by security personnel the world over. Of course, it's equally possible that Gedalia could have done the damage all by himself, without the benefit of shot-stuffed gloves. Gedalia—Gadi to his friends, "Gotti" to one very confused court reporter—was a school-bus driver and the coleader of the Crown Heights Shomrim Rescue Patrol. He was the second-oldest brother in a powerful, well-known Lubavitch family. A big guy. Compared to Braunstein, who was thick through the shoulders but relatively short, Gadi was a giant, six foot two, maybe six foot three.

*G-d, I hope Beliniski is getting this on camera*, Braunstein thought and covered up his head like a boxer, his forearms shelled over his eyes. He blundered around for a moment, hearing but not seeing.

Q: While you were raising your hands to cover your head, what
    happened?
A: At that moment Lifshitz caught me in the shirt and started
    shaking me.

All of that shaking loosened Braunstein's shirt, the shirt buttons popped off, exposing Braunstein's belly and white-fringed *tallit-katan*. Before he knew it, Braunstein was standing pretty well near naked in the middle of the room. He would later recall that the second punch hit him in the kisser, splitting his lips and knocking loose a tooth. The third, he claimed, hit him in the nose, jarring loose some cartilage and sending a river of blood out of his nostril. The fourth punch hit him in the eye, he testified, shattering his glasses and knocking the frames off his face. And the fifth punch? Hell if Braunstein knew. Somewhere in the head. He said that he spat and, looking into his palm, saw two shards of tooth, bound together by a streamer of saliva.

Schneur Rotem, strong and blond and wild-eyed, had been one of the first kids in Room 107, an hour earlier. Now he was one of the first to hear the sirens on Eastern Parkway. "Police," someone yelled, and for a moment the room was enveloped in a wet, anticipatory silence. Then the cops rushed across the threshold in waves, tossing some kids up against the wall and herding the rest out into the hallway as if they were stray dogs. Rotem was well aware of the precariousness of his situation. Unlike the Shomrim, who spoke cop English—and were even then helping the NYPD with evacuation—Rotem didn't speak any English at all. If he tried to appeal to the police, he'd end up with his tongue tied in a bow. Around him, his friends wheedled, prayed, bled, struggled to be heard. *Please, officer. This guy was hitting me. Please help me. My hand is broken.* Or: *My nose is broken.* Or: *I lost my tooth!*

But Rotem stayed quiet, weighed his options. Bided his time. He considered following the example of the *bochur* Yaakov Shatz, who had literally chucked himself out the window and was now climbing like Spider-Man along the wall of the air shaft. Instead, Rotem gave himself up to the crowd. Went loose. A cop grabbed him by the shoulder, steered him toward the door, and Rotem obeyed. He had never seen the dormitory in such a state. Water spilled out from the bathroom and coursed through the hallway. Handprints and boot prints covered the walls. He stumbled, turned left, and fell into Room 108.

It remains to this day unclear whether Rotem had company in 108, which was not his room but the room of an acquaintance from Israel. Had other *bochurim* sought refuge there? Perhaps. Rotem testified only that he got into the room and shut the door, waited one minute, two minutes, three minutes. A period of waiting that felt interminable.

From under the crack of the door came the suck and slop of rubber soles, the circuitous clucking of Hebrew, the whir of the fleet of vehicles parked on Eastern Parkway. By now, the ambulances would have arrived—trucks provided by the city of New York, and the buses that belonged to Hatzolah, the official ambulance service of the Lubavitch community. By now, the cop cars would have lit up Eastern Parkway as if it were Broadway. By now, the newsmen would be snapping photographs.

From the testimony of Schneur Rotem:

Q: Now, how long were you in Room 108?
A: A minute or two or three. And when the noise and the talk in the corridor died, went away or ended—

Rotem eased the door open with his toe and pressed his eye to the inch-wide gap. Where did he think he was going? Rotem, for his part, remembered that he wanted to talk to his friend Jonathan Gorichnick. Others say that Rotem only wanted to run. Run down Eastern Parkway. Run toward Brownsville. Run until his shoes fell off.

Either way, he got only to the first-floor landing, in sight of the front door and the sidewalk beyond. There Schneur Rotem, a long-time resident of 749 Eastern Parkway, ran smack into Gedalia Hershkop, the leader of the Crown Heights Shomrim Rescue Patrol. "I want him," Gadi allegedly said, echoing the order issued minutes earlier by Binyomin Lifshitz.

Rotem later recalled the ensuing scene thus: First, he and Hershkop did a little dance on the landing—a little ballet. A Tom-and-Jerry routine. Rotem, big but not as big as Hershkop, ended up pinned to the door frame of Room 102, Hershkop holding him in place with an outstretched palm. Over Hershkop's shoulder, Rotem saw more Shomrim members, fanning out in what he later described as "a form that I couldn't escape." He remembered panicking and pushing back, but Gadi smacked Rotem square in the face, hard enough to send Rotem's glasses spinning off into the darkness.

Rotem slipped on the wet tile, landed on his side, and balled himself up into the fetal position. Unfortunately for the detectives and the prosecutors who would investigate the incident at 749 Eastern Parkway, Rotem had rendered himself blind. His glasses were gone, his chin was tucked.

Yes, he did feel fists and the hard toes of boots. He remembered being kicked in the legs, in the ribs, in the head. He remembered more than one person doing the kicking. More than two. More than three. He remembered dropping his guard, peering up, and seeing Chaim Hershkop, Gadi's little brother, holding a fire extinguisher in the air as if it were a battle ax. He remembered seeing his friend Shalom Cohen attempt to pull the fire extinguisher from Hershkop's hands, hold onto it for dear life. He remembered rolling out of reach of the fists and the feet, rolling down the hallway, past Room 102, past Room 103. He remembered pulling himself to his feet and stepping in the first-floor bathroom, and he remembered pulling a stall door shut, and he remembered standing on the toilet so he wouldn't be found, and he remembered standing like that for a very long time.


Aron Hershkop, the co-coordinator of the Crown Heights Shomrim and the younger brother of Gedalia Hershkop, arrived at the yeshiva dormitory just in time to see an ambulance loaded with *bochurim* peel off in the direction of Kings County Hospital. In the courtyard of 749, an army of cops from the local precinct were doing the mop-up work: interviewing witnesses, writing out the summonses and the tickets, steering the remaining students back through the front doors of the dormitory. On Eastern Parkway, a couple of taxis barreled down from the intersection of Brooklyn Avenue and jammed on the brakes just as they neared Kingston, the drivers rubbernecking, going googly-eyed at the phalanx of NYPD units lined up along the curb.

Like his older brother, Gadi, Aron Hershkop was tall and barrel-chested; he usually pushed his shoulders forward when he walked, as if he were marching into a cyclone. He rarely dressed in traditional Lubavitcher garb, preferring instead grease-stained canvas pants, big work boots, wool caps, or his heavy blue Shomrim jacket, the bottom hem deliberately hiked up and over his Shomrim radio. He worked full time down at the auto shop he owned in south Crown Heights, and all of that time wrenching under broken-down cars—all of that time outside in the hard Brooklyn winters—had hardened his skin.

Around strangers, he could be taciturn and unforgiving, his answers stripped to the barest number of syllables. But when he was around his friends, his wife, his employees, his kids, he was a different man— warm, welcoming, downright effusive. For this reason, his friends referred to him as a *sabra*, the sharp Middle Eastern cactus with an interior like liquid candy. "Aron would do anything for us," the other members of the Shomrim crew often said about Hershkop, and as far as Hershkop was concerned, that was true.

For more than a decade, he had lived and breathed for the Shomrim. He saw the other members as protectors, fighters; together, they were a force for good in Crown Heights. They tracked down thieves and home invaders—they fixed flat tires and escorted the old biddies back and forth from the bus stop. They did the work that the

NYPD should have done. And yet in the years since Hershkop had taken the reins of the Shomrim—he was a teenager back then, just a kid—the organization had been repeatedly and sorely tested. Tested sometimes by petty criminals and other troublemakers, but more often by elements within the community, who wanted the Shomrim put out of business for good.

Hershkop looked up to see a couple of Shomrim guys bounding across the sidewalk. Breathlessly, they filled him in on the details of the brawl: the punches thrown, the taunts exchanged, the way the riled-up *bochurim* had surrounded the Shomrim, closing in from every side until the Shomrim guys had crawled up on the beds to get away from the scrum. Worst of all, Paul Huebner, a local Lubavitch lawyer, had apparently accompanied the *bochurim* to the hospital, which could mean that he was helping them prepare charges against the Shomrim guys. Which could also mean the cops would be dishing out arrest warrants later tonight.

The Crown Heights Shomrim had weathered a hell of a lot in the last ten years, and after every disaster—after every brawl and restraining order and arrest warrant—the members had bounced back. It was a resilient organization, composed of some of the most principled men Hershkop knew. But standing on the sidewalk outside of 749, listening to the saga of the brawl, he couldn't suppress the sneaking suspicion that his brother and his friends had just stumbled into something very different—a kind of trap sprung by the *bochurim* and their supporters in Crown Heights. And the Shomrim were the target.

# 2

The report landed on Officer Brian Duffy's desk on a Wednesday, two days into the New Year. It was a traditionally quiet time in Crown Heights, which would remain a ghost town for at least another twenty-four hours—the partiers holed up with hangovers and everyone else dodging the deep freeze. Inside the 77th Precinct House, Duffy flipped slowly through the pages of the incident report, noting the names, noting the times, taking stock of the parameters of the mess he was stepping into.

In late December, several units had responded to reports of a major brawl at 749 Eastern Parkway. The cops had barreled in, cleared the place out, and, later that night, arrested two yeshiva students for assault. The victims were members of a community patrol called the Shomrim; the alleged assailants were issued Desk Appearance Tickets. A judge would likely parcel them out some sort of community service. Problem solved.

But the form Duffy had in his hand told a different story. The complainant, a gentleman named Schneur Rotem, claimed to have been sucked into the melee in Room 107, kicked, punched, and threatened. Later that night, Rotem's friends had taken him to Kings County Hospital, where he was treated for a fracture of the metacarpal bone.

According to Mr. Rotem, his attackers were the members of the Crown Heights Shomrim Rescue Patrol, a freelance anticrime unit made up entirely of local Hasidim. If Rotem was telling the truth, the police had collared the wrong guys on December 29.

Duffy, block-faced and blond, had been stationed at the 7-7 for only a year or so, but he had already become used to its sprawl, its peculiar patterns of life, the way things stayed interesting but not so interesting that you needed a bulletproof vest to get a cup of coffee. Cops will often rank neighborhoods on a three-point scale. "C" is a shit show, a place like Brownsville, where half of the population is cooped up in multistory projects and bodies accumulate at an alarming rate. "A" is a bedroom community in New Jersey. The place a certain kind of cop pines for. Where the worst you had to deal with was a flat tire and a fistfight at the local watering hole. Where you could doze off in your squad car, watching YouTube clips on your city-owned Dell laptop.

In the '80s and the '90s, Crown Heights had been a "C." The criminals were exceptionally bold back then, thinking nothing of popping off on Eastern Parkway in the middle of the day; the murder rate was high. These days, Crown Heights was a solid "B." The 7-7 was just another regular old inner-city beat, thick with low-level dealers and purse snatchers. Not that there weren't reminders of the way things used to be.

A couple of weeks earlier, a mother had been walking down Eastern Parkway in the early evening and had caught a bullet meant for someone else. Her son was sitting in a nearby car. SHOT SHATTERS B'KLYN KIN read the all-caps headline in the *New York Post*. The *Times* had run a story about how technically crime was way down, but people were still scared—as if they couldn't let their guard down. As if being guarded had become part of who they were. "Crime around here, I guarantee you, it's going to pick up," a resident told the *Times*. "This year it's going to pick up. I have a gut feeling."

Ray Kelly, the police commissioner, had rented out space at a SUNY satellite campus in mid-December, ostensibly to introduce a new community partnership program for Crown Heights and Flatbush but really to soothe everyone's nerves—to let them know that the NYPD was paying attention.

For Brian Duffy, a complaint from the Hasidic community would have been a relatively rare occurrence. The 77th was wide and short, bounded by Atlantic to the north, Ralph Avenue to the east, and Flatbush—all the way over in Prospect Heights or Park Slope, depending on whether you were talking to a real estate broker or a Brooklyn lifer—to the west. The southern precinct border was Eastern Parkway, which was really the northern border of Jewish Crown Heights, so the 77th got none of the calls from the shops on south Kingston Avenue, for instance, or from the old row houses on Union and President and Crown. Those belonged to the 71st Precinct, whose members could talk Lubavitch politics as well as the Lubavitchers themselves.

The Hasidic settlement in Crown Heights, even at its most dense, accounted for only about 30 percent of the population in the neighborhood, but the Lubavitchers, for a variety of reasons—political and fiscal—got the full-time attention of the NYPD, and nine times out of ten, it was the 71st that provided it. Pictures of the rebbe hung inside the 71st Precinct House on New York Avenue and Empire—pictures of the rebbe with a prayer shawl draped over his head, pictures of the rebbe officiating a service at the main Lubavitch shul, pictures of the rebbe with his trademark fedora pulled down over his sharp blue eyes.

By comparison, the men and women of the 77th only had to worry about the Chabad institutions on Eastern Parkway: 749, the shul, the offices of the Lubavitch emissaries. Which wasn't to say that they weren't occasionally treated to a crash course in black hat culture. In 2006, a major riot had broken out in the basement of 770 Eastern Parkway. By the time the cops got there, the floor looked like a mosh pit. One contingent of Lubavitchers had climbed up on the stage, where they threw books at their enemies down below; others played tug-of-war with heavy wooden benches. Blood was everywhere. Hasidim were wandering through the lobby, their hats knocked askew, their faces flushed. In the end, there had been a couple of arrests, including one for felony assault.

But once the suspect—a member of the Shomrim—had been booked and put through central processing, the Brooklyn DA had dropped the case for lack of evidence. Not that anyone could blame him. The Lubavitchers had their own form of "Don't Snitch"—their own take on *omerta*—and getting a Jew to testify against a fellow Jew in secular court was uphill work indeed.

Duffy had secondhand knowledge of the 2006 incident, and staring at Rotem's complaint, he may have figured he'd stumbled his way into a related fracas. Some sort of spillover. Another chance for the guys who hadn't gotten enough the first time around. He put down the file and listened to the crunch of the Crown Vics rolling south down Utica, toward Eastern Parkway and the whole of Brooklyn beyond.

Three days later, Duffy was driving through the back streets of Jewish Crown Heights, the weather relatively warm for January, the skies bright, the radio idly spitting chatter. He turned onto Nostrand, passing Carroll and Crown and the countless sunless nameless access roads, and left again on Montgomery, until the asphalt dropped downward, and he was barreling past a used car lot, the front doors of the 71st in sight.

Paul Levi Huebner. That's how the guy had introduced himself on the phone—Levi the Jewish name, Paul the given name. The call came in on Thursday. Duffy had never heard of him.

"Listen," Huebner had said, "these kids don't speak English very well—I mean they speak a little English, but it's broken. You're going to need someone to translate for you. I can do that." There was protocol for this kind of thing, a list of preapproved translators. But it was a real hassle getting anyone good when you needed them, and in practice, most cops went with whoever was on the scene. A family member, a friend, the guy in the bodega across the street. So Duffy had accepted, and Huebner had offered to host a sit down at his home on Malbone Street.

Duffy parked, locked up. By the time he got to the stone apartment building at the end of the street, Huebner was standing at the front door, his arm extended, a million-watt smile plastered across his face. Six feet tall, give or take, he had silver-black hair and a beard that sprang at all angles from his face as if he'd stuck a finger in a socket. His eyes were big, restless, and kind. He and Duffy shook hands, nodded, exchanged pleasantries. Huebner, interestingly enough, spoke regular old American English, infused with that Brooklyn slang.

He could have been a Midwesterner or maybe a California native—somewhere neutral.

In court, Officer Brian Duffy never specified as to the full extent of his knowledge of Hasidic culture. But like all local cops, he would have known the basics: That Lubavitch Hasidism was a missionary movement. That it regularly recruited from the ranks of unaffiliated or Orthodox Jews. That it had plenty of political sway, in Brooklyn and farther afield. That its adherents were bound by the same codes of modesty, or *tznius*, as other Hasidim but were considered to be slightly more outgoing, more liberal. That the married women wore the same wigs, kept their real hair to the same two- to three-inch cut as their counterparts in other Hasidic communities but were not opposed to faux leather boots or designer handbags; that men often talked sports, cranked cigarettes, kept up with state politics.

Duffy followed Huebner through the front door of the apartment complex and into a unit on the first floor. The first thing Duffy saw was a big long table, with a blond kid sitting at one end, his hands in his lap. The kid was stout, broad through the shoulders, with a neck like a college wrestler's. He wore a starched white shirt, open at the chest, and a black yarmulke rolled back across his head. A ginger wisp of beard hung off his chin. Schneur Rotem. Duffy nodded to Rotem and walked around the table. Flanking the table were two heavy bookshelves, each filled to the spilling point with leather-bound books.

The remaining wall had been covered, gallery-style, in an array of portraits—there were family portraits of Huebner's kids in the traditional black fedoras and suits, portraits of the late Menachem Mendel Schneerson, portraits of the six Lubavitch rebbes who had come before him, and a faded black-and-white photograph showing a woman clutching her children in her arms. The photograph appeared to have been taken a lifetime ago. Huebner left to fetch water and coffee, leaving Duffy with Rotem, who was staring expectantly out the window at the grassy abandoned lot next door.

Duffy sized him up. The kid was vibrating with an electric kind of energy; he couldn't seem to keep himself still. He was clutching a single sheet of paper, but when Duffy tried to read the writing at the top of the page, Rotem ripped it backward. "Okay," Huebner said, dancing back into the room, his timing impeccable. "Let's get started."

Few Israeli *bochurim* speak English—unlike local Lubavitchers, they rarely interact with outsiders—and Rotem spoke almost none at all. This worked to his advantage. The kid was able to collect himself between each question, accept advice from Huebner, and prevent Duffy from issuing any kind of rapid-fire follow-up. Meanwhile, he held on tight to that piece of paper, which turned out to be a hand-written list of the names and addresses of all of the men in the Crown Heights Shomrim. Rotem, in other words, was working off a script. Duffy did his best. He leaned across the table, pressing Rotem for more—for the details that would help him pull this case together.

From the Informational Report later filed by Officer Brian Duffy [all sic]:

> Mr. Rotem stated that on December 29, 2007, at approximately 2130 hours, he was inside of 749 Eastern Parkway Brooklyn NY when several males entered apt 107 and attacked Mr Rotems friends. . . . I inquired if Mr Rotem knows who these individuals were and he advised me that these individuals are members of the Shomrim and that he does know who they are. It was during this altercation that the police were called. Mr Rotem stated that when the police showed up and the fighting stopped and the men then left the residence. Mr Rotem stated that after the incident he was speaking with his friend Jonathan Gorichnick in the hallway when the four of the men re-entered the building and proceeded to attack him. Mr Rotem stated that he received several bruises as well as a fractured hand during this altercation. Mr Rotem advised me that four of the men that attacked him were Gedalia "Godi" Hershkop, Yehudah "Yudi" Hershkop, Chaim Herschkop and Nossi Slater.
>
> By five in the afternoon, Duffy was back in his car.

Every criminal investigation is a matter of mathematics. A cop starts with a hundred variables, a thousand, a million. The variables stretch out in all directions, because everything is a variable. The way a shoe sits on the sidewalk. The pattern of the blood splatter on the wall. A witness who gets cagey at the mention of the perp's name. From these variables, a cop whittles. Tosses out what doesn't belong. Keeps what does. Eventually, he arrives—via gumshoeing if he's lucky or paper-pushing if he's not—at a simple equation. $A + B = C$ because $A$ is the actor and $B$ is the motive and $C$ is the dead guy on the sidewalk. From myriad possibilities he produces one possibility; from abstractions he provides proof.

By the middle of January, Duffy had his equation: six suspects and four complainants. He interviewed Rotem at Huebner's home on Malbone Street; Shatz and Gurfinkel and Braunstein were kind enough to present themselves at the 7-7, thus saving Duffy some legwork. Duffy ran point on the interviews but got some help from a couple of detectives, including Detective Edgar Bourdon. All four complainants were spinning variations on a single yarn: Two men had argued over a mattress. At some point, the Shomrim were called; the Shomrim had proceeded to bust heads. A guy named Gurfinkel, the brother of the resident of Room 107, had been swung around like a piñata; a guy named Shatz—aka the Hasidic Spider-Man, the one who had booked out the window as soon as he heard the sirens on the Parkway—had been strangled; Braunstein had been punched, and Schneur Rotem had nearly been trampled to death.

Duffy had limited experience with the Shomrim. Bourdon, a detective, would have understood a little more. He would have known that the Shomrim served as intermediaries between the police and the Jewish residents of Crown Heights, who often spoke broken English and weren't always wild about going to the police with their problems. They drove small police-style carts with police-style decals and wore police-style uniforms. They even had a riot van, a big bulking bus, festooned with lights and filled with all sorts of police paraphernalia—the riot van purchased at auction and the paraphernalia purchased from online police and military supply stores.

Privately, plenty of cops thought the Shomrim were hilarious. A kind of sideshow that brightened up their days. Hasidic vigilantes! You couldn't *make* this shit up. Or they found the antics of the Keystone Kops to be enraging. They'd seen some crazy scenes: A scrum of

Shomrim members, kitted out in navy blue, piled on top of a terrified homeless black man, everyone screaming, and the Shomrim saying they were only helping hold the guy until the real cops showed up. Or a couple of Shmira guys, their radios flopping around loose on their belts, pacing up and down Kingston Avenue as if they were gunslingers at the OK Corral.

But everyone understood that the Shomrim and the Shmira were basically untouchable. Word from the top was that these community-minded individuals could be a help, if only the 7-1 and the 7-7 would let them. Catch them doing something, and maybe you could lock them up. Until then, you know, work out any way you can. Bide your time, stiff upper lip, keep calm and carry on, look the other way, grin and bear it.


Crown Heights is big. Hasidic Crown Heights is small. Even by the most generous measurements, the Jewish settlement is seven blocks wide and six blocks deep. Some set the boundaries more stingily: the Jewish settlement is really four blocks wide—New York Avenue to Troy Avenue—and five blocks long. Either way, the place is a speck in the sprawling Brooklyn sea. A countable number of buildings in a borough of millions.

Right away, Brian Duffy, kicking around Jewish Crown Heights in search of his suspects, would have sensed the parameters of the world on the south side of the Parkway. Compared to the varied and eclectic architecture of North Brooklyn—the brownstones and the prewar beauties and the modernist glass high-rises—Crown Heights really had only three kinds of buildings. It had mansions. It had plenty of mansions. On President Street, you could still lose your breath staring at those mansions—those absurd conglomerations of brick and glass and bent metal that seemed a better fit in Westchester than in Brooklyn. The lawns large enough to actually *roll*; the Mercedes-Benzes gleaming in the driveways; the chandeliers sparkling through the wide bay windows. Houses that still went for $1.5 million, $2 million, more.

Then there were the apartment buildings. Five floors or less, five apartments to a floor, four rooms to an apartment, the good ones with three windows overlooking the street. The standard starter unit for a young Hasidic family. Cheap, easy to heat, anonymous. Most of the complexes were on the outskirts of the settlement—on New York or Troy or even on Utica or south near Empire. But the standard building block of Hasidic Crown Heights was the limestone row house. East of Kingston on President, the row houses were polished, clean, and gleaming white like freshly cleaned teeth. Farther out, they were chipped, musty, and bruised by the passing seasons. All of them were a neat three stories tall and pressed together, wall to wall, each one resembling the last, the only distinguishing characteristics the color of the door, the shape of the front porch, the color of the flag flapping in the breeze.

January 16, 2008. Eighteen days after the assault at 749 Eastern Parkway, and the case was finally coming together. The mathematical equation nudged toward its proof. In his hands, Duffy held the complaint forms and the names and addresses of the seven alleged assailants. A grand total of six Shomrim guys, three of them brothers: Gadi Hershkop, Yudi Hershkop, Chaim Hershkop. Nothing particularly unusual there. In Hasidic culture, it was considered a great blessing to have a big family. The bigger the better. Many Lubavitch women quickly settled after marriage into a decade of child-making and child-rearing, six kids a respectable tally, and seven or eight even better. The kids stuck around the home—sharing bedrooms with their siblings—until they hit their twenties and then set off to make their own families. So although the Hershkop brothers were relatively young—Yudi in his early twenties, Gadi in his early thirties, and Chaim somewhere in between—all were busy with families of their own and had scattered to their respective corners of the Lubavitch community.

In what order did Officer Brian Duffy visit the homes of the alleged assailants? On the stand at the Brooklyn Supreme Court in the fall of 2009, he never specified. He said only that not a single one of the men was home. Of course, it's possible—and indeed probable, considering that word of a possible arrest was already circulating around the shops of Kingston—that the men *were* home. That they were peering out from behind the curtains on the second floor, watching Duffy knock. It's also possible that Duffy had made the error of visiting the parents' homes, which are often the only listed addresses for young Lubavitchers—the younger generation preferring to fly under the radar, using cell phones and e-mail and Facebook and not land lines. And those parents? They certainly weren't going to open the door.

Among older Jewish residents of Crown Heights, distrust of the NYPD was a time-honored tradition. The reasons varied: Some Lubavitchers had fled Russia or Eastern Europe, where they learned the hard way not to obey men in uniform. Some worried that justice could never be served in a secular court. Others had been unlucky enough to get a front-row seat to the Crown Heights race riots, which forever sullied their opinion of New York's finest. In 1991, a car in the rebbe's caravan had veered off course and struck an apartment building near the corner of Utica and President, knocking over a stone pillar, killing a small Guyanese boy, injuring his cousin, and setting fire to the neighborhood. The neighborhood had burned for three days. The police counted 225 incidents of robbery or burglary; 152 cops were injured, along with 38 civilians; 27 NYPD vehicles were damaged or destroyed. An elderly Jewish Holocaust survivor, fearing the worst, threw herself out her window to her death, and 129 people were arrested for crimes ranging from criminal possession of a weapon to assault. Most were black.

All of that corked-up fear and loathing had finally found an outlet. All of that friction from years of cohabitation had finally given way to flame. Could it have been otherwise? Depends on whom you asked. The idealists argued that blacks and Jews were brothers in suffering. That they had both been trampled and, having been trampled, had risen up again; they understood each other better than they thought. The realists denounced the humid rhetoric of the idealists and argued that a disturbance of some sort was only a matter of time. Blacks and Jews were just different, the realists counseled, and the sooner everyone realized it, the better it would be for Crown Heights.

And so it went, on TV and on the radio and in the newspapers and the newsmagazines, with everyone dying for a chance to say something meaningful about the riots, anything meaningful, because you couldn't turn on the TV and see blacks and Jews squaring off in the middle of New York City and not have an opinion. What did it mean? Nothing. Everything. It was proof that political correctness was bullshit or proof that political correctness was everything, and America wasn't PC enough. Crown Heights was a crucible, a battleground, it was water cooler gossip; it was exhibit A in the race wars.

Wire stringers and local network videographers descended on Crown Heights, slithering between the piles of ignited trash, sniffing in all of the chaos, popping up from behind storefronts just in time to catch the rioters lining up on the asphalt, like the English archers at Agincourt. A reporter got a rock in the face. The Iranian owner of the Utica Gold Exchange watched his storefront go up in smoke and told *Newsday* that Crown Heights was "worse than Iran. There, if someone tries to burn your store, the people wouldn't allow them to do it." Here, in Brooklyn, your store could burn forever, and no one would bat an eye.

Black protesters were bussed in from every corner of the Bronx, Harlem, Queens. A troubled sixteen-year-old kid named Lemrick Nelson Jr. heard a heroin addict named Charles Price screaming about "going up to the Jew neighborhood," and Nelson followed Price, fingering in his pocket a folding knife with the word "killer" on the handle. Around 11 p.m., on August 19, 1991, Nelson was one of several blacks who set upon Yankel Rosenbaum, an Orthodox Jew from Australia. Nelson stabbed Rosenbaum several times; Rosenbaum later died in Kings County Hospital.

His death was ruled a homicide, and to Lubavitchers, the city of New York was just as culpable as Nelson or Price was. The cops, the mayor, the Brooklyn DA—all of them had watched as blacks enacted a full-scale "pogrom" in the middle of New York City. Posters bearing the picture of Mayor David Dinkins went up around Crown Heights. "Wanted for the Murder of Yankel Rosenbaum," the posters read. Speaking to a reporter from the *Jewish Press* in September 1991, Governor Mario Cuomo appeared to confirm that Dinkins had bungled the management of the riots. "The Mayor," Cuomo opined, "said that the night before"—August 19—"had been a sort of day of grace to the mob, and that wouldn't happen a second day because it was abused and because there were crimes perpetrated that were not prevented."

A day of grace! For murderers and thieves! In Crown Heights, the Lubavitchers seethed. How could they ever be expected to trust a bunch of cops who had once left them to die?

On January 17, 2008, Officer Brian Duffy was back at his desk, staring at enough paper to power a Kinko's joint for six years. He had struck out on the Shomrim guys—struck out on all of them—but it wasn't as if the flood of paper stopped, just because you were hot on a different case. It never stopped. A cop was drowning in paperwork from the day he got on the job until the day of his retirement. Push a complaint one way, push it another. Whole days could pass this way. Whole careers.

Late in the afternoon, Duffy's phone lit up. He took the call at his desk. The guy on the other line, a "Mr. Moses," identified himself as a member of the NYPD Clergy Liaison, a department created a while back to help facilitate a back-and-forth between the cops and the members of certain religious communities. There were something like five hundred liaisons posted to precincts all over the five boroughs, all noncops but trained by the NYPD in crisis mediation, counterterrorism tactics, community politics. And although some liaisons could be a real hassle—sometimes you just wanted to pull a guy into interrogation, delicate religious sensibilities or not—they could help get an investigation into gear, open up lines of communication where a regular beat cop couldn't.

"Can you give me their names?" Moses asked, and Duffy did, knowing each one by memory now. There was a pause, the sound of pencil on paper. "Okay," Moses said. "I'll call you back." And then, on the morning of Tuesday, January 22, 2008, in they came, sullenly walking single file off Utica and through the scarred metal doors, a late holiday present for the 7-7. They might as well have been wrapped in big red bows. Gadi Hershkop, Ben Lifshitz, Nussi Slater, Schneur Pinson, and Chaim Hershkop. Yehuda Hershkop, who was out of town, showed up the week after that. One by one, Officer Brian Duffy read them their rights, and put each man under arrest.

Later, the Hershkop brothers would blame Duffy for actively participating in what they considered a wide-ranging conspiracy to put the
Shomrim permanently out of business. But save for a 2009 appearance in Brooklyn Supreme Court—where he reiterated the details
of his investigation—Duffy had no further contact with the Crown
Heights Shomrim. He turned his reports over to the district attorney
and turned back to the stack of papers on his desk. Paul Huebner, on
the other hand, was far from finished. He had successfully laid the
groundwork for a case against the Shomrim. Now he could sit back
and watch the fireworks.

# 3

In 1874, the architects Frederick Law Olmstead and Calvert Vaux finished work on a fifty-five-foot-wide boulevard called Eastern Parkway, which rolled out like a red carpet from the tip of Prospect Park and toward the tenements of Bedford-Stuyvesant and Brownsville. Among the first families to travel east on the parkway were Jewish émigrés, fleeing persecution in Europe and Russia. They were rich, or relatively rich by the hardscrabble standards of contemporary Brooklyn; they were strivers and dreamers; they knew enough of the good life to want to recreate it in America. Many settled in Crown Heights, a Brooklyn neighborhood nestled between the borders of Flatbush and Bed-Stuy.

In his memoir, *A Walker in the City*, the writer Alfred Kazin remembers the residents of Crown Heights as "middle-class Jews, *alrightniks*, making out 'all right' in the New World." Compared to the Jews of Brownsville, the immigrant slum where Kazin was raised—and still a place paralyzed by economic inertia—the Jews of Crown Heights lounged in a gilded shtetl. They prayed in temples of stained glass; at dusk, they strolled hand in hand under the dappled light of Eastern Parkway. To the young Kazin, these Jews seemed wondrous and distant. In fact, he wrote, they were like "Gentiles to me."

Crown Heights grew in fits and starts. A line of brick mansions dubbed "Doctor's Row" went up on President Street; the limestone row houses on Union Street were commandeered by servants. Ebbets Field—that great hitter's paradise—was completed in 1913, on the embers of a collection of shanties formerly known as Pigtown. A fifteen-hundred-seat "deluxe" cinema opened on Eastern Parkway.

By 1940, Crown Heights had come to encompass a brick-shaped chunk of north-central Brooklyn, bounded by Atlantic Avenue to the north, Lefferts Avenue to the south, Washington Avenue to the west, and Ralph Avenue to the east. Those borders, ratified in the 1960s, made Crown Heights at least a mile long and more than two miles wide. The neighborhood included the dense Jewish settlement around Eastern Parkway and also thriving Irish, Italian, and Scandinavian enclaves. It was predominantly white.

But the history of New York City comprises hundreds of small-scale real estate revolutions—colonizations and recolonizations, incursions and retreats, the exodus and the return. And in the years after World War II, the alrightniks, gentrifiers themselves, began to lose their grip on the neighborhood. Thousands of Southern blacks arrived in Central Brooklyn in search of warehouse or factory work; many settled off Eastern Parkway. An incursion from the Bedford-Stuyvesant ghetto to the north brought street crime to the once-hushed streets. The alrightnik enclave might have remained intact had it not been for the passage, in 1965, of the Hart-Celler Immigration and Nationality Act, which eliminated nationality quotas—before 1965, the vast majority of citizenship slots were offered to residents of the United Kingdom, Ireland, and Germany—and opened the floodgates to a wave of immigrants from Asia, Africa, and the Caribbean.

In Crown Heights, the bulk of the new arrivals were West Indian. "Every jack-man buying a swell house in ditchy Crown Heights," Paule Marshall wrote in her novel *Brown Girl, Brownstones*, which documents Caribbean immigrant life in Brooklyn. Soon, bakeries and seafood restaurants had sprouted up alongside the kosher eateries; talk in the park turned from baseball to cricket. Crown Heights became the seat of the Brooklyn West Indian Carnival, the biggest ethnic parade in New York City. The alrightniks took their cue. Many fled for Upper Manhattan; others for bedroom communities in New Jersey and Connecticut.

And yet the Jewish presence in the neighborhood was by no means erased. Many apartment complexes and synagogues remained in the hands of the Lubavitchers, an ultra-Orthodox Jewish sect with roots in White Russia. In 1969, the seventh Lubavitcher rebbe, Menachem Mendel Schneerson, commanded his Hasidim to fight for their foothold in Crown Heights. Schneerson had fled Europe in 1941. His youngest brother had been killed by the Nazis; his father perished in exile in Kazakhstan.

He was tired of running.

The Hasidic tradition as we know it today—the mystical faith, so concerned with matters of light and darkness and the transcendence of the soul—is usually traced to a man named Rabbi Israel ben Eliezer, who was born in 1698 in the Ukraine.

Ben Eliezer, or the Baal Shem Tov, "the master of the good name," maintained no single residence, preferring instead to travel the land by foot, preaching a gospel that infused Talmudic lore with an appreciation for the miracles of the everyday world. He was born to humble origins, and perhaps as a result, the Baal Shem Tov's Judaism was proximate, attainable, *democratic*. He saw God in everything. There was God in death and life and also God in the way an outstretched hand waits for the first drops of water. There was God in the poor and God in the rich and God in the doctor and God in the diseased. According to the Baal Shem Tov, God did not make himself available only to the learned. "The coachman who kisses the holy scrolls of the Torah pleases God more than the angels who praise Him and do nothing else," he advised.

A tale is often told of a "robust and earthy" man visited by the Baal Shem Tov. As far as anyone could tell, all the man did was eat. He ate from the morning through the afternoon and into the evening, at which point he stopped, fell asleep, and rose to eat again. Finally, the Baal Shem Tov demanded to know what prompted the man's voracity. The man explained that his father, an exceedingly pious *tzaddik*, had recently been captured by bandits. When the old man refused to kiss a cross produced by the bandits, the bandits lit the old man on fire; because the old man was so thin, he burned quickly, like a "miserable skinny candle." His "robust and earthy" son was filling himself with food so that if he was ever captured, he would burn for hours, days, weeks.

"All my energy, all my passion is devoted to eating," the son told the Baal Shem Tov. "Not that I am hungry, you understand."

The moral of this tale, which appears in Elie Wiesel's *Souls on Fire*, a lyric retelling of the central Hasidic myths, hints at the core of Hasidism: Every gesture must be purposeful, prayerful. Every Jew must burn with fervor. And only in the burning can one truly know God. For large portions of European Jewry, the Baal Shem Tov's message was irresistible. It promised a crushed people the possibility of divine communion. It "brought back to the fold large numbers of Jews," Wiesel wrote, "who faltering under the weight of their burden, came close to conceding defeat." It reinvigorated Judaism. It spread across the villages and the towns of White Russia, Poland, and Lithuania. The poor seemed especially receptive to the Baal Shem Tov's teachings. Wiesel again:

> He told them what they wanted to hear: that everyone of them existed in God's memory, that everyone one of them played a part in his people's destiny, each in his way and according to his means. He assured them that simple but sincere prayer has as much merit as a mystical incantation, that the fervor born in a pure heart is greater than the one born of a complex and unfathomable thought.

In 1760, when the Baal Shem Tov passed away, the flag of Hasidism was picked up by a new generation of disciples. Among them: Rabbi Yaakov-Yoseph of Polnoye, Rebbe Pinhas of Koretz, Rebbe Nahman of Kossov, and Rebbe Nahman of Horodenko. Hasidism duly splintered, evolved. The Baal Shem Tov had left little, if any, written record of his teachings, and his disciples were left to interpret the words they had heard him speak. There were disagreements over subtext, context, the precise meaning of a parable.

There were feuds. Some feuds were worse than others; they were remedied or else they split families and towns apart. There were also accords. Dynastic courts were born. The Belzers made their court in Belz, in Western Ukraine. The Breslov in Bratslav. The Lubavitchers in Lyubavichi, in Russia. Distinct customs, traditions, and even "uniforms" developed among the courts.

And just as each Hasidic court followed its own interpretation of Hasidism, each rebbe further shaped the message and intent of his court, like a master potter working wet clay. For instance, Rabbi Schneur Zalman, who founded the Lubavitch court, stressed a particularly rational approach to Hasidism—the "mind ruling over the heart." He called his doctrine Chabad, an acronym for *Chochma* (Wisdom), *Bina* (Understanding), and *Da'as* (Knowledge). In *Tales of the Hasidim*, a collection of kabbalistic tales edited by the scholar Martin Buber, Rabbi Zalman warns his followers of the dangers of an overly ascetic life. "There are two kinds of men—those with black gall and those with light," he said. "The dark-tempered sit over the books of the teachings and are of miserly disposition. The light-tempered love company and are generous."

Zalman also believed that the lessons of past Jewish mystics—and especially of the Kabbalah—were there to be wrestled with. His great book, the *Tanya*, offers what the journalist Lis Harris has identified as "a system of contemplation." To Zalman, all of life was in essence a struggle between the animal soul and the divine soul. Only with intellectual rigor, he wrote in the *Tanya*—only with unstinting faith, study, and service to God—could a pious Jew rise above his base impulses and finally experience true transcendence.

The seventh Lubavitcher rebbe, Menachem Mendel Schneerson, was born in 1902 in the Ukraine. As a young man, he married Chaya Mushka Schneerson, the daughter of the sixth rebbe. The couple spent time in Berlin and Paris, where Menachem Mendel received a degree in engineering from the Sorbonne. In some early pictures, he appears to wear his beard short—something of an affront to ultra-Orthodox tradition, which requires all men to let their facial hair grow. Menachem Mendel certainly lived a relatively cosmopolitan lifestyle. He enjoyed strolling through Berlin and Paris with his wife, and although there is evidence that he immersed himself in Hasidic theology from a young age, he did so with none of the overt piety of his peers. (He and his wife never had children; later, Chaya Mushka would say that Menachem Mendel's Hasidim were children enough.) In 1941, the couple, with the help of the U.S. State Department, fled France on a ship called the *Serpa-Pinto*. They arrived in New York on June 23.

Behind them, all was death and destruction. The Hasidim unlucky enough to not have decamped for American shores found themselves trapped by the Nazis on one side and the Soviets on the other. Menachem Mendel's youngest brother, born mentally handicapped, was killed by the Nazis; his father died in exile in Kazakhstan. "Mendel's whole world had collapsed," Menachem Friedman and Samuel Heilman wrote in *The Rebbe*, their biography of Schneerson. "Now he was a childless refugee in America nearly forty years old with little or no English facility, with no job prospects in what had been his chosen field." Initially, Schneerson seemed loath to devote his life to the Lubavitch court. He and Chaya Mushka moved into a modest house on President Street, a few blocks south of the bustle of Eastern Parkway, and he apparently found a job at the Brooklyn Navy Yard. (Friedman and Heilman are somewhat skeptical that the job existed; scant evidence remains of it.)

In 1950, when the sixth rebbe died, many Lubavitchers assumed the mantle would go to his grandson, Barry. But modern Lubavitch lore—strengthened by hindsight—has it that Menachem Mendel Schneerson, a blood relation to the third rebbe, was the logical and even the divinely preordained choice. Schneerson himself certainly wasn't convinced. His initial talks as rebbe were marked by a distinct modesty. He deferred to the spirit of his father-in-law, regularly telling his Hasidim that Yosef Yitzchak Schneersohn was "in the room," listening to their prayers. "Know that father did not die, and whoever wants to make requests [of him] can still do so. I too have done so," he said. His confidence came to him gradually. And yet when he began to build his legacy, he built it quickly and tirelessly and with an alacrity that surprised even the most devout Hasidim.

Schneerson's greatest skill was in outreach. Outreach work was not unheard of in the Hasidic world, but Schneerson made it a priority, envisioning and then enacting a network of Chabad houses across the globe. Compared to the harsh rhetoric of his predecessor, the seventh Lubavitcher rebbe's message was decidedly benign. Enough Jews had perished in Europe. Now was the time for rebuilding—for the kindling of the Jewish spirit. Schneerson threw open the doors of Chabad to all Jews, regardless of their affiliation. He welcomed lapsed Jews, secular Jews; he welcomed Jews who had long since forgotten their heritage and Jews who spoke not a word of Hebrew. He told all Jews that they would have a role in welcoming the Messiah, if only they would devote themselves to a life of kindness and *yiddishkeit*, or the Jewish way of life.

Much to the chagrin of other Hasidim, who believed that the "oracle of Crown Heights" was betraying the cloistered, rigorous spirit of Hasidism, Schneerson's *mitzvah* campaign was a success, and by the mid-1960s, the Chabad movement spilled across borders, time zones, and continents. Chabad membership swelled; the Lubavitcher coffers expanded. On the last day of Passover, Schneerson opened a *farbrengen*—a kind of group religious discussion—by commanding his Hasidim to stay in Crown Heights, now the anchor of the Chabad community worldwide. "In recent times, a plague has spread among our brethren—the wholesale migration from Jewish neighborhoods," he explained. "One result of this phenomenon is the sale of houses in these neighborhoods to non-Jewish people. Even synagogues and places of Torah study are sold. Furthermore, the livelihood of many members of the community becomes undermined or completely destroyed by this precipitous flight."

To drive home his point, Schneerson quoted from Deuteronomy: "Do what is right and good in the sight of the Lord, so that all may go well with you and that you may be able to possess the good land that the Lord your God promised on oath to your fathers, and that all your enemies may be driven out before you." (Schneerson spoke to his Hasidim in Yiddish, but the comments from this *farbrengen* were printed and disseminated in Hebrew; the first and longer quote here was translated by the journalist Edward Hoffman, and the second by the anthropologist Henry Goldschmidt.)

So it was settled, and in fact it was divinely ordained. If not Israel, then Brooklyn. If not Jerusalem, then Crown Heights. From a basement shul at 770 Eastern Parkway, in the midst of the growing black community, Rebbe Menachem Mendel Schneerson would conduct his mission of *yiddishkeit*. But first the enemies of the Jews would have to be driven out before them. During the 1960s and the '70s, the Lubavitchers consolidated their control of the ten-square-block area surrounding Kingston Avenue—the new High Street of Jewish Crown Heights—in some cases bribing families that refused to go quietly. If Lubavitchers could no longer dominate all of Crown Heights— they were vastly outnumbered by the West Indians and the African Americans—they could adopt a policy of demographic consolidation. (The scholar Jerome Mintz estimates that there were probably between three and four thousand Hasidim in Crown Heights in 1960 and possibly twice that number by 1975.)

By the late '70s, a Hasid could shop for kosher food, purchase a fedora and a black suit, pray at shul, and visit his rebbe, all without walking more than half a mile. The Jews had successful diners, bookstores, yeshivas, and hotels for the thousands of pilgrims who came to Crown Heights to visit Schneerson's court. A volunteer Jewish ambulance corps, Hatzolah, was pressed into service. There was a *beis din*—a Jewish court—to adjudicate internal community matters, including divorces and financial disputes.

The anthropologist Henry Goldschmidt relates the efforts of the Lubavitch leadership to secure the borders of the Hasidic settlement to the Jewish legal doctrine of *daled amos*:

> Lubavitchers often mark their Rebbe's geographic centrality by referring to Crown Heights as "the Rebbe's *daled amos*," a phrase which draws metaphoric significance from the technicalities of Jewish law, where it refers to the minimum required breadth of a private home—four cubits, or *daled amos*. To describe Crown Heights as "the Rebbe's *daled amos*" is to define the entire neighborhood as the Rebbe's home—a private Jewish space, and a uniquely holy place for Hasidim.

Lines were drawn, invisible barriers erected. Eastern Parkway became the "Green Line," Goldschmidt notes, a nod to the borders established by Israel after the 1948 war. When a Hasid walked north, into Caribbean Crown Heights, he told his friends he was crossing into "Beirut." Some Lubavitchers went so far as to declare that the rebbe was *Moshiach*, or Messiah, and that their neighborhood was the event horizon—the cornerstone of the space-time continuum, the place from which all light spilled across the universe. Hasidic Crown Heights, in this sense, came to obviate traditional understandings of geography. As the Lubavitchers had hoped, the settlement had become a world within a world. Or maybe it was the world itself, stripped of the rind.

You never needed a map.

# 4

On May 29, 1964, the *New York Herald Tribune* carried on its front page a three-column photograph of two men, sitting together on the front bench of what appeared to be a police cruiser. One was idly fingering a police radio. Both were wearing yarmulkes. Over their shoulders, the *Herald Tribune* photographer had captured a gritty urban landscape—a sun-splashed boulevard, a pedestrian waiting for a light, rows of faded apartment buildings that appeared to recede into infinity. The caption identified the two men as Sidney Gordon and Rabbi Samuel Schrage—top-ranking members of the Maccabees, an all-Jewish anticrime patrol based in Crown Heights.

"When Greeks and Syrians oppressed them in Pre-Christian days, the Jews struck back through the Maccabees, a vigilante-type group of warriors," the caption read. "Now, with the crime rate rising in the Crown Heights section of Brooklyn, the ultra-orthodox Hasidic Jewish community has formed a band of modern-day Maccabees, unarmed but equipped with roaming patrol cars and two-way radios."

Schrage, who typically appeared in public wearing a sleek black suit—his dark beard neatly combed, his hair painstakingly lacquered—had for many years served as the administrator of the United Lubavitcher Yeshiva, a school on the north side of Eastern Parkway.

He had never considered vigilante action, preferring to press his case through legal means. But in April 1964, four Hasidic students leaving a yeshiva on the north side of Eastern Parkway had been provoked and allegedly assaulted by at least fifty black youths. Two weeks later, a black man had broken into a Crown Heights home and attempted to rape the wife of a popular Lubavitcher rabbi. The woman managed to beat back her assailant; in the process, she received several slashes across the face and the neck. Both crimes were touted as proof that Jews were no longer safe in Crown Heights—that the growing black population had begun to eclipse the Hasidic settlement.

Schrage's choice of the name Maccabees was not accidental. It evoked the spirit of ancient Jewish strength—of protest in the face of a vast and fearsome enemy army. Judah Maccabee had once used guerrilla warfare to reclaim Jerusalem. Schrage hoped to use guerrilla warfare to reclaim Crown Heights. For those who scoffed at the mention of the long-dead Maccabees, Schrage unearthed a modern precedent for his cause: the brave young paramilitary organizations that had battled the Bolsheviks in Russia and the Hashomer, a Jewish defense group founded in Palestine in the early twentieth century.

During the darkest periods in history, Schrage explained, "many of our men went underground, to fight the enemy back. And they did a good job." In Brooklyn, Schrage allowed, the enemy would not be the "government or the general population," but the "individuals who do not have the respect of the government or the population. We are defending ourselves against criminals." The Lubavitchers are what has been called a "survivor sect"—the movement had survived the trials of life in the Pale of Settlement, the perils of the Russian Revolution, and the incomprehensible violence of the Holocaust. They had not made it to Brooklyn only to lose their kingdom on a hill to a bunch of hoodlums.

In April, Schrage convened a meeting of five hundred Jewish leaders, including the heads of all of the yeshivas in Crown Heights, and asked that the Maccabees be formally recognized by the community. His argument—which he would reiterate many times in coming years—was simple. "What are people to do when their wives and children are afraid to walk the streets because of muggers and rapists?" he later asked.

What are people to do when the sanctity of their own homes are being violated by thieves who break in in the still of the night? After they install window bars in their windows, what next? What are they to do? Naturally, they have to call upon the police, but what are they to do when the police tell them that they don't have enough policemen for the job? That they understand their problems, that they have every feeling for their concerns, yet they don't have enough to police to help them? Are they just to wait and wait? I say no. I say they must act in their own interest and in the interest of the community.

The vote was nearly unanimous. The next week, Schrage rented a low-slung, musty former corset shop at 459 Albany Avenue in south Crown Heights and converted the first floor into a dispatch office. With help from a few wealthy donors, he purchased four squad cars, four two-way radios, and a hulking metal base unit. He bought maps and telephones and first-aid kits. He trained his men in rudimentary self-defense and in the art of the capture; he demonstrated how to drive a fleeing assailant to the ground and how to keep him there.

The rebbe had ordered his Hasidim to remain in Crown Heights, but he had not promised that life amid the tumult of Central Brooklyn would be easy. Every Lubavitcher—every man, woman, and child—would have to do his or her part to sustain the health of the Jewish community. Some prayed. Some organized fund-raising efforts. Some erected shuls. Others built schools and bookstores. For his part, Schrage took to the streets. Organized resistance to him was just another kind of *davening*—every crime prevented by a Maccabee was as good as a prayer. It was a *mitzvah*.

Schrage carved up the neighborhood into numbered districts and gave every volunteer a call sign. He saw Crown Heights as being like a checkerboard and the members of his patrol as the plastic pieces. During the height of the summer of '64, while violent crime rates continued to corkscrew upward, he had four cars working the neighborhood on a grid pattern, criss-crossing east to west on Eastern Parkway and Crown and north to south on Utica, Kingston, and New York Avenue. Schrage bragged that no block in Crown Heights ever went unsurveilled for more than two minutes. He said that all of Crown Heights knew the name of the Maccabees, and that the word of the patrol was enough to make a hardened criminal quiver in his sneakers. Schrage was an inspiration to all of Crown Heights, and decades later, young men like Gadi and Aron Hershkop—both born long after the disbanding of the Maccabees—would proudly remember the example that Rabbi Samuel Schrage had set.

The number of volunteers in the Maccabees swelled. A dozen, two dozen, a hundred. They came from Crown Heights but also from Bed-Stuy and Flatbush and even from Park Slope. The majority were married, with families of their own; others were young and brash and looking for a fight. Schrage warned every recruit that the work of a Crown Heights Maccabee would often be mundane. One day, a member might be walking an old woman home from the super-market or fixing a flat tire. The next he might be driving for hours across the whole of Central Brooklyn, passing darkened storefronts and empty streets, peering blearily out rain-soaked windows, praying for the shift to end. Only rarely would he be afforded an opportunity to barrel down an alley after some knife-wielding criminal. Officially, Schrage said he abhorred the word *vigilante*. He said he did not con-done violence. Publicly, he said that the Maccabees would always notify the police before pursuing a criminal. He handed out fliers and magnets and stickers adorned with the logo and the number of the Crown Heights Maccabees: Slocum 6-5100. He urged residents to call dispatch whenever they were in danger, no matter the time of day. Privately, he told his troops that they would sometimes have to take matters into their own hands—nothing less than the fate of Crown Heights Jewry was at stake.

In the fall of 1964, as Schrage's star rose, producers from a short-lived television program called *Survival* arrived in Crown Heights to profile the Maccabees. The segment was largely positive and fea-tured plenty of footage of the Maccabees careening around Central Brooklyn like a bunch of cops on *Dragnet*. In one clearly posed shot, Schrage stands in the living room of his Montgomery Street home, cradling his baby and *davening* under a traditional Jewish prayer shawl. The narrator, James Whitmore, explains that "the cities of America are under attack. Crime is on the increase, in some cases overwhelming the resources of law enforcement agencies. While sociologists and politicians ponder the causes, one group of victims fights back. This is the story of a neighborhood under attack—a story of survival." The melodramatic string score surges.

Attack! Victims! Survival! The phrasing was dramatic, indelible: Americans were fighting against persecution, and they were fighting well. In fact, the *Survival* segment featured only two opposing views, one from a black woman who seems baffled by the very existence of an all-Jewish security organization. "I don't see how you can just draft a lot of people and say you're just going to patrol areas," the woman said. "Because after a while you're going to get to the point where the white people say, 'You're not going to come into my neighborhood,' and the Negroes are going to say, 'You can't come into my neighborhood,' so you're still going to have race violence, and you're still going to breed more trouble or discontent."

The next dissenter was a young black lawyer, who stood in front of a Bed-Stuy law firm, clad in a smart suit and spectacles. Someone has to be responsible for the actions for the Maccabees, he told the camera:

> Who's going to control individuals in these groups, some of whom might not have all their senses, who may not be responsible, who may want to fight, who may want to pursue someone—who's going to control them? Who's going to be responsible? Who's going to avoid the body contact that leads to all kinds of confusion? Even with the police department, you see, we have individuals who creep in and who may not be balanced, and there's trouble between the police and the people. I'm afraid of any group, whether there are Negroes in it or not, which is not controlled for all of the people by all of the people.

Unlike James Whitmore, the lawyer did not see the Maccabees as victims. He saw them as agitators. And much of the black community concurred. In the late months of 1964, scores of black leaders—most preachers and reverends from Bed-Stuy and Crown Heights—used every available opportunity to excoriate Schrage and his "Jew police." The black leadership did not disagree that crime had risen in Crown Heights, nor did they believe that the New York City Police

Department was doing enough to tamp down on the criminals. But to allow a bunch of untrained, unvetted patrolmen to take to the streets—well, that was injudicious at best and exceedingly dangerous at worst. There was simply not enough oversight. Moreover, by recruiting exclusively from the ranks of the Lubavitch community, Schrage was helping to cement the racial barriers that divided Crown Heights.

On a brisk Saturday in early April 1987, a crowd of four hundred black men gathered on the campus of Medgar Evers College on Bedford Avenue and marched east through Crown Heights, toward the Lubavitch shul at 770 Eastern Parkway. Most were students. They walked in lockstep, holding aloft signs bearing an array of slogans: "Africans fight back," or "No more racist attacks," or "Johannesburg, Howard Beach, Crown Heights." They were there to be seen. They smiled at the journalists with the telephoto lenses and they smiled at the police, who followed the crowd on horseback and in squad cars and on foot. There were 2,000 cops assigned to the march—just 500 fewer than the 2,500 cops assigned to the post–World Series ticker-tape parade for the Mets a year earlier—and every cop was told to be prepared for violence. On orders from City Hall, the subway station at Kingston Avenue had been temporarily shuttered and half of the side streets from Bedford to Utica were cordoned off with sawhorses and yellow tape.

The procession moved slowly, past green lawns and regal brick mansions and clusters of black-hatted Hasidim, who leaned with curiosity over the police barricades. At 1304 President Street, the home of the Lubavitcher rebbe, the crowd parted way, and a handful of community leaders stepped forward. The first to speak was Dr. Vernal Cave, the former president of Medgar Evers College.

"We are here not in any violent way," he said, "but to make a peaceful statement." Over the murmuring of the protesters, Cave put loud voice to the grievances of the black community in Crown Heights: the poverty, the rising crime, the drugs and the guns, the increasing sense of helplessness—and above all, the inequality.

It had been a particularly tumultuous year for Crown Heights. In July 1986, four Hasidim, all between the ages of nineteen and twenty-three, were arrested for beating a black teenager with a hammer, a hose, and a baseball bat. The victim had managed to escape to his Empire Boulevard home, where his mother jotted down the plate number of the assailants' car; all four men were later convicted of assault. The Brooklyn District Attorney called the attack "a racially motivated crime."

The following February, a house belonging to a black woman named Willie Mae Reddish was firebombed; a witness told the police that one of the arsonists was wearing a black coat and a black hat. The Lubavitchers vehemently denied involvement, and the police failed to turn up any leads, but to blacks, it was reasonable to assume that a Jew was behind the attack. After all, it was widely believed that the Hasidim were attempting to snatch up all of the real estate immediately surrounding Kingston Avenue, and that they were doing it with the implicit backing of New York City officials.

According to one survey taken in 1987, more than 60 percent of black homeowners in Crown Heights had been approached with unsolicited offers from potential buyers. Black residents were allegedly threatened or harassed when they refused to leave; when they complained to the police, they were ignored. "Sometimes I feel like we are living in an apartheid state where a tiny minority is controlling our state," a woman told the *New York Times*. "They have to accept the fact that we are here. They have to respect our beliefs, just as we are bound to accept theirs."

The term *apartheid* was everywhere in the spring of 1987—in the newspapers, on the street, on the lips of community organizers. Certainly, it was true that Jews were the minority in Crown Heights. According to the 1980 census report, of the 96,892 people residing in the neighborhood, 78 percent were black, and 9.5 percent were Hispanic. Only 9.3 percent were white. It was also true that the Lubavitchers were unabashed in their attempts to maintain control over the houses and the storefronts surrounding Kingston Avenue. In the '70s, the Jewish Community Council had created an organization called Chevra Machazilei Hashchuna, or the Coalition to Strengthen the Neighborhood. Chevra was enormously successful in securing government grants for low-income housing, most of which went directly to Jews; the organization was eventually dismantled in the 1980s, amid charges of fraud and discrimination.

And yet even if black leaders could publicly denounce the under-handed tactics of organizations like Chevra, they had a difficult time making the larger case that the city of New York favored Jews over blacks. As U.S. representative Major Owens admitted in 1987, the Jewish community in Crown Heights was exceedingly well organized; Lubavitchers had proved adept at working the New York political machine. "Every advance that they make seems to build up new resentments in the black community, which is less able to cope with the system," Owens said.

Lubavitchers voted in higher percentages than did other Brooklyn residents and usually in predictable blocs, and for this reason, Crown Heights became—and remains today—a regular stop for politi-cians on a local and a national level. In his book *Race and Religion among the Chosen Peoples of Crown Heights*, Henry Goldschmidt wrote that blacks have long been split on whether the political clout of the Hasidim represented "an attack on their neighborhood's black majority, a model of community empowerment to emulate, or both."

There was less ambiguity when it came to the matter of the civilian anticrime patrols. In the early 1970s, the Lubavitch leadership had reluctantly disbanded the Maccabees—a move intended to appease black leaders and bring a modicum of peace to the neighborhood. But a few years later, a fresh crime wave swept through Central Brooklyn, and several former Maccabees re-formed as the Crown Heights Shmira. By 1987, when Dr. Vernal Cave gave his speech on the front lawn of the rebbe's residence, the Shmira was a well-known, well-orga-nized—and much feared—institution.

Locals regularly reported being stopped and asked for identifica-tion; several men said they had been collared and shoved into the back of a squad car, for no discernible reason other than the fact that they were black. "Periodically, one of their patrol cars that has a searchlight will feel no compunction about flashing that light at someone," said Cheryl Anthony, a black woman who worked on Nostrand Avenue, well outside the borders of Jewish Crown Heights.

In 1978, the black leader Reverend Herb Daughtry had attempted to create a patrol to rival the Shmira, but after several months, the group, dubbed the Men of Crown Heights, dissipated, and blacks were forced to resort to pleading with city leaders for help. Help was a long time coming. Lubavitchers were able to argue that they had the right to protect their own streets, just as a homeowner has a right to protect his own backyard. That the majority of the perpetrators apprehended by the Shmira were black made sense to the Hasidim—it was the blacks who were doing the robbing and the shooting, not the Jews. To the astonishment of the black community, the city seemed to agree.

"In my meetings with the black community, I have spoken candidly about the fact that crime in their neighborhood is overwhelmingly committed by young blacks and is predominantly directly against the black citizens of the community," Mayor Ed Koch wrote in a letter to the *New York Times* in May 1987. The facts, he added, "do not justify the illegal acts of the Hasidic patrols, but the fear of black crime is nevertheless real."

In the same letter, Koch announced that he had found a point of consensus: Rabbi Josef B. Spielman, a leader of the Lubavitch community council, and Reverend Heron Sam, a black minister from Crown Heights, had agreed to form an integrated unit under the auspices of the NYPD. Reverend Sam had only one precondition: the Shmira had to hang up their uniforms and leave the streets of Crown Heights for good. "There's got to be an end to any kind of partisan patrols that exist in that community if there's going to be a joint patrol," he said. "That is part of the agreement. If that is held, I think we have a chance of success."

And so on a rainy evening at the tail end of August, off they went, Rabbi Spielman and Reverend Sam, sitting two astride in the bench seat of a rusting old Dodge sedan fitted out with a rack of official-looking police lights. The pair crawled carefully up and down the streets of Crown Heights—the standard-bearers of a new age of racial unity. They saw nothing. Or close to nothing. They claimed to be looking mostly for "potholes, broken street lights and abandoned vehicles," and that's what they found. They investigated a hit-and-run—the investigation was unsuccessful—and jotted down notes on cracks in the Brooklyn cement.

They were an odd pair, certainly. In a portrait of Spielman and Reverend Sam that ran in the *New York Times* two days later, it is a smiling Sam who has the wheel. Spielman, thickset and wide-faced, is looking on with what appears to be amusement. "There were no rooftop chases with helicopter gunships," Spielman later confided to reporters. He wasn't telling them anything they didn't know. The press had been tailing the Dodge sedan for hours. It was a hell of a story: a battered neighborhood, a strangely matched team of crime fighters, the vague possibility of violence.

In fact, the only people more enamored by the adventures of Spielman and Sam were the politicians, who used the occasion to pontificate grandly on the future of Crown Heights. "It's the first time you will see a Hasidic [sic] and a black riding in the same car together," announced Joan A. Gill, a Democratic district leader in the 43rd Assembly District. "I'm proud to see it happen." But Gill was wrong. Blacks and Jews had attempted once before to integrate the anticrime patrols—and the experiment had ended badly. In 1964, the Maccabees had taken onboard a handful of white Christian members and a pair of black Crown Heights residents, including David Simmons, a seven-and-a-half-foot-tall mechanic. "This is a community problem," Simmons said at the time, "and it affects both black and white."

Within a year, Simmons was gone, as were the other non-Lubavitcher members of the patrol. The problem had nothing to do with animosity—Simmons and the rest of the Maccabees got along just fine—and everything to do with differing goals. The primary mission of the Jewish anticrime organizations has always been to serve the Jewish community. Everything else was ancillary. Once black members caught on, they tended to flake away. For that reason, many Lubavitchers remained skeptical that an integrated patrol headed by Sam and Spielman would last longer than two months.

One of the skeptics was Israel Shemtov, a headstrong local rabbi. On August 29, the *New York Times* asked Shemtov if it was true that the Shmira members were prepared to call it quits. No, Shemtov scoffed. The Lubavitch patrols are "expanding, not disbanding." Even as Sam and Spielman were piloting that rusty Dodge around Crown Heights, a group of protesters was parading down Eastern Parkway, holding signs that read, "We want armed, trained vigilantes in our alleys, not you."

The protesters got their way. Soon, Spielman and Sam—like Simmons and the Maccabees—had stopped participating in the patrols, offering platitudes about a lack of support from the residents of the neighborhood. Their work ended up a footnote in the history of Central Brooklyn—a brief lull in the battle for Crown Heights. By 1988, Shemtov and the Shmira were back on the streets, bigger and stronger than ever.

Tina Haynes knew her assailant. Or if she didn't know him personally, she knew of him—had heard word of the thief who wandered from apartment to apartment, hunting for crack, a pistol shoved into his waistband. Later, the police would ID the shooter as Eban Robbins and charge him with the slaying of four Brooklyn residents. He would be caught attacking a gypsy-cab driver in East Flatbush, Robbins nearly shooting his own fingers off in the scuffle, at one point taking a chunk out of the cabbie's nose with his teeth. He would be known in the tabloids as the 9-mm Madman or the One-Gloved Killer, on account of the rubber glove he wore on his shooting hand, perhaps to keep the powder burn off his skin.

The police would explain that Robbins, who was thirty-two in 1993, had been shooting people since at least 1980, but he'd slipped out of the grasp of the cops, eventually enlisted with the army, and shipped out to Germany. He was arrested in 1982 and convicted of first-degree manslaughter, but he was paroled in 1988; by December of that year, he was back on the streets, this time packing a 9-mm pistol. All of this would come out in court, in press conferences, and in interviews attributed to "inside sources" at the New York City Police Department. But for the time being, Tina Haynes knew the guy only as "Kevin." And she knew to stay the hell out of his way.

In the early morning of August 12, 1993, Haynes was in the bathroom of an apartment at 1616 President Street in Crown Heights. The memory of the riots still hung over the row houses like a burial shroud. In 1992, a jury had given Lemrick Nelson a free pass; it would be several years before Nelson and Charles Price were indicted again, this time for violating Yankel Rosenbaum's civil rights. Violent crime was up. Drug use was up. The police were overwhelmed. Crown

Heights was bubbling over with crack fiends, and when vice broke up one den, the dealers simply moved to a different apartment, drew the blinds, and waited to move again.

The apartment at President Street belonged to two men, Floyd Moore and a guy nicknamed "Old Joe." Joe and Floyd didn't officially deal, but they did allow friends to smoke crack in the apartment, and occasionally, if they were in a good mood, they might trade sex for drugs. According to the police, around 2 a.m., Haynes was in the basement bathroom. Moore was a room away, a crack vial in one hand and a five-dollar bill in the other.

Robbins hit Moore first. He needed only one shot, the bullet entering Moore's skull and killing him instantly. When Haynes got out of the bathroom, she saw Moore slumped on the floor, a blossom of blood circling his head like a halo. She screamed. Robbins took no chances. He unloaded the rest of his clip in the direction of the bathroom, hitting Haynes seven times in the stomach, the arms, and the neck. But she kept approaching, her hands outstretched as if to catch the oncoming bullets.

When Robbins turned heel and ran, Haynes followed him out of the apartment, staggering up the stairs, clutching her stomach, her shirt and pants soaked with blood, her head on fire. She made it as far as the basement door, and then she dropped to her knees, now crawling hand over hand down the sidewalk of President Street, sucking the wet summer air, thinking she was dead for sure.

A few blocks away, the Lubavitcher rabbi named Israel Shemtov sat in the driver's seat of his Mercury Sable, idly spinning the AM dial on his car radio. Shemtov was fifty-three. He was an unlikely crime fighter: not much more than five feet tall, slender, and possessed of a spectacularly frazzled red beard, speckled with white, which had once earned him the nickname "The Red Baron."

For more than a decade, Shemtov had been patrolling Crown Heights, sometimes with an organized Hasidic safety patrol and other times on his own. His rap sheet was long and illustrious. His first arrest came in '83. The cops had showed up near 770 Eastern Parkway, looking for a Hasid who had allegedly ripped the mirror off a city school bus, and Shemtov was arrested for starting a riot. A few years later, he yanked a suspected mugger off a passing bicycle and beat the kid into the ground, allegedly with a hammer. In 1989, a Hasidic woman was slashed by a razor blade–wielding mugger, and Shemtov and his son, Mendel, pulled together a gang of men to track down the assailant. The Shemtovs found their man, and the Brooklyn DA charged the pair with assault. A grand jury failed to indict.

Samuel Schrage may have been the first Hasidic vigilante in Crown Heights, but Shemtov was the first to publicly revel in the role. Like all American folk heroes, he was a master of image management. Where other Hasids shirked press attention, he embraced it, regaling reporters from the *Post* and the *Daily News* with tales of bloody brawls and daring midnight takedowns.

He said he derived his strength from his rebbe, Menachem Mendel Schneerson, and from his God. He compared himself to Charles Bronson, circa *Death Wish*. "There will not be a crime in the neighborhood because they know they will be dead," he said. When reporters asked him whether he worried about being hurt, he shook his head. "A woman in the kitchen who cooks twenty good meals is going to have one little cut," he said. "It doesn't mean she stops cooking." When reporters asked if he owned a gun, he shrugged. He might have been carrying anything "from an Uzi to a handgun," but until he was asked for a permit, he wasn't going to confess to anything. He called Crown Heights a "war zone," and for decades, he fought toward an always distant peace. And when Israel Shemtov became too old to prowl the darkened corridors of Crown Heights by himself, he passed along the vigilante mantle to a new generation of Hasidic crime fighters, one led by the Hershkop brothers.

Now Shemtov heard the crack of a pistol, and, rubbing his fists against his eyes, he gunned the Sable down Carroll Street, running scenarios in his head: a domestic disturbance, a holdup gone wrong, a drug dealer, a couple of punks test-firing a stolen handgun. The streetlights quivered like broken disco balls overhead. He steered east, toward Utica Avenue, where two years earlier, a Guyanese boy had been crushed under a stone pillar, and reversed up Schenectady, his head hanging out the window, his yarmulke askew, his red hair mussed. At the corner of President Street, he saw a black woman inching toward him, her nails scraping the concrete. "I decided there wasn't enough time to wait for the police or ambulance," he would later say. With the help of an anonymous onlooker, Shemtov wrapped Haynes in a blanket and hustled her into the backseat of the Sable. She was moaning, clinging to consciousness, muttering nonsense. The Red Baron held his foot to the gas. Within minutes, he was at the front door of the Kingsbrook Jewish Medical Center. Haynes underwent three surgeries that night, but she survived, and the doctors credited her life to Shemtov, who became—for at least a few days—the most famous man in New York City.

The *New York Post* gave Shemtov all of the front page of its late-city edition and proclaimed August 12 "the day hate died." Shemtov was photographed bedside at Kingsbrook Jewish Medical Center, clutching Haynes's hand. "Outside of God, I owe my life to that man," Haynes said, her body wrapped in gauze and bandages. "He's a brave man who didn't hesitate one second to help me, even though he could have been shot himself." The *New York Times* interviewed Tina's mother, Dorothy Haynes-Martin, who said Shemtov was proof "that you can't judge all people and that you can't solve all problems by talking about it. He proved that actions really do speak louder than words." Tina Haynes remained in the hospital for weeks, recovering from her wounds. At some point, she made the acquaintance of a handsome young chemotherapy patient named Ernesto Ellis; when Ellis and Haynes were married, less than a year later, Rabbi Shemtov was invited to officiate at the wedding.

The man formerly derided as a headstrong vigilante received commendations from Mayor Dinkins—Shemtov had demonstrated "that what unites us is stronger than what divides us," Dinkins said—and by Brooklyn borough president Howard Golden. *Newsday* cautioned that New Yorkers "shouldn't make too much of this act" but said that "the kind of help Rabbi Israel Shemtov gave Tina Haynes last week can act as a powerful salve for the racial wounds of Crown Heights."

The events did seem freighted with symbolism. For one, as the press was fond of pointing out, the apartment where Robbins shot Moore and Haynes was remarkably close to the scene of the accident that had started the riots. And the timing lined up: The rioting had begun on August 19, 1991. Shemtov saved Haynes on August 12, 1993. Writing in the *Jewish Week*, reporter Steve Lipman predicted that Shemtov's actions, "exactly one week before the second anniversary of the Crown Heights riots, may hasten the healing of interracial relations in the troubled Brooklyn neighborhood and improve its image outside the borough." Shemtov was called an "angel," a superhero, and a "symbol of unity."

He was lauded for having taken an important first step in brokering a peace between the black community and the private Jewish security patrols. In the past, black leaders had complained—not at all unreasonably—that they were being targeted, harassed, and beaten by the "Jew police." Now a member of the "Jew police" had saved a member of the black community. As Rabbi Shemtov seemed to acknowledge in an interview in late August 1994, a kind of olive branch was being extended.

"Sometimes you have to be a vigilante," he said. "Sometimes you have to save a victim. Sometimes you just have to act to protect yourself and others." His words were a neat paraphrase of Ecclesiastes 3: "There is a time for everything, and a season for every activity under the heavens." And at that moment, after almost three decades of war, it was "a time to embrace and a time to refrain."

# 5

At five in the afternoon, Levi Huebner shut the last of the manila folders and wandered outside, where the air was sludgy and surprisingly sweet. He passed a gaggle of uniforms milling near the front door of the 7-1, and at the corner of Empire, he tipped his fedora down against the bright spring sun. May 22, 2008. For weeks, the phone had been ringing, blaring that three-note symphony at all hours of the day. Not that Huebner minded the work—he certainly wasn't in a position to turn any of it down—but the pace was murder. He was working now six days a week, morning to night, breaking only to eat, and spent most afternoons in front of his computer, compiling files, organizing his notes. In the mirror he saw blue creases under his eyes and an appalling gauntness in his cheeks.

He shook his head. Well, maybe it was to be expected. Crown Heights was a very different place from what it had been in the 1970s, when Huebner had first arrived in Brooklyn, enamored by the grand ideals of Chabad, by the mysticism of it all—by the promise that a tangled mass of mathematics and numerology and acts of *loving-kindness* could finally redeem the mess of the everyday world. That's how it had seemed to him, anyway, a *boychik* from California, born Jewish and raised Orthodox but not Hasidic.

As a kid, Huebner had run with a bad crowd. He didn't deny it. He was raised by his mother, who was a poet, and his stepfather, who was an artist and a professor at UCLA. Ann Rice was a family friend. His parents knew artists, writers, even a few members of the Symbionese Liberation Army. The whole crowd had milled around the kitchen of Huebner's childhood home, all of these hippies and beatniks and prognosticators; they drank beers and strummed guitars and talked about revolution. Huebner, meanwhile, was kicking around the streets of Oakland with a gun in his pocket. Did he ever have occasion to use the gun? When he was asked this question—and he was asked, by friends and journalists—he'd twist one hand through a strand of beard and smile. In the past, he'd say. All in the past.

Because in the mid-'70s, Huebner experienced his own revolution. Like thousands of other disaffected Jews, he had trekked east, to Crown Heights, to hear for himself firsthand the teachings of the grand rabbi, the rebbe, the "Oracle of Crown Heights." At first, Huebner crashed on couches and in grimy sublets, meeting in the evening with his fellow converts, many of them raised secular Jewish or in some cases without a religious education at all—all drawn by the centrifugal power of the rebbe. Suddenly, he had brothers and a mission, and a cause. He would have a hand in the redemption of mankind. Who could fail to see the beauty in that?

He *davened* ceaselessly. He attended classes and *minyans*, ten-man prayer groups. He married a woman named Suri, the daughter of a family of Eastern European immigrants—old world Chabadniks. For Huebner, the union offered a kind of validation, and an entree into the inner circles of Lubavitch life.

Suri, for her part, found Levi's newfound religious fervor endearing. She told her friends that she had never seen a man buy so many books. At the end of every week, as soon as Huebner had even a bit of pocket change, he'd walk straight to the bookstore on Kingston Avenue, returning with a new leather-bound tome, which he'd dutifully add to the already overflowing shelves.

Levi and Suri rented an apartment on Crown Street. Huebner was offered a job as a jeweler, and he quickly proved to be an exceptionally fine artisan. He acquired black suits, black fedoras, a closet full of polished black Oxford shoes. He slogged through the nine to five in Midtown Manhattan, returning via the number 2 train every evening to his growing family. For the first time in his life, Huebner was comfortable. He was happy. During the riots, while the rest of Crown Heights was up in arms, he calmly pulled the mattresses from the bed and propped them up against the windows and the door. He and Suri and the kids slept on the floor. When the noise didn't subside, Huebner walked out onto Kingston Avenue. He found his fellow Hasidim pressed shoulder to shoulder on the steaming asphalt, watching the storefronts burn.

Some counseled violence—an eye for an eye—but Huebner had a better idea. He'd been raised by hippies; he knew his way around a protest. So he led a few friends out to the middle of Eastern Parkway, which had been shut down by the police. "Listen," Huebner told his friends. "We're going to sit down in the street, and no matter what happens, we are not going to fight back. We are going to *sit*." He prayed that their resolve would be enough. Of course, as soon as the blacks started jeering, the guys around him lost their cool, and then everyone was fighting, throwing rocks and elbows and fists. Huebner had walked back home, disgusted.

It was one of the first times his faith in the power of prayer was tested. It was not the last. The death of the rebbe in 1994 had hit all of Crown Heights hard—it was said you could hear the wailing from heaven, beyond—but it hit the recent converts hardest of all. Because let's face it: a convert is drawn by a religious message but also by the charisma of the messenger. It was the rebbe, with his sharp blue eyes, who had convinced Huebner to believe. Without the rebbe, where would he turn for inspiration? He felt like a swimmer trapped in the shallows, pulled back and forth by the current, desperately feeling with his toes for purchase.

In the end, he muddled through. They all did. They put down their heads and accepted that they were being tested—that the bleak days would eventually be replaced by days of light. But it was a strange new world they'd inherited. No longer was their neighborhood a fortress, its hard stone shell protecting the Hasidim from the perils of the secular world. The walls were collapsing. To the east, you had the yuppie onslaught—the writers, the artists, and the Web workers, priced out of Park Slope and drawn to the proud stone balustrades of the row houses off Eastern Parkway. More of them showed up every year. Rents were spiraling upward. Even the cost of food was jacked up. It was ironic, when you thought about it: The Lubavitchers had remained in Crown Heights in the sixties and the seventies, long after the other whites had fled. In 2008, many of those same cowards wanted back in—and it was going to be the yuppies, not the blacks or the West Indians, who finally did the Lubavitchers in.

Twenty years ago, a Hasid could find a job at a grocery store on Kingston Avenue and raise his whole family on the proceeds. Real estate back then was cheap. So was the cost of living. The rebbe was safely ensconced on his throne; hardly anyone—save for the *shluchim*—had left Crown Heights. Now you couldn't even support yourself on less than 25K a year, and plenty of people were decamping for gentler shores. Who could blame them? Compared to the suburbs of upstate New York, the place was a ghetto.

The smartest of the young men from the community were signing up at the local community colleges, in hopes of landing a profitable job in Manhattan, New Jersey, or even California. They were marrying later—enjoying their lives while it was still theirs. Huebner's own children prided themselves on being "global citizens." One son had attended school in Argentina and moved down to Florida, and, hey—Huebner was proud of him. His son wasn't constrained. He was alive. He was plugged in.

In fact, it was rare these days that you visited a home in Crown Heights that wasn't littered with laptops, desktops, BlackBerrys. The *rabbonim* had spent so many centuries explaining how to keep the secular world at bay, and now here it came, rushing in at a gazillion bytes a minute—Facebook, YouTube, MySpace, iTunes, whatever.

To Huebner, many of these changes were natural ones—he figured he was observing not just the evolution of a community, but the evolution of the Chabad movement itself. What he hated—what really made his blood bubble—was the infighting that had consumed 770 Eastern Parkway since the rebbe's death. There was no leadership on the council, no leadership from the *rabbonim*. People were just flailing, looking for someone to lead them out of the morass and toward the promised land. A *vacuum*. He had heard that word a lot recently, and to Huebner, it made sense. Not that anyone could fill the rebbe's shoes. But it was 2008, fourteen years after the rebbe had succumbed to that final stroke, and the feuding was worse than ever.

Exhibit A: This ridiculous spat between the Shomrim and the Shmira. Back in the '70s, there had been only one anticrime patrol, a group called the Shmira, which operated under the auspices of the Jewish Community Council. Huebner had even signed up with the organization, taken a few spins through the neighborhood in the passenger seat of someone else's busted-up sedan. He understood the thrill involved—a thrill that had to do with danger and darkened streets but also the simpler, more understated thrill of serving one's community. Huebner had been proud to strap on that two-way radio. He'd been proud to answer distress calls. He'd been proud to visit a friend's home and be able to point at the Shmira sticker on the refrigerator, lean over toward his host, and tell him, "You know, I belong to the Shmira." And his friends would nod appreciatively, pat his back, and express their thanks. "Well, someone's got to do it," they'd say, "and I'm glad it's you."

But the real world eventually caught up to Huebner. He had a job to do, a family to raise, children to put through yeshiva. So he'd cut back on his tours of duty, putting himself forward in a strictly *on-call* capacity. Still, he'd kept in touch with his friends on the patrol, and he'd followed with a good deal of interest the evolution of the Shmira. The Crown Heights Shmira patrol—formerly known as the Maccabees, and redubbed the Shomrim in the years after the riot of '91, in order to better integrate with the other Shomrim organizations that were then springing up in Williamsburg, Flatbush, and Borough Park.

And then in the '90s, the Shomrim itself had split apart, making Crown Heights the only Hasidic community in the world with *two* anticrime organizations. In public, Huebner claimed not to know the details of the feud; if he did know, he never said. Kept it to himself. Still, in Jewish Crown Heights, there were two official versions of the split, and most people were inclined to believe one or the other. Which version you backed depended on whether you were a Shmira

man or a Shomrim man. And Huebner was a Shmira man, through
and through.


It was all a failed putsch, the Shmira said. It came down to bruised
egos—to grown Lubavitch men acting like little yeshiva boys. During
the '90s, community anticrime efforts had been led by a small circle of
Lubavitchers, which included Yanky Prager, Aron Hershkop, and his
brother Gedalia Hershkop. The men were all roughly the same age—
in their twenties and thirties at the time the feud began.

Gedalia Hershkop was the largest. He wore his dark hair long and
shaggy. His little brother Aron was smaller than Gadi but also big
through the shoulders and the chest. He had buttery brown hair and
soft, overwide eyes. He kept his beard trimmed closer to his chin.
Prager was shorter than both Hershkops and also rounder; he often
caught shit from the rest of the Shomrim guys for being overweight.
"How are you going to catch anyone with that paunch hanging off
your waist?" they'd ask with a smile. But Prager turned out to be fear-
less. The darkest of alleys was no obstacle; neither was the brawniest
of suspected felons. He enjoyed the pursuit—enjoyed playing hero. In
a Polaroid picture later posted to the Internet by the Shomrim boys,
Prager is shown pinning a black kid to the ground in some sort of
wrestling hold. Prager, dressed in a maroon shirt—his glasses still
perched perfectly straight on the bridge of his nose—is snarling, not
unhappily. His tongue hangs out of the side of his mouth. The black
kid looks terrified.

They were close, the Shomrim. They played poker together, drank
together, patrolled together. They carried their radios everywhere
they went. Showed off their blue Shomrim uniforms, their Shomrim
police-style patches, and their Shomrim squad cars, obtained for a
few thousand and trussed up by Aron Hershkop, who was a master
wrench. Even more than Huebner, the Hershkops and Prager found a
deep reward in defending their fellow Jews against the outside world.
They were all of the same disposition: stubborn, fiery, self-righteous.

At least two of them already had criminal records. In April 1994,
Aron Hershkop and Prager—then seventeen and twenty-one,
respectively—had been arrested at Beth Israel Medical Center in

downtown Manhattan. Along with Aron's eldest brother, Jack, Aron and Prager had apparently attempted to fight their way into the room where Rebbe Mendel Schneerson was recovering from a massive stroke. The alleged victim, Chaim Halberstam, had required stitches to close a cut over his left eye. So, yes, back then, the three men had even fought together. But after the adrenaline rush of the riots had subsided—and after the rebbe was dead and gone—the Hershkops had decided to take the reins of the organization. They'd allegedly brooked no dissent: you were either in or out. And plenty of members were out. The Hershkops had picked up their radios and dispatch gear, moved their office down to south Crown Heights, and dubbed themselves the Shomrim. This, anyway, was the Shmira party line. It cast the Hershkops as sore losers—as power hogs, unable to share the duties of running a neighborhood patrol.

But ask the current Shomrim members, and you'd get a very different answer. A tale of a botched safe robbery in Montreal, deep in snowy Canada, 370-plus miles from the row houses of Brooklyn. The story went like this: A few Lubavitchers had been renting cars up in Montreal, scraping off the serial numbers, and driving them back to New York, where they'd be repainted and resold. Eventually, they'd decided to get a little more bold, ratcheted up the stakes. They settled on an office complex at an industrial park in Saint-Laurent, west of Montreal.

On the evening of January 10, 1999, three men—known to the Montreal police as Samuel Green, Yani Yota, and Chaim Stern—had allegedly made their way into one of the buildings and attempted to throw a loaded safe out the window. Unfortunately, the safe door had not opened—maybe the safe wasn't thrown hard enough—and the three would-be robbers screamed out of Saint Laurent with their tails between their legs. A witness called in a report, and the authorities put out the Canadian equivalent of an APB; on January 11, two Montreal officers had pulled over a broken-down van, tossed it for evidence, found masks and gloves inside, and arrested the driver and the passengers—Stern, Yota, and Green.

All three men might have been found guilty, but the witness had not actually seen the safe go out the window—he'd only heard the crash—and the prosecutors had trouble concretely connecting the suspects to the robbery. In the end, Green pled guilty to breaking and entering; he paid a relatively small fine. Yota and Stern were released. It sounded simple enough: idiot criminals who'd gotten lucky. The world was full of those, right? But to the Shomrim, the botched robbery in Montreal was proof of something much more sinister. Chaim Stern was actually Shmira member David Rogatsky, they said. Moreover, they believed that Rogatsky and Prager had been in on the safe robbery together—Prager was there the night of the botched robbery, but he'd managed to escape the net cast by the police and return safely to Crown Heights.

In the early months of 1999, Gadi and Aron Hershkop reportedly convened a meeting of the Crown Heights Shomrim. They demanded the ouster of Rogatsky. Prager refused, and together with his friend Yossi Stern, he formed—or re-formed, because the name had been used by anticrime organizations in the past—the Crown Heights Shmira. A year later, in 2000, Yanky Prager pled guilty in a New York Court to threatening to burn down Aron Hershkop's home. Aron Hershkop—Prager's old poker buddy, his old brother in arms—was now his mortal enemy.

Since the days of the Baal Shem Tov, Hasidic culture has comprised myth, happenstance, and legend. As Elie Wiesel hints in *Souls on Fire*, one could make the argument that much of Hasidism is nothing *but* a series of stories, most brightly and boldly told:

> To the disciple who had transposed his verbal teachings to paper, the Master said: "There is nothing of me in your pages; you thought you heard what I didn't say." Also: "I said one thing, you heard another, and you wrote a third." For the Baal Shem, imagination gains in impact with each passing moment. Until finally its power is perhaps greater than that of any testimony. The real and the imagined, one like the other, are part of history; one is its shell, the other its core.

In many ways, the story of the Shmira and the Shomrim feud came to outgrow fact, testimony, and verbal record. It acquired a mythic quality—a house divided. Former friends, turned against each other. A story older than Shakespeare, as old as the Bible. Was any of it true? Yes and no.

Prager had certainly threatened Aron Hershkop. And Rogatsky was certainly a veteran member of the Crown Heights security patrols, as was his brother, Eli Rogatsky. And yet it seems much more unlikely that the safe robbery had played out in exactly the way the Shomrim boys described.

For one, the Montreal police had obtained U.S. passports and fingerprints from all three would-be robbers—and the passports checked out. Unless the documents were forged, Yota, Stern, and Green were who they said they were. Moreover, all charges were eventually dropped against Chaim Stern—even if Rogatsky was playing dress-up, he was not a convicted felon, as the Shomrim alleged. Still, the Shomrim persisted, and the Shmira denied—it went on like this for years. By 2008, the feud was a decade old. No resolution was in sight.

Late on the evening of December 27, 2007, Huebner had been awakened by the sound of his cell phone skittering across the bedside table. He considered not answering at all. But then he started to feel strangely guilty—what if one of his kids were hurt?—so he opened the handset and grunted, listened. "They've got a couple of the *bochurim* down at the 77th Precinct," his friend had told him. "They could use your help." Now Huebner was really awake, and he weaved through the darkened bedroom, matching a suit and a pair of pants to his body and dashing out the door into the heavy darkness. At the precinct house he signed in at the front desk and demanded to be taken to his new clients, Jonathan Gorichnick and Motti Cohen, who were sitting in a holding cell, tousled and a little bruised and obviously terrified.

Taking their cue, the catching detectives began to rattle off the long list of possible charges against the two *bochurim*, which included assault in the third degree, menacing in the third degree, and harassment in the first degree. For what? Huebner demanded. For what is all of this? The cops, smirking as they talked, explained that Cohen and Gorichnick had been arrested earlier that night, following a scuffle at the yeshiva dormitory at 749 Eastern Parkway. Cohen and Gorichnick were in the middle of it, the detectives said—they'd apparently launched some sort of ambush against the Shomrim. Was Huebner familiar with the Shomrim? Yes, Huebner said. I am very much familiar with the Shomrim. He glanced at Cohen, who was slumped in the corner of the cell, examining his hands. Huebner felt himself on the brink of some gigantic outburst, and quietly, he reeled himself back in. He and the Cohen family went way back—he'd attended his first Shabbos dinner in Crown Heights with the elder Cohen—and he knew Motti to be sensible, alert, and totally incapable of being a party to this kind of nonsense. As for Gorichnick, well, Huebner had only met him a couple of times, but he doubted that he was capable of assault.

"I'm getting them out of here," Huebner said, finally. And he did. He snatched up Cohen and Gorichnick right before they were to be shipped to central booking, where they would have been surrounded by real criminals—dealers, robbers, rapists. Yes, Levi Huebner had saved them from that indignity. His process had included some fine lawyering—in his own humble opinion—plus the production of a pair of passports to stop the kids from going rabbit and a little bit of wheedling, which Huebner was not above. Not this time.

During the next few weeks, he had set about turning the tables on the *boychiks* of the Crown Heights Shomrim. First, he paid a visit to 749 and interviewed several *bochurim* who had been present on the night of December 27, 2007. From that group, he found four *real* victims—Elkon Gurfinkel, Yaakov Shatz, Gavriel Braunstein, and Schneur Rotem. He arranged for the kids to file a complaint at the 7-7, and then he followed up with Brian Duffy, the young officer who had caught the case. Supporters of the Shomrim would later argue that Huebner had never really identified himself as a lawyer. He was just Levi Huebner—proud Lubavitcher, Hebrew and Yiddish translator, friend of the *bochurim*, friend of the police.

But not even Huebner could have predicted the maelstrom that descended on Crown Heights in the spring of 2008—a disaster big enough to almost drown out all memory of the 749 assault. It began on mid-April, a little more than three months after Duffy placed the six Shomrim members under arrest. The alleged victim was twenty-year-old Andrew Charles, a sophomore at Kingsborough Community College and the son of Moses Charles, a longtime cop in the 70th Precinct, down near Borough Park. The media had picked up on that relationship right away and for good reason: any case involving a relative of a police officer—even a distant relative, even a cousin, seventeen times removed—was guaranteed to get fast-tracked by the NYPD and treated with the utmost sincerity by the pooh-bahs at City Hall. And true to form, by April 15, Andrew Charles was a media celebrity—a walking, talking example of the latest blast of racial tension in Crown Heights.

You had to hand it to him: Charles certainly had his story straight. He knew how to talk to the media, how to rile up a crowd. "Every day I attempt to function normally [but] it's impossible because there is so much confusion as result of this incident," he told a gaggle of demonstrators in May. He begged the cops to act. To bring down the Hasidic anticrime patrols. Even his mother, Wendy Craigg, got into the act. "I can't even function," Ms. Craigg said. "My child's life was almost taken from him. Where are the police now?"

According to Charles, on the afternoon of April 14, he'd been walking with a friend near Albany Avenue, on the fringes of the Lubavitch settlement. It was late afternoon, the weather cooperating, the sky overhead smudged a black-blue. Up toward Eastern Parkway—and again, this was all in Charles's telling, which had an action movie feel to it— Charles had been approached by two men. Both men were wearing yarmulkes. There had been a stare-down. Maybe an exchange of a few choice words. One of the Jews had apparently pulled a canister of Mace from his pocket and blasted Charles in the face. Charles felt the spray searing the soft skin under his eyelids, and he collapsed to the pavement.

Before he could haul himself up again, a black GMC Envoy SUV barreled down Albany, and a third kid hopped out, this one allegedly wielding a nightstick. Charles said he took several blows around the back. He had limped down to Kings County Hospital, registered a report with the police, and given the requisite interviews to the tab-loids, taking pains to note that his attackers were Jewish. And thus, for the first time in decades, had the residents of Brooklyn become aware that there were teams of Hasidic vigilantes working the streets of Crown Heights. Driving cop cars, SUVs, scooters. Wielding night-sticks, pepper spray. "We will not tolerate vigilantism," Brooklyn councilwoman Letitia James announced. "I urge them"—the patrol members, presumably—"to be regulated and licensed and trained by the local police. This way, you can avoid conflict and avoid these types of incidents."

That night, April 14, 2008, the manhunt had begun. A helicopter hummed over Crown and President and Carroll streets, and the cops worked apartment to apartment, house to house, alley to alley. They slow-crawled their Crown Vics up and down Kingston. And just to make sure everyone got the message, they parked a giant command post near Eastern Parkway. They had two targets. One was Menachem Ezagui, a Shmira member and the owner of a black GMC Envoy. The other was a Hasidic EMT named Yitzhak Shuchat, also linked to Shmira.

But Shuchat, tipped off that the cops were hot on his tail, had booked it upstate and then crossed the border into Canada; from Canada, he took a flight to Israel. The rumor mill churned. The *Daily News* ran a report alleging that Shuchat had once been in an auxil-iary NYPD unit at the 77th Precinct, but that he'd been discharged five years earlier for undisclosed reasons. Meanwhile, the Shomrim claimed that Shuchat had been aided in his escape by his pals on the Crown Heights Shmira. Whatever the case, Shuchat was gone. He never returned to Brooklyn.

In late May, Yossi Stern appeared on the NPR program *News & Notes* to discuss the Andrew Charles incident. The appearance was a notable one, not least because Hasidim often avoid speaking to secular media outlets, for fear of drawing unwanted attention to the commu-nity. Stern was full-throated and often even prickly in his defense of the Crown Heights Shmira: he admitted to host Farai Chideya that Shuchat was a member of the group but maintained that the fight had been nothing more than a scuffle between two groups of boys. "Here is one incident," he said, "that's an ugly incident, where a Jew is being charged for hitting a black boy and that has to be addressed not in the media, it should be addressed in the courts of New York, and each side should have their day in court and resolve the issue."

He continued,

I do know that there is a person of interest that [the police] do want to talk to, and he is a member of our patrol. He is also a member of the NYPD auxiliary force, and we all know who he is. He is a nice kid that lives in the neighborhood. If in fact he was involved in this situation, then he should be punished if there was a crime committed. The Crown Heights Shmira clearly does not condone violence of any sort, to anyone. We are only the eyes and ears for the police, we act as a passive patrol, and we have been doing so for 40 years. We have hundreds of members that volunteer in patrolling the streets, or responding to our hotline to all sorts of domestic situations, and emergencies. We assist the police in many situations.

Stern told Chideya that the Shmira would welcome black recruits and even recited his home phone number on the air. "Contact me," he said. "We can set up a meeting." Still, the mood in Crown Heights remained tense. On May 14, a sixteen-year-old Hasid named Alon Sherman had been ripped off his bicycle and beaten by a pair of black teens, possibly in retaliation for the Charles incident. Lubavitchers paraded up and down Eastern Parkway, hefting signs that read "Jewish blood is not cheap," or "Every Jew a .22." A police observation tower—a "cop in a box"—went up on Eastern Parkway. Officers from ten precincts were asked to pull double duty on Kingston, and unmarked police cars were assigned to tail Lubavitch school buses to and from yeshiva. Crown Heights had begun to resemble, in the words of a *Times* reporter, an "armed camp."

Two months earlier, everything between the Shmira and the city had been copacetic. The police hadn't exactly invited the Shmira to join the ranks of the 7-0, but Eliot Spitzer, then the attorney general of New York, had presented the group with the Neighborhood Watch 2000 Award of Excellence. Michael Bloomberg had mailed the Shmira an official commendation, praising the members for "their continued good work" and noting that "we cannot depend on government alone to meet the challenges facing our communities." In 2003, the Shmira had even won an award from the Caribbean community for "excellent community service."

Now, the city was ratcheting up the pressure on the Shmira. The Brooklyn DA, Charles Hynes, empaneled an investigative grand jury to look into the Charles assault. "You can't have a group, whether it's the Bloods, Crips or Shmira, acting like vigilantes," Hynes told a reporter for the *Jewish Week*. A week later, Huebner and a lawyer named George Farkas, who had worked extensively in the Lubavitch community, met with Hynes, in an attempt to broker some sort of deal for Shuchat. But Hynes demurred. As an anonymous city employee told the *Daily News*, Charles was "first Maced and then hit by someone with a nightstick. It is not a misdemeanor assault no matter how you cut it."

If only they could make an arrest. Many politicians said that the Lubavitch leadership was helping shield the Shmira from prosecution. At a press conference in May, Councilman Charles Barron urged the Shmira to surrender Shuchat and any other involved parties to the police. The police are quick to investigate crimes allegedly committed by blacks, Barron pointed out. But it had been a month since Andrew Charles had been clobbered, and the NYPD had made absolutely no progress.

Officially, the police were hedging their bets. Speaking to the *Times* in May, Police Commissioner Raymond Kelly acknowledged the existence of the Shmira but stopped short of condemning the organization. "There has been talk of a group that is not officially sanctioned or recognized. But that there is a group of young males in that community that do patrol. If that is the case, we certainly frown on that. There is a group there that is recognized, that we work cooperatively with. Those are the groups we want to work with and continue to work with." He meant the Shomrim—at the time the "only recognized" freelance patrol organization in Crown Heights.

# 6

In the long weeks and months after the trial of the six Shomrim members had concluded, many in the Lubavitch community would marvel that the case had made it to a secular court at all. Did it not go against the Torah? Were there not holy laws in place preventing one Jew from sullying the reputation of another Jew before a goyish judge? Was there not one rabbi in Crown Heights who could prevent this *Hillul Hashem*—this desecration of God's name? Certainly, it was true that even twenty years earlier, the feud would never have been allowed to become so acrimonious. Twenty years earlier, the feud might not have started at all. Back then, the leaders of the Shomrim and the Shmira would have quickly been told by the rebbe to make nice. Either that or representatives for both patrols would have argued their cases in front of a *beis din*—a rabbinical court—and politely accepted the ruling, no matter which way it fell.

The *beis din* is not a concept unique to Hasidism. Rabbinical courts have been a part of Jewish culture for centuries, from the temples of Jerusalem to the battered outposts of the Diaspora. The words *beis din* translate literally from the Hebrew as "house of judgment." Most rabbinical courts consist of three rabbis, who are given authority to issue a ruling in line with halacha, or Jewish law. (The word *halacha* is derived from the root "to walk" or "to go," which yields some hint of the importance of halacha in Jewish culture—it is not only a law or a collection of judicial rulings but the very way in which a Jew moves through the world.)

In centuries past, the findings of the *beis din* were binding above all other laws, and *dayans*, or judges, could rule on everything from minor squabbles to allegations of murder; in most of the ultra-Orthodox world, the rulings of the *beis din* remain sacrosanct. The court decides matters of marriage and divorce, helps oversee *koshering* operations in the community, and resolves small-scale spats.

Under the dictates of the halacha, a Jew must first attempt to adjudicate any dispute internally, usually with the help of a rabbinical council. If he fails to do so and instead approaches a secular court first, he has technically committed the sin of *mesira*, or "informing"; he will henceforth be known as a *mosser*. A snitch. The bearer of a scarlet letter.

And yet Lubavitchers, like most Americans, have become extremely litigious in recent years, and in Crown Heights alone, dozens of cases that would have once been handled by a *beis din* regularly spill into secular courts. Central Brooklyn has its own cottage industry of lawyers—most of them secular Jews—which serves the members of the Lubavitch court, and Lubavitch news services regularly report on community cases that have reached state, supreme, and appellate courts. Partly, this is a consequence of the widening reach of the Chabad movement, which puts Lubavitchers in ever greater contact with nonreligious Jews or Christians and opens the doors to litigation with parties beyond the walls of the settlement. Partly, it is a matter of the vacuum left in the wake of the passing of the Rebbe and the partisan bickering that has reached even the bench of the *beis din*.

And partly, it is a matter of precedent.

Asked to justify his presence before a secular judge, a Lubavitch litigant will often cite the case against Barry Gourary, the grandson of the sixth Lubavitcher rebbe, Yosef Yitzchak Schneersohn, and the nephew of the seventh Lubavitcher rebbe, Menachem Mendel Schneerson. In 1950, when Yosef Yitzchak Schneersohn was felled by a heart attack, many community leaders had assumed that the mantle of grand rabbi would be passed to Gourary, who had served for decades as a trusted assistant and aide in the Lubavitch court. Yosef Yitzchak Schneersohn was rumored to have hinted as much. Years earlier, the sixth Lubavitcher rebbe had reportedly blessed Gourary with the hope "that this child grow to be the greatest of his brothers, and stand firmly on the same basis on which his grandfather is standing." Schneersohn asked that God "grant that he tread the same path that was boldly trodden by my holy forebears, for in his veins flows holy blood that is bequeathed from a father to his son, to his grandson, and to his great-grandson."

The lineage, in other words, would be writ in blood: from father to son, or from grandfather to grandson. But by 1951, Menachem Mendel Schneerson had showed himself to be a more charismatic leader than Gourary—he was also an especially deft diviner of Hasidic theology—and following a year of mourning and prayer, he took his place at the head of the Chabad Lubavitch movement. Gourary, a graduate of Brooklyn College, eventually moved to Montclair, New Jersey, and found a job as a management consultant. For several decades, Gourary had little contact with his uncle. But he often visited his mother and father, who had remained in Crown Heights, in a third-floor apartment above the shul at 770 Eastern Parkway.

In 1984—driven perhaps by revenge or simply fiscal necessity— Gourary began removing hundreds of volumes from the main Chabad library at 770 Eastern Parkway. He took old books and new ones— essays on Lubavitch theology; the testimony of past rebbes; histories of Hasidism; biblical exegeses. He brought the books back to his home in New Jersey, compiled a computerized catalogue of the rarer volumes, and sold a stack of texts to various dealers; in the end, he made $186,000. Several years later, in an interview with the scholar Jerome Mintz, Gourary claimed that Chaya Schneerson, his aunt—and the wife of the seventh Lubavitcher rebbe—had given him permission to take the books:

> In 1984, my mother and my aunt had reached an accommodation on the library. They were the two heirs. My aunt had been depressed by grandfather's death. She said: "I'm not going to

read those books. Why don't you take what you want?". . . I took the things that had no emotional value for the movement to sell them.

But the volumes did have great value to the Lubavitch movement, as Gourary soon discovered. Over the centuries, Hasidic courts traditionally compile great libraries of their central texts and treatises, which are passed from one rebbe to the next. In the early twentieth century, Soviet authorities had confiscated the Lubavitch library; the Soviets offered to sell it back to the Lubavitchers, but Rebbe Yosef Yitzchak Schneersohn was unable to meet the terms of the ransom.

In 1925, Schneersohn opted—with the help of several wealthy backers in the United States—to purchase instead the private library of a man named Shmuel Wiener, who had at one time served as the head of the Asiatic museum in Leningrad. When the Nazis began their march across Europe, Schneersohn fretted that the new library would suffer the same fate as the old. In 1939, in a last-minute bid to stave off disaster, he wrote a letter relinquishing control of the library to Agudas Chassidei Chabad, the Crown Heights–based organization that ran the Lubavitch empire.

"I have no apartment, and I find myself living with friends with my entire family in one room; consequently, I have no space for the books which Agudas Chabad loaned me for study," Schneersohn wrote. "I would be pleased if Agudas Chabad were to take these books back."

The ploy was successful—the letter was passed along to the U.S. State Department, and much of the library was spirited out of Poland in a diplomatic pouch. Unfortunately for Barry Gourary, Schneersohn's letter cast some doubt on whether the books belonged to the rebbe and his direct descendants or to the Lubavitch leadership.

In 1986, Agudas Chassidei Chabad filed a suit in civil court, seeking to block the sales of future volumes from the Lubavitch library. "These books were not taken for sentimental reasons, but because [Gourary] wanted money. Some people rob banks, and some steal books," Lubavitch spokesman Yehuda Krinsky said. "He's a thief, an outright thief." The Lubavitchers were chastised by other Hasidim, who argued that the squabble over the books should be settled—as was custom—by a rabbinical court. To bring suit in a civil court, in front of the media and the goyim, was to embarrass all in the Hasidic world.

"Lubavitch Hasidim don't want to go to a [rabbinical court]. They just want to go to a [secular court]," Jacob Cohen, a virulent critic of the Chabad movement, told Jerome Mintz. Cohen called the decision of the Lubavitch leadership a "desecration" and argued that "anybody who goes to a non-Jewish court for Jewish matters is desecrating God's name."

The Lubavitchers, for their part, argued that in the case of the library, a civil suit was a necessary evil. The Shulhan Arukh, or the code of Jewish law, forbids a Jew from taking a case before "heathen judges" unless the other litigant is unlikely to abide by the ruling of the *beis din*. For instance, an ultra-Orthodox Jewish businessman who has been defrauded by a Christian businessman would not be bound to present his case before a group of rabbis. Instead, he could—and indeed probably should—proceed directly to a secular court.

The Lubavitch leadership worried that Gourary, who had long ago abandoned the Hasidic lifestyle, would be unlikely to hand over the volumes on the basis of a *beis din* ruling alone. Furthermore, Gourary was in 1985 in the *active* process of selling off the library. If he was permitted to continue—if Agudas Chassidei Chabad waited around for a ruling that was duly ignored—the books would be scattered into the hands of dozens of different collectors. They would be impossible to retrieve.

In the spring of 1985, the rebbe went public with allegations that Gourary was looting the sacred library of Lubavitch, going so far as to call the missing books "bombs," which would detonate unless they were immediately returned to their rightful owners.

Gourary certainly didn't do himself any favors. He continued to maintain that about a third of the books he had taken were not sacred and were actually secular texts. "Grandfather was a collector and he enjoyed collecting," he explained. "Some [books] were sacred and some were not. Books that I had taken were far from sacred in the Jewish sense—the Old Testament printed by missionaries, with notes by priests in beautiful handwriting."

He was also quoted as saying that Chabad had "acquired many characteristics of a cult." Although he told Jerome Mintz that he had never been interested in the job of rebbe, the library case "reopened"—in Mintz's phraseology—"old wounds that had existed since the death of the old rebbe in 1950." Gourary lashed out at his uncle, noting that at "one time, Chabad was concerned with joyful worship of God." No longer:

> Nowadays the group is primarily interested in proselytizing. My uncle organized the outreach movements, and some of this is good and some is bad. He became power hungry. He began to measure his achievements. After a while he began to encourage anyone who would treat him as the Messiah.

These were incendiary charges, and Gourary quickly found himself the target of threats and intimidation. A strange car attempted to run his daughter off the road, and a group of thugs broke into his parents' residence at 770 Eastern Parkway, leaving his mother with a fractured hand, nose, and palate. (Community leaders blamed the attack on Hanna Gourary on a deranged man, who they claimed had since escaped to Israel.) "My uncle never said anything about it, and they took this as a sign of approval," Gourary said later. "Three weeks later, they started the case against us."

In the fall of 1985, District Court judge Charles Sifton ruled that the library ownership issue would be resolved by bench trial. Agudas Chassidei Chabad, which alleged that the books were the legal property of the Chabad Hasidic movement, was the plaintiff; Barry Gourary and his mother, Hanna Gourary, were the defendants. The Gourarys issued a counterclaim, arguing that the books removed from the library—along with some of the volumes that remained at 770— were the legal property first of Yosef Yitzchak Schneersohn and now of Barry and his mother.

News of the trial consumed the Jewish settlement in Crown Heights. Every day, the courtroom swelled with Lubavitch spectators, the men assembled in neat rows in the front of the gallery and the women in the back. Because so many Lubavitchers wished to watch the proceedings, a lottery system was devised by the leadership on Eastern Parkway—the winners would be ferried to and from Crown Heights in a school bus.

As Jerome Mintz noted in *Hasidic People*, there was much more at stake than the fate of the library, "a precious (if little used) archive." There was also the issue of the rebbe's authority, which might be seen as greatly diminished if the defendants were awarded the decision. Schneersohn had lectured regularly and loudly about the missing books; his Hasidim believed that God himself wished the whole of the library restored to the rightful hands of Agudas Chassidei Chabad.

"Gourary's contention of familial rights was a poisonous thorn threatening the Rebbe and the well-being of the community," Mintz wrote. "Gourary's actions could undermine Chabad and retard the spread of Yiddishkeit," or the Jewish way of life. In this way, Judge Sifton was seen by Lubavitchers as presiding over not a secular problem but a divine struggle: the pretender versus the rightful king. A win for the plaintiffs would be proof that God was on the side of the Chabadniks.

The Agudas Chassidei Chabad case was relatively simple: a rebbe's library traditionally belonged to his Hasidim and to the movement at large. Yosef Yitzchak Schneersohn himself accepted this truth, the organization's lawyers said. As evidence, the plaintiffs cited three letters: the 1939 note that signed over the collection to Agudas Chassidei Chabad; a missive to Rabbi Israel Jacobsen in Brooklyn, reiterating that the library belonged to the Chabad movement; and a request mailed in 1946 to the scholar Alexander Marx, requesting Marx's help in getting the remainder of the Lubavitch library to Crown Heights. At the time, many volumes were still in Poland, and Schneersohn evidently thought that Marx—a respected historian, librarian, and translator—would be able to convince the U.S. State Department to take action on behalf of Chabad.

"In order that the State Department should work energetically to locate these manuscripts and books in order to return them to their owners, the State Department needs to understand that these manuscripts and books are great religious treasures, a possession of the nation, which have historical and scientific value," Schneersohn wrote.

He continued,

> Therefore, I turn to you with a great request, that as a renowned
> authority on the subject, you should please write a letter to the
> State Department to testify on the great value of these manu-
> scripts and books for the Jewish people in general and particu-
> larly for the Jewish community of the United States to whom
> this great possession belongs.

The Gourarys acknowledged the veracity of the letter to Marx,
but they claimed that the letter itself was a necessary lie on the part
of the rebbe, who knew that his request would not be honored unless
the retrieval of the library was seen as important to the whole of the
Hasidic world. Sifton duly refuted this claim. "It does not make much
sense that a man of the character of the sixth rebbe would, in the circumstances, mean something different than what he says, that library
was to be delivered to the plaintiff for the benefit of the community."

On January 6, 1987, Sifton rendered his verdict:

> The conclusion is inescapable that the library was not held by the
> Sixth Rebbe at his death as his personal property, but had been
> delivered to plaintiff to be held in trust for the benefit of the reli-
> gious community of Chabad Chasidism.

The counterclaim against Agudas Chassidei Chabad was dismissed.
The defendants, Sifton wrote in his ruling, had no rights to the library.
Gourary filed a cursory appeal, but the appeal was denied, and in
1987, Chabad headquarters dispatched an armored car to pick up the
missing books from Gourary's New Jersey home.

In Crown Heights, news of the ruling was greeted with a daylong
celebration. The NYPD helped cordon off the pavement in front of
770 Eastern Parkway, and jugs of vodka and soda were quaffed. Later
in the day, the rebbe himself marched into the basement shul and
joyously linked Sifton's ruling to the 1798 release of Rabbi Schneur
Zalman, the first rebbe of Chabad, who had been confined to a
tsarist prison for allegedly supporting the Turks in their war against
the Russians. On being freed from prison, Schneerson pointed out,

Zalman had redoubled his outreach efforts—and now Schneerson, on the day of the emancipation of the Chabad library, would widen the reach of the Lubavitch movement.

"We will spread more Yiddishkeit," he said. "We will publish these writings and we will start more Chabad houses. . . . The obstacles we have faced have been overcome. They are no longer obstacles. They show us how far we can go in our devotion. They show us how hard we must work."

In the end, the implications of the library trial were felt in every sector of Chabadnik life. Mintz noted that the case helped establish the legal rights of the Lubavitch community. It also helped demonstrate that the Crown Heights *beis din* could not adjudicate every internal conflict. Sometimes, a secular judge would have to be called on—and Sifton's ruling was proof that an outside court could sometimes get it right. It was an important landmark. The doors of the Lubavitch kingdom had parted. In 1994, on the death of the rebbe, they would be flung wide open.

# 7

David Steingard was the first one out of the car, and he stood for a moment on the sidewalk outside the yeshiva dormitory, imagining the asphalt as it must have looked on the night of December 29, 2007, lit up by the erratic strobe lights of the emergency vehicles, the curve of this part of Eastern Parkway basically just a hollow between two hillocks, probably acting like an amplifier, sending those shrieks and shouts and protestations all the way to Bed-Stuy. Steingard peered up at the dormitory. Four stories, the typical finely wrought ornamentation over the door, which hung loose on its hinges. The windows from the ground up were bruised a deep gray and in some cases stuffed with detritus—pillowcases, yellowed newspapers, tattered clothing. Steingard knew a little bit of Hebrew, and he made out the words on the white banner that was plastered on the stone above the fourth-floor windows: "Long live the Rebbe, King Messiah." He smiled and made his way toward the sagging front steps of the dormitory, passing piles of trash and empty black plastic bodega bags, which drifted underfoot like tumbleweeds.

"Beautiful place," Steingard said, and David Weiss, a couple of paces back, nodded. They made a good team, the two of them. Many assistant district attorneys had a thing about splitting the work—and thus the potential reward—on high-profile trials, but Steingard had been pleased to find out that Weiss would be riding shotgun on the Shomrim fiasco. For one, it was an exceptionally complicated case— six defendants, hundreds of pages of documentation, decades of tangled Hasidic politics to explicate for a jury that would probably be made up mostly of non-Jews. Moreover, Weiss had spent a couple of years in Israel. He spoke Hebrew fluently and understood some Yiddish; he'd be invaluable when it came to the state witnesses.

Of the two prosecutors, Weiss was taller and stouter, with narrow, bright eyes. He'd graduated from law school in the city, spent some time interning with the Brooklyn DA, and pounced at the opportunity when a full-time job opened up. He wore his dark hair short to the scalp and spoke with a soft, undisguised lisp. A few months later, when the Shomrim case finally hit Brooklyn Supreme Court, the defendants would make the mistake of confusing that lisp with weakness. But Weiss was really running circles around the Shomrim kids, picking up on everything—the chatter from the gallery, the most fleeting smirk, a whispered aside.

Unlike the average lawyer at the Kings County office, who used the DA post as a stepping-stone to a lucrative gig at a Manhattan firm, Weiss saw himself as something of a career prosecutor. He reveled in the arrest reports, the mug shots, and the screen sheets, the summaries of potential cases passed along by the catching officers. And he was invested—invested enough, anyway, to really put his heart into a case and to be busted up if things went pear-shaped. He was also savvy enough to revel in his work. At thirty-two, he was already a favorite of the court reporters for the tabloids and the broadsheets, who flocked to him for insider dirt.

Steingard admired him. They were teammates, friends. When they weren't working, they'd pound out quick text messages on their BlackBerrys or meet up for coffee in the city. Both Weiss and Steingard lived in Manhattan, but it was Steingard who was the lifer.

He had been raised in the same building where he still lived— a converted Tribeca warehouse his father had bought way back when Tribeca was a wasteland. Now the neighborhood was among the best in all of New York City, and the building was worth a fortune. Steingard and his wife lived a couple of floors up by private elevator—not exactly the typical digs for a young Brooklyn ADA, but Steingard was good at being self-effacing about the whole thing, smiling when visitors commented on how *lucky* he was to live where he did—and then quickly changing the subject, feinting, as if he were on the courtroom floor.

Steingard hadn't initially planned on a career in law. He'd worked first in marketing, a job that ended up helping his courtroom demeanor—he was a natural actor and quick to read people's moods. He'd saved a little bit of money, eventually gotten burned out on the whole thing, and signed up at New York Law School. It wasn't exactly Columbia or New York University, but it was a solid school nonetheless and a good jumping-off point for a gig in the city. After graduation, next stop was an internship on the Homicide desk at the Brooklyn DA's office, followed not long after that by a full-time gig working the orange zone.

For the sake of convenience, the borough of Brooklyn is split into five colored prosecutorial zones. Each zone encompasses a set number of police precincts. A prosecutor assigned to the gray zone, for instance, would be responsible for Bushwick, Williamsburg, and Greenpoint, plus a random splotch of Kensington and most of Borough Park. (The zone map was arranged on the strangest of rubrics, in a way that grouped together sections of Brooklyn that were geographically separated by dozens of blocks.) Steingard and the rest of the orange zone team had the 62nd, the 73rd, the 77th, and the 78th precincts, which boiled down to Bensonhurst, Bath Beach, and Gravesend—relatively residential neighborhoods, with plenty of well-manicured lawns and whitewashed duplexes—and the narrow North Brooklyn corridor stretching from Park Slope in the west to Brownsville in the east.

Naturally, little of the action came from Park Slope, a hyper-gentrified grid of brownstones and coffee shops, which had once played host to a large Puerto Rican and black population and was now dominated by bankers, stroller-pushing nannies, and the "creatives"—writers, artists, actors, graphic designers—successful enough to pay upward of a grand and a half a month for a worn studio apartment with a window and a half and a broken stove. Prospect Heights coughed up a few more interesting cases than Park

Slope—drug-related, most of them, along with the occasional mugging and bar fight—but even the far corner of Prospect Heights was
stable now, the poorer families already pushed out and bound for
south or east Brooklyn.

The real excitement for the orange zone came from the 7-3 and
the 7-7—from Brownsville and north Crown Heights. These were
higher-risk sectors, heavy on projects and street crime. In 2009,
Hollywood producers searching for an appropriately dangerous
neighborhood to film a few scenes for a cop movie called *Brooklyn's
Finest* had settled on the projects of Brownsville. In the papers,
the place was sometimes identified as "Little Iraq," the regular title
owner of Most Murders in the Borough, and by extension—because
Brooklyn is the most murderous borough in New York—Most
Murders in the City. Steingard and Weiss, of course, didn't see a lot
of these cases. Just as NYPD detectives have a catching order, based
on seniority and experience and rank, so, too, do assistant district
attorneys. Homicides, crimes against children, and sex crimes are
typically optioned to special prosecutorial units, which can take the
case or, less frequently, pass it back to the zone where the crime was
committed.

Younger prosecutors, on the other hand, start by clearing lower-
level drug raps, assaults, and breaking-and-entering charges. Each
case is doled out by the precinct supervisor—who is in turn super-
vised by the longtime Brooklyn district attorney Charles Hynes—
and if the fledgling ADAs prove themselves in the courtroom,
they are often kicked up the food chain. It is for this reason that
many private practice or corporate lawyers in Manhattan fondly
remember their time as prosecutors. From the very beginning,
ADAs are trying cases—not just assisting, but helping to build the
whole thing from the ground up, from the order of the witness testimony to the summations. The city prosecutors are in the trenches
from the start.

Steingard and Weiss caught the Shomrim case in the summer of
2009. It had originally belonged to another, more senior prosecutor,
but that prosecutor had decamped for a job in China. Their first step
had been to give the documents a once-over, processing the immensity
of the arena they were stepping into. They'd independently handled a

few cases involving Lubavitchers—the orange zone covered only the north side of Eastern Parkway and did not extend toward the heart of the Jewish settlement in Crown Heights—but nothing so politically charged.

So they'd sat a few times with Levi Huebner, who seemed to Steingard to be a relatively sensible guy, maybe a little nosy—a little insistent on being present at every step in the investigation. It had clearly thrown Huebner that Weiss spoke Hebrew, in effect negating the need for a translator and making Huebner superfluous. But to his immense credit, it was Huebner who offered to link Steingard and Weiss up with a Lubavitch tour guide, a kid named Cohen, who had been present on the night in question and would be more than happy to show the fine gentlemen from the Office of the Brooklyn District Attorney around the dormitory.

Steingard reached the front steps of the dormitory a few paces ahead of Weiss. He cupped one hand over his brow and peered through his reflection and into the darkened lobby. Half of his view was obscured by a three-foot-high bright-yellow poster of the rebbe, one frail white hand raised in solemn benediction. A few yards out, Steingard could see more stickers and posters bearing Schneerson's image—they were plastered over the cracked cement walls and all over the stairwell, running up to the top three floors and down to the first floor, where the assault had taken place. Weiss arrived behind Steingard. "Should we call him?" Weiss asked. "Nah." Steingard shook his head. He didn't have Cohen's number, and even if he did, he would have preferred to wait here for a moment, sussing the place out. The dormitory gave off an otherworldly vibe, as if it were a radioactive device, a hulking piece of Kryptonite.

In his attitude toward Crown Heights, Steingard was no different from hundreds of thousands of secular Jews in New York. Crown Heights, which was really just a neighborhood—a slab of concrete, a bunch of row houses—seemed to promise some sort of cosmic revelation about life as lived by generations of Jews. At the same time, Crown Heights might as well have been the surface of Mars. The black hats and the long black coats, the pounds of fresh fish pressed wetly to the windows of the stores on Kingston, the women in wigs and high leather boots, the dancing and the singing, the proselytizing, the outreach work, the promise of the arrival of a *messiah*, for God's sake, the veneration of the rebbe—this was not the Jewish tradition in which Steingard had been raised.

He rapped a few times at the glass, losing himself for a moment so deeply in thought that he didn't see the gaggle of *bochurim* burst through the door until it was almost too late. The four of them were all dressed nearly identically—the pressed white shirts, yellowed near the collars and the armpits; the black coats; the yellow pins, each bearing a blue ink illustration of a crown. The tallest of the students, broad shouldered but skinny at the waist, smiled at Steingard and Weiss, and removed his black fedora, exposing a black velvet yarmulke, ringed with yellow Hebrew script.

"Can I help you?" the kid said, his English thick with a chewy Israeli accent.

Steingard had read up on the dormitory, not exactly wasting hours on research but digging through enough blog posts and Wikipedia entries and Chabad news site articles to understand that the vast majority of the boys living at 749 were members of the messianist faction of Lubavitch Judaism. *Mischistizn*. Technically, of course, all Lubavitchers are messianists, in that they believe that a messianic age is imminent, and that it can be ushered in with piety, prayer, and unstinting adherence to the 613 *mitzvoth*, or commandments, identified in Holy Scripture.

But amid the chaos following the rebbe's death, the Lubavitch community had cracked open along messianist lines. The *Mischistizn* announced that it was their duty to spread the word of the Messiah's arrival. Moderate Lubavitchers, on the other hand, worried that if the messianists came to dominate the Lubavitch movement, they would scare away prospective converts. For a decade and a half, the two factions had been fighting what amounted to a cold war, with the moderates retaining control of the office of the *shluchim* and Agudas Chassidei Chabad, and the messianists clinging to their collection of strongholds, including the dorm at 749 Eastern Parkway.

In 2006, in one of the most violent incidents involving the messianists, a group of *shluchim* in town for an annual conference, had poured into the basement shul of 770 Eastern Parkway, apparently to hold a *farbrengen*, or religious discussion. In the rebbe's day, the shul had belonged to all Lubavitchers, but in the late '90s, the messianists had assumed control of a large portion of the floor, which they used to sing, dance, and wave yellow flags. On this night, the *shluchim*— a caste of Lubavitch society known to be politically moderate—had decided to temporarily evict their messianist counterparts.

Things came to a head immediately. Competing factions jostled for space in the crowded room; at some point, a *shaliach* from Chicago jumped on a table held by the messianists and began kicking books onto the floor. Pictures from that night, snapped by members of the messianist faction, showed sweaty, red-faced Hasidim screaming, shoving, ripping down opposition banners, and playing a calamitous game of tug-of-war with a heavy wooden bench. Eventually, someone was brained with the butt end of a fire extinguisher and hauled out on a stretcher.

Steingard took a step forward, bringing himself within spitting distance of the tall, skinny *bochur*. He was twenty-two, twenty-three years old, not much more than that. Couldn't be. Because at twenty-three, many Lubavitchers are already on the marriage track, which for the *bochurim* of 749 meant heading back to Israel and working with a matchmaker to find a suitable wife. Either that or hitting the singles circuit, hoping that luck and prayer were enough to get you the girl of your parents' dreams.

This kid seemed more confident than most *bochurim*, more aloof. He held his jacket forward proudly, so Steingard could inspect the yellow pin he was wearing on his lapel, the symbol of the crown a reference to the rebbe's status as King Messiah, the redeemer of all mankind, the descendant of King David—the blessed leader who would finally rebuild the ruined cities of Israel, fill every mind with the wisdom of God, destroy the weapons of war, raise the dead. Almost everything the *bochur* was wearing was an advertisement for the messianists, right down to the yarmulke, which read, "Yehi Adoneinu Moreinu v'Rabbeinu Melech haMoshiach l'olam vo'ed," or "Long Live our Master, our Teacher, and our Rabbi, King Messiah, for ever and ever." In Crown Heights, the motto was known simply as *Yehi*, its two slick syllables enough to raise eyebrows. It was a catchphrase, a password, proof that you were a True Believer and possibly—depending on who you were talking to—unhinged.

"We're looking for Cohen," Steingard said.

"Inside. Second floor."

"Thanks," Steingard said and began walking back toward the door. At the top step, he turned and saw Weiss was standing with the *bochur* Past the courtyard, Eastern Parkway was filling with westbound traffic, the sleek black SUVs and the gypsy cabs and the graffitied supply vans jostling door to door, with little margin for error in the four narrow lanes, horns and shouts and the hiss from the subway grates winging toward the courtyard.

Steingard was about to reverse course, pull Weiss with him into the building, but then a short, squat Hasid was barreling down the staircase and through the lobby at a lunatic clip, his mouth open, his hand pinning his black yarmulke to the top of his head. Steingard opened the door for him. "I'm Cohen," the guy said and extended a hand. "Come inside, please." Steingard whistled for Weiss, and they both followed Cohen through the glass door of the dormitory.


They'd tussled over the messianist thing from the beginning, Weiss and Steingard. Not an outright fight but a series of friendly disagreements, stretching back almost to the moment when they'd caught the case. Weiss was fascinated by the idea that a group of twenty-first-century New Yorkers could be actively waiting for the arrival of Armageddon, and not just waiting in the way you wait for a cross-town bus or something, but waiting in the way that you put everything else away, delayed vacations and Major Life Events, because within a few days and maybe even sooner the skies were going to part, and a long-dead guy was going to come back to life and start putting back together the cities of Israel as if they were Lego sets. Weiss had done his homework. He'd bought the right books, read the right Web sites, talked to the right folks—he was immersed.

There were plenty of prosecutors like that, Steingard knew. Great lawyers who became enraptured with the context of a case. In reality, although you might be lucky enough to get the rare juror who was willing to follow you down the rabbit hole—who might treat an opening argument as if it were a master lecture from a Princeton professor—most juries operated by a simple internal schematic: the members rigorous, dutiful, responsible, and eager to get back to their lives. Steingard had long considered pulling together a coffee table book called *Oath*, which would feature pictures of lawyers, doctors, cops, jurors, and large-scale reprints of the Hippocratic oath, the ethical oath for police officers, the fireman's oath of office, the juror's oath, and so on. Point was, people took oaths seriously. If you watched carefully enough, you could see a witness's entire demeanor change the second after he took his hand off that leather-bound book—one minute he was a comedian, all laughs and smirks, and the next minute he was a morally invested and stern-faced instrument of the legal system of the United States of America.

Still, there were limits. Jurors were mothers, fathers, teachers, employees, bosses. They wanted to be helpful, they wanted to believe and to adjudicate, and they wanted things kept relatively simple. Steingard sought in all cases to comply, to boil the immensity of the most intricate trial to a simple causality: the suspect, the motive, the charges. It was not that he was not fascinated by the milieu in which he worked—New York was the most fascinating city on the planet— but Steingard was a firm believer that an actor was either guilty or he wasn't. A guy was either going to jail or he was going home to his cat and his television and his house plants. That was all Steingard needed to know, and that was all a jury needed to know.

"It's connected," Weiss had said, a week before they trudged out to 749 for the first time. "The Shomrim came to that dormitory for a reason. It was political," Weiss added, and Steingard found himself nodding reluctantly along with his partner. Weiss was right.

The cops had initially treated the assault at 749 like your garden variety fistfight. In fact, the whole mess was a manifestation of a schism in the community, the fault lines swallowing everyone eventually, from the rabbinical courts right on down to the yeshiva students. Yes, the immediate cause for the fight might have been a spare mattress, an argument over an extra body in the room. But the resident of Room 107 had been a moderate in a house full of *Mischistizn* sticking out like a sore thumb. It would be useless to pretend that the *bochurim* hadn't been fighting over something much bigger—something as big as God himself.

Still, Steingard had tried to concentrate on the video. He knew that these days a trial was often in trouble from the get-go unless the state could present DNA, tox screens, snapshots, video, fingerprints, whatever. Too many jurors watched *CSI: Miami* or those pseudo-science showcases on the Discovery Channel. They had been schooled to expect nothing less than unassailable proof. Luckily, Steingard and Weiss had it. Or they thought they'd had it until they got a good look at the Beliniski video. There was plenty of action on the tape, but at several points it appeared as if the Shomrim guys were the ones who were cornered, outnumbered, and outgunned by the *bochurim*. Steingard could still hear the wails of the Shomrim member Binyomin Lifshitz, digging around in the scrum for his missing glasses. There wasn't a mother alive who wouldn't wince at that.

Bottom line: There was plenty of material that he and Weiss could exploit, including an indelible image of Gedalia Hershkop, clad in some serious-looking black gloves, which might or might not be packed with shot, shaking around the *bochurim* as if they were wet towels. Or that sequence of the rest of the Shomrim team attempting to barrel into the already crowded room, shouting orders and showing off their heavy Motorola radios.

But much of the fiasco had not been captured by Beliniski, and even if the jury bought that the video footage was proof of the Shomrim members' guilt—or at least of their intent—the defense team would likely have a field day with the state witnesses, few of them speaking much English, and all of them having a religious stake in the outcome of the trial.

Incredibly, the grand jury had come down with a charge of gang assault, and Charles Hynes, the Brooklyn district attorney, had pressed his prosecutors hard to go after the max. In Steingard's humble opinion, there was no way they'd be able to stick the gang assault rap. They'd be lucky to get simple assault.

"We've got to streamline this thing," he'd told Weiss, finally.

"I'm with you," Weiss had said. And that had been that.

• • •

Cohen had at first promised a quick whirlwind tour of Room 107, where the assault had gone down, enough time for Steingard and Weiss to get a feel for the place, take a few photos, maybe ask a few questions. But it quickly became apparent he seemed intent on giving the grand tour, and he was impervious—or perhaps immune—to what Steingard considered to be a pretty damn obvious display of body language. So up they went, climbing into the darkened stairwell, the blunted planes of Cohen's face almost reflective with perspiration, Steingard and Weiss trudging complacently behind him, their eyes directed toward the corrugated cement steps.

There were about a hundred kids in the dorm in any given month, two or three to each bedroom, five or six bedrooms to each floor. Theoretically, the dormitory was under the direction of the rabbinical leadership at 770 Eastern Parkway, but in practice, these boys ruled themselves—established rooming assignments, adjudicated disputes, dictated house rules. Steingard had heard Lubavitchers refer to the place as the equivalent of a third-world tenement. A Taliban stronghold. Choose your metaphor. The dilapidation of the place was certainly remarkable, but Steingard chalked it up to circumstance. Put a hundred boys of any background in their own house and give them free rein, and they were bound to end up trashing the place. You needed only take a spin down the fraternity row of your local state college to know it.

"So let me ask you," Weiss said. "I'm curious. You know, let's say you're walking down Kingston, and a guy punches you in the face."

"Yeah, okay." Cohen querulous now, possibly playing out this hypothetical assault in his head, or maybe the hypothetical assault wasn't so hypothetical—Jewish kids got the shit kicked out of them in Crown Heights all the time, had been getting the shit kicked out of them for decades, it went with the territory.

"So there you are, getting assaulted," Weiss said. They had stopped now at the end of the hallway, and the fire escape door hung loose on its hinges, bringing with it a much welcome gust of breeze. While Weiss talked, Steingard edged out onto the rusted fire escape, teetering suddenly over a sea of trash. Across the alley, Steingard saw a woman standing in her kitchen, scrubbing a dish, and for a moment he was able to imagine this place as it must have looked decades ago, a century ago, Crown Heights then a middle-class suburb, acres of grand old apartment buildings, maybe a doorman standing out front, his maroon suit finely pressed.

"Who do you call first?" Weiss asked.

"My friends."

"No, like, yes, maybe your friends, but also you probably call the police, right?"

"Shmira first, and then police," Cohen said more confidently, this pretty much par for the course in Jewish Crown Heights. It struck Steingard as incredible: a part of the United States where the populace distrusts the police so much that they will call a private army of uniformed vigilantes before they call the NYPD.

"Why not the Shomrim?" Weiss said.

"As I understand it," Cohen said, deepening his voice, as if he were a professor addressing his students, "there is one group that is authorized by the *rabbonim* and one that is not. I call the authorized patrol."

Cohen had more or less outlined the DA's case against the Shomrim: there was one authorized patrol and one unauthorized patrol, and it had been the unauthorized patrol that had showed up at 749 Eastern Parkway on that night in 2007. An unauthorized patrol made up mostly of political moderates—not a single member of the Shomrim was affiliated with the messianist cause—who had good religious reason to crack skulls and a long history with the *bochurim* at the dormitory. Case open, case shut.

"Are you scared of the Shomrim?"

"Everyone is scared of the Shomrim. In Israel, before we arrive in Brooklyn, we learn to be afraid of the Shomrim. We hear that there is a group that hates us . . ."

"Hates you."

"Wants us gone. They hate us politically."

"Because they are not *Mischistizn*?"

Weiss had left it wide open for Cohen, but the kid was still stonewalling.

"If you had to join one of these groups, which one would you join?"

"I would not join either, but if I had to join, I would join Shmira."

"How many people in Crown Heights do you think pay attention to the Shmira and Shomrim thing?" Steingard asked, stepping back into the hallway. "Like, how many people really care?"

"People who are involved care."

"And no one else?"

Cohen shrugged.

A few days earlier, a friend had sent Steingard a link to a blog called "Who is Shmira?" that turned out to be a Lubavitcher Perez Hilton or TMZ, a cartoonish shout-fest, portraying the Shmira guys as thugs and Huebner as the Shmira's consigliore—Tom Hagen to Yankel Prager's Don Vito Corleone. The site—anonymously written but obviously controlled by the Shomrim—received a hefty amount of traffic, most of it presumably coming from inside the Jewish settlement. Steingard had seen one post with an image of a patrol car used by the Shmira squad, over a three-line caption: "If you see a fellow Jew driving this car, know this, he is NOT there for your protection. He is not there looking out for you! The people driving this car are not looking out for their fellow Jews!" Dozens of comments had piled up under the post, some commenters denouncing the Shmira, others calling the Shomrim guys *mosers*, rats, snitches—the Web just another place for the supporters of both groups to bicker like little kids.

"So, how about it?" Steingard said. "Can we see the room?"

They walked back downstairs. Using the heel of his hand, Cohen pounded hard on the door of 107. A moment passed—a heartbeat, two—and there was a squawk and a great rustle, and presently a *bochur* emerged in segments from the room, appearing first as an explosion of uncombed brown hair, frazzled and curving up into one gigantic cowlick, and then a bare chest.

Steingard got up on his toes and looked into the room, seeing shadow and not much else, hearing the faint sound of a Hasidic chant piping out of a cheap stereo system. The way he understood it, the average *bochur* lived a little like a college student on the brink of finals week—buried in the books from morning to night, sleep stolen at odd hours, the only fuel a few gallons of coffee and greasy food. Two years of that, maybe three, and then you were a rabbi, and you could get

the hell out of Crown Heights, join the rest of the "Rebbe's Army"—
the Lubavitch emissaries that every year peeled off to Argentina,
Mongolia, God knew where, with their prayer books and *mezuzahs*.
So much of Lubavitch culture seemed infused by militarism, down to
the Mitzvah Tanks, actually big RV vehicles, covered in pictures of the
rebbe, the words "*Moshiach* Is Now," enlarged clip art of menorahs. It
was something to see, that fleet of Mitzvah Tanks, rolling up through
the silver and chrome canyons of Midtown Manhattan, the tourists
looking on as if New York were under attack by an alien army.

"The Shomrim," Steingard heard Cohen say, followed by something
in Yiddish, and then Cohen pointed back at the two attorneys.

"Okay," Cohen said. "He says it's fine. Come inside."

The room turned out to be not much more than a dimly lit cube
overlooking the air duct, the walls a burned beige, the ceilings deco-
rated with cobwebs and blue balls of lint. There were two beds in the
room, both of them up on cinder blocks, and a pair of bureaus. No
desk, no chairs. Steingard peeled away from Cohen and peeked into
the closet on the right side of the room, which was overstuffed with
white shirts and jackets, the dirty laundry stacked precipitously on the
floor, boxer shorts and a couple of ties barfed out across the floor. The
kid who had let them into the room stood watching Steingard.

"Mind if we take some pictures?" Steingard asked. The kid flipped
on the light switch and held his palms up toward the sky, the universal
gesture for *Yeah, whatever, just don't break anything*. In the bed to the
left of the window, a second boy was curled up under the top layer of
sheets, pretending to ignore his guests.

Weiss began snapping photos, starting from the hallway and then
working his way around the room. Cohen pressed himself against the
wall so Weiss could get a better view, and Steingard wondered what
Cohen got out of his tour guide duties—a slap on the back from
Huebner or maybe just a sense of pride at helping seal up the case
against the *boychiks* of the Shomrim.

For a bunch of supposedly holy men, the Hasidim sure did know
how to fight. In some ways, of course, all of these petty feuds—the
messianists versus the moderates; the Shmira versus the Shomrim—
had to be a by-product of the tight-knittedness of the community. The Lubavitchers spent decades consolidating their control of

the area around Kingston Avenue, which had been great when the rebbe was alive, but once he'd passed away, the proximity had made it exceptionally easy for fights to fester, spread, consume whole families.

"These two guys," Steingard said, gesturing at the residents of 107, "they weren't here when the fight happened, correct?"

"That's right," Cohen said. "Back then, it was just Gurfinkel and Wilhelm." Both Gurfinkel and Wilhelm had since left the dormitory, as had a good number of the other boys present that night, although Huebner had promised that he'd get everyone back by the time the thing went to trial—pay for their tickets from Israel, arrange for the passports, if that's what it took.

"Does he know Wilhelm and Gurfinkel?" Steingard asked, nodding toward their host.

"Sure."

"So, how did the Shomrim end up here that night?" Steingard asked, knowing the answer but wanting to see how Cohen would handle the question. The *bochur* in the bed sat up and began chattering, set off by the word *Shomrim*, this one at least wearing a white undershirt, looking halfway presentable.

"Wilhelm," Cohen said. "Wilhelm called his uncle, and the uncle called the Shomrim."

"Right," Weiss said, snapping a few more pictures of the window, the flash reflecting back into the room. "But why the Shomrim? Why not Shmira?"

"The Shomrim and Wilhelm—they are friends." Cohen shrugged, as if the whole thing were self-explanatory. Steingard turned his attention again to sizing up the room, really not much more than a prison cell, a wonder that so many bodies had fit in here—squirming, wriggling, punching bodies.

On the video, you could see Frankel and Lifshitz in the middle of the room and the rest of the Shomrim guys trying to push into 107, the hallway outside just as congested, forty bodies, maybe more. The tape at least gave the illusion of space, just a fraction of the room caught by Beliniski, so that you thought maybe the room keeps going, opens out somewhere to the right of the closet. But that fraction of the room was all there was.

You heard all the time about people getting trampled on their way out of concerts or sporting events. Had anyone started a stampede in 107, at least a few guys would have gone down underfoot. Steingard remembered the report from the hospital—some fractures, some bruises. Coupled with the video, it might be enough to convict a couple of the Shomrim guys, but he was struck once more with the thought that gang assault rap was going to be tough to prove. Maybe the defendants would plead out, but they probably wouldn't, not these guys, not in Crown Heights, where fights had a habit of going on forever and ever, with no one smart or cool enough to step away from the fire, so everything just burned.

# 8

That week the weather was good, and Aron Hershkop worked with the door open. In the back of the shop, he could hear a couple of his guys chattering happily under a rusted Dodge Caravan, their voices swirling up and over the sounds of the radio, which was tuned to a local Caribbean station. Like many young Lubavitchers, Hershkop held no particular animosity toward the local blacks. You walked up and down Kingston Avenue these days, and you saw blacks working in the hat stores, the grocery stores, the fish market. Israel Shemtov, the former Red Baron—and now a haberdasher with a nice little basement store up on Empire—even had an African American tailor operating a sewing machine in the front room.

And why not? It wasn't the 1990s anymore. The days of the riots, when Hershkop and his big brother Gadi had sat up on the roof of his folks' place, watching the blacks march up and down Carroll and Crown streets—those days were over, and thanks be to God for that. Besides, Hershkop knew that the riots hadn't been caused by locals. It had been the out-of-towners, shipped in by Al Sharpton to stir things up in Crown Heights. There was a distinction. Most people didn't realize there were the Jamaicans and the Guyanese and the Haitians, and then there was Al Sharpton's crew. The real instigators.

"I'll be right back," Hershkop shouted toward the back of the shop, getting a couple of weary nods in return. The garage was long and narrow—it could accommodate two cars bumper to bumper and enough spare parts to build six more. But the space was tight, and even with the front door open, the air carried a thick chemical humidity, all fluorocarbons and acrylic sweetness.

When he'd first decided to open up a repair shop—this back in his late twenties, the idea coming to him naturally, as if it had been there all along—Hershkop's friends and family had worried aloud that he'd get burned out too quickly. They'd said the repair market was already crowded enough, which was true, and yet business had been brisk almost since the first year. Hershkop had started out with a small circle of clients and then expanded outward, until he was wrenching for half of the Jewish families in South Crown Heights. He got a kick out of the job, too, not just the management stuff, the paperwork—he left that to his wife, mostly—but the hours spent on the floor of the garage, the way the grease and the dirt became a second skin.

In fact, the only downside to the garage work was the time it took away from his duties as Shomrim coordinator. Hershkop was no longer free to roll around at all hours in the Shomrim vehicles, looking for trouble. He had this problem in common with his good friend Schleimy Klein, who worked at a grocery store during the day and the Hunts Point market every night, leaving him barely enough time to sleep, let alone patrol the neighborhood. Hershkop had a family now, a business, obligations.

He stepped out onto the sidewalk and peered west down the boulevard, in the direction of his own apartment. He had been savvy about his real estate investments back in the day, buying up a lot of the property around East New York when the area was only a slum, just razor wire and vacant lots. The lots and the wire were still there, but Crown Heights was now gentrifying just like the rest of Central Brooklyn, the yuppies coming out from Park Slope in their Mini Coopers, set on raising families in what was once a war zone—and in the process making Hershkop a relatively wealthy man.

In five more years, ten years, the area around East New York would likely be booming—the evidence was there, and in fact, the neighborhood had already changed, filled in a little, losing that look of desolation that had dogged it for so many decades. Twenty years out, who knew what South Crown Heights could become, maybe a Park Slope Junior. Fifty years out, it might revert to the bedroom community it had been in the early part of the twentieth century. Hershkop understood the history of Crown Heights, had studied it carefully. Part of his family had moved off to Israel, but Hershkop had trouble picturing himself anywhere but New York. Something about the sedimentation of the city appealed to him—the predictable cycles of change and rebirth, the way a neighborhood could evolve just like a human being, coming full circle in the end.

Across the street from the shop, a pair of Shomrim scooters sat under a tent of plastic sheeting, one of the scooters with a stone-size dent in the hood and the other with a busted wheel, the rim in silhouette now resembling Pac-Man. Well, Hershkop would get to the scooters when he could. The logjam was bad enough as it was.

"Doing pretty well for yourself over here, huh?"

Hershkop bounced on his toes, thinking that the last thing he had time for right now was the police. But there he was, Bobby De Luca, standing on the other side of East New York, clearly not just stopping by for a courtesy call, waiting to be invited in for a chat. "Officer De Luca," Hershkop said. "Always a pleasure."

De Luca trotted across the street, holding up his palm to the passing traffic. He was out of uniform today, a baggy nylon jacket not doing much to hide the bulge of the waist holster. Hershkop liked De Luca. Knew him to be intelligent, personable.

De Luca had started out as a regular old beat cop, back when Crown Heights was bad news—back when the only place worse was Brownsville or Bedford-Stuyvesant or maybe East New York—and he'd returned in recent years to act as a community affairs officer, the meat and potatoes of the job being politics in the Jewish settlement and outside. To his immense credit, De Luca seemed to actually care—he knew the basics of Lubavitch politics as well as most Lubavitchers and even kept a few pictures of the rebbe in his second-floor office at the precinct house.

"Aron." They shook hands. Aron peered down at De Luca, the guy preternaturally tan, his dark hair shorn close to the head, his eyes looking more tired than usual. "Can we talk?" De Luca said.

"Of course." Aron nodded. He wondered for a moment if the visit had something to do with Shuchat. It could definitely be Shuchat. Hershkop couldn't help much with that. He knew Shuchat had probably hoofed it to Israel—Israel by way of Montreal—but everyone in Jewish Crown Heights knew that, which meant De Luca did, too.

"I'm assuming you know we've got a new precinct commander up there," De Luca said, turning his square head up the hill, in the direction of Empire Boulevard. "Simonetti. You heard of him?"

"Yep," Hershkop said, noncommittally. He had a bad feeling about this conversation. He could see a couple of ways it might play out, and judging by the grimace on De Luca's face, none of them were good for the Shomrim.

In June, the NYPD brass had replaced longtime commander Frank Vega with Captain Peter Simonetti, who'd previously been stationed in Sunset Park. Word on the street was that Vega had been forced out by Jewish activists furious at the 7-1's inability to crack down on bias crime. Even before the news of the Charles case broke, the rumors were circulating: the cops, afraid of a second riot, were actively burying cases that appeared to be racially motivated. On January 28, 2008, *Jewish Week* had published a long story on the allegations, topped by one of those can't-look-away headlines: "CROWN HEIGHTS COVER-UP?" The reporter gave the lead quote to the Lubavitch politician Barry Sugar, who fumed that "the Jews in this community are not being adequately protected. The police department has to [properly] characterize crimes and not play politics with my people," he continued. "There have been hate crimes against our people, and the police department characterizes them as robberies."

Sugar had provided the *Jewish Week* with a small laundry list of alleged assaults: A black man who had clobbered a Lubavitcher in the head, before announcing that he was going to "complete what Hitler started." Two black men who attacked a Lubavitcher with a metal object, sending five broken teeth skittering across the pavement. A brick thrown through the skylight of a Lubavitcher home. A five-gallon can of tar tossed onto the porch of a second Lubavitcher home. A sixteen-year-old boy beaten by a crowd of black teenagers, who called the boy a "fucking Jew," declared that Crown Heights belonged to the blacks, and promised the boy that he was about to die. That assault had lasted almost five minutes, enough to leave a gash in the Lubavitcher's head and bruises across his chest and arms.

The police had responded to the alleged incidents as they always did: by deploying a few extra patrols and sending one of the bigwigs—in this case, Ray Kelly—down to Crown Heights to mingle with the natives and dispense platitudes. But then in April the Charles case had hit the news, and by May, Crown Heights was a media circus, with everyone prognosticating about the possibility that this could turn into another riot. In June, Vega was gone. Maybe it was true that he had left of his own accord—or finally gotten the assignment he wanted—but to plenty of Hasidim, Vega's departure was long overdue. They looked forward to working with Simonetti, who was welcomed on Kingston with open arms, given the grand tour of his new precinct, written up in glowing profiles in the Lubavitch press. It was supposed to be a fresh start.

At first, Hershkop had shared in the optimism. In the last few months that Vega was on the job, Hershkop had become convinced that the 7-1 meant to get the Shomrim off the streets—the *Shomrim*, after all they'd done for Crown Heights.

On a cold morning back in March, for instance, the Shomrim had been called to the scene of a mugging and helped chase down and apprehend a couple of young thugs, nearly killing themselves hopping over fences and through backyards as if they were U.S. Marines in the battle of Fallujah, and finally driving their targets facedown into the dirt. But then when the cops showed up, the victim had gotten confused and blubbered that he wasn't *sure* that the Shomrim had the right guys pinned to the ground. Maybe these guys were the ones who stole his cell phone, and maybe not. So the cops had let the thugs go and arrested a Shomrim member instead—cuffed him right out there on Lefferts Avenue, not far from Everything Automotive, for all the world to see. No, Hershkop would not miss the leadership of Captain Frank Vega.

And yet he wasn't sure he could warm to Simonetti, either. A week after Simonetti took office, Hershkop had heard a disturbing report from Ben Lifshitz, who moonlighted snapping photos for a few of the tabloids in town. Lifshitz had a nice little side racket going: he kept a police scanner in his office, and when a particularly interesting call came in—murder or armed robbery or even a traffic accident—he'd hop in his Shomrim scooter and usually make it to the scene long before the regular shooters showed up and sometimes before the police.

Lifshitz had the kind of telephoto lens used by professional sports photographers, and his technique was good, certainly up to the standards of the *Post* or the *Daily News*. If no one ended up buying the shots, Lifshitz would simply upload the files to his own website, CrownHeightsInfo.com, where they were guaranteed to help drive traffic sky high. For Lifshitz, it was a win-win kind of situation.

In late June, not long after Simonetti took the reins at the 7-1, Lifshitz caught word of a stabbing on the east side of Prospect Park, out near Lefferts and the Q subway stop. By the time he arrived on the scene, the police had cordoned off the body with sawhorses and yellow tape, a white sheet and a puddle of blood the only signs that something had gone down. Lifshitz had gone straight to work, crouch-walking around the perimeter of the crime scene, his pointer finger light on the shutter release, the flash lighting up the block. Lifshitz had heard the footsteps but assumed it was just one of the CSI techs watching him work. "Turn that thing off," the guy said.

Turning around, Lifshitz saw that it was a uniform, an older guy, small eyes, his cheeks flushed even in the half-light. Lifshitz flashed his press pass.

"I know who you are," the cop said.

"Officer—"

"Captain Simonetti."

"Captain Simonetti. I'm just taking some photos. For the newspapers," Lifshitz added.

"Sorry."

Lifshitz, apoplectic but wise enough not to prolong the argument, had nodded, jammed the camera into his case, and steered the scooter out through the darkened streets, furious. "The Shomrim— we help people," he later fumed to Aron, the two of them sitting in the Shomrim dispatch in East New York, surrounded by photos of the Shomrim in better days—the Shomrim at city hall, the Shomrim

BBQ, the Shomrim lending a hand at the scene of a four-car pileup. "How can they do this to us?"

Hershkop had in the end counseled patience.

"Let's just wait and see," he said. "We don't know what Simonetti has in mind. He's still got the Shmira to deal with, right? We're the least of his problems."

Lifshitz was young—only twenty-two years old. He had no wife, no children, no family. Unlike Klein and Hershkop, he could afford to make the Shomrim Rescue Patrol the centerpiece of his life. He had let the job consume him, and Hershkop had figured that Lifshitz was being a little dramatic with all of this Simonetti business. "Give it a few days," he said, and Lifshitz had obeyed, or at least he'd stopped pestering everyone with his prophecies of imminent doom. But now here was Bobby De Luca, his body all hunched up like a question mark, clearly prepping himself to say something that Aron Hershkop didn't want to hear.

"I've got an offer for you," De Luca said. "This whole little argument, between you guys and Prager and Stern and them," De Luca clearly not wanting to say the word "Shmira," probably figuring—rightly—that it would set off Hershkop as if he were a Roman candle. "We want to end it. Simonetti wants to end it. Now hold on . . ." He held two open palms face out toward Hershkop. "I want to say first that we have not yet approached Mr. Prager. This offer comes to you first, and it comes in good faith."

"I haven't heard an offer."

"I'm getting to it. The offer comes to you guys first because we trust you guys. You've done good in the community. You've been a help. Hey, this neighborhood? It's a tough place, and I just want to say, from my perspective, I'm grateful that you guys are here. Now, Simonetti, he's only been here a few weeks, but I've been here for years, you know that . . ."

"Let's get to it," Hershkop said.

"Fine." De Luca nodded. "You want us behind you? We'll be behind you. You can even keep the Shomrim name. But there are some conditions: First of all, this feud shit stops today. You absorb some of the Shmira guys, you undergo some cursory training with the police, you go through some background checks, and you'll have our full support—100 percent."

"And if we don't?"

"I have to tell you, Aron, this is a hell of an offer. You turn it down, and we'll be watching you guys like hawks. You step out of line, we'll be there. And these things?" He pointed at the scooters. "You guys will have to stop parking them all over town. We'll start ticketing."

Hershkop was smart enough to read between the lines. It hadn't been so long ago that six Shomrim members, including his brothers, Gadi, Chaim, and Yudi, had surrendered themselves at the 77th Precinct. If Hershkop did accept De Luca's offer, De Luca could probably help get the charges against the Shomrim downgraded or even dismissed altogether. He could grease the wheels. And in exchange for giving up some of their autonomy, the Crown Heights Shomrim would save themselves the trouble of a criminal trial, with all of the bad publicity and the *lashon hara*—malicious gossip—that a trial would entail.

Still, surrender was out of the question. That's what it amounted to, Hershkop knew: surrender. For decades, reaching all the way back to the halcyon days of Samuel Schrage and the Maccabees, the Jewish community had produced squads of soldiers, guardians, warriors. Men unafraid to risk their own necks for the betterment of the community. And never, as far as Hershkop knew, had a Jewish anticrime force in Crown Heights ever acquiesced to the will of the NYPD.

Mostly, this was because the average Hasid preferred to be policed and protected by his own. A security patrol vetted and trained by the city would really just be a proxy for the city and therefore somehow tainted. Schrage had known this, and so had Israel Shemtov. This knowledge is what made them such effective crime fighters.

The Jews of Kingston Avenue had a healthy respect for history. They understood that in the past, the severest threat had often come not from their fellow citizenry but from the state itself. No, the mayor of the New York wasn't Hitler—not by a long shot— but as a practical matter, it was wise never to put too much trust in bureaucracy. It was better to develop your state, your own city within a city, your own country within a country, and to burrow deep, to resist the grasp of the government. Hershkop thought of a quote that Lifshitz had hanging on his office wall: "When a good man is hurt, all who would be called good must suffer with him." The line belonged to Euripides, the ancient Greek dramatist, but for Lifshitz, it might as well have been written by one of the Shomrim. The words embodied the possibility of martyrdom—the idea that the good men of the Shomrim would suffer and, through suffering, be proved right.

Well, Hershkop thought, there was something to that. "What you are asking us to do," he said, "is make a deal with a bunch of criminals."

De Luca smiled.

"Okay, so you've heard that story," Hershkop said. "But what you're asking for, in effect, is for the Shomrim, which is a law-abiding organization, to absorb a bunch of thugs and felons. Is that what you're asking us?"

"I'm asking you to keep an open mind."

"With all due respect, I don't think you understand what's going on here."

"This is the last chance you're going to get. You say no, I'm going to have a sit-down with the Shmira, and I'm going to offer them the same thing I'm offering you right now. And guess what? Unlike you, they're probably going to say yes. You understand?"

"I guess I do," Hershkop said, looking right through De Luca.

"So I'm assuming we have your answer."

"You assume right."

"Okay," De Luca said. "Well, thanks, Aron. I appreciate you taking the time." When Hershkop looked up again, De Luca was bounding back across East New York, his hands jammed into his pockets.


During the next few days, Hershkop repeatedly played back the details of De Luca's visit, trying to suss out whether he could have handled the situation more deftly. He daydreamed about receiving a summons from some pinch-faced court officer, the white slip slapped onto his open palm with relish. He imagined the possibility of one of the Shmira guys getting it into their heads to do something *really* stupid, like setting the entire shop on fire. He didn't put it past either of them. There was precedent.

More than a half decade earlier, not long after the Shomrim split, Prager and Stern had come after Hershkop and come hard. They started with simple verbal harassment, jumped quickly up to low-level intimidation—trailing Gadi and Aron through the streets, hollering slurs from the windows of their cars, trying to psych him out. Hershkop had at first managed to keep his head down, but by the spring of 2000, he was getting fed up with the crank calls, the men phoning in to his East New York office, muttering threats to his family, and eventually, he filed for an order of protection.

He couldn't prove Yanky Prager was behind everything, but he did manage to convince a New York judge to grant his request. The criminal court order of protection—docket number 2000KN030761—extended through June 2001 and forbade Prager from "assaulting, harassing, menacing, intimidating or threatening" Hershkop. It turned out to be one of the wisest things Hershkop had ever done. A month before the order of protection against Prager was due to expire, Prager and his Shmira buddy Mendel Chuditov had rolled up on Hershkop while he was walking home down Kingston. From a complaint report later filed by Hershkop at the 71st Precinct:

> At T/P/O compl. states above perps approached him in a gold Acura. Comp/witness states both perps shouted to them that they were rats and that they are going to kill him. Comp. also states he has an order of protection in criminal court against perp #1. Above perps fled northbound on Kingston Avenue. No injuries.

A few weeks later, Yaacov Prager was charged by a Brooklyn court with criminal contempt and harassment, both in the second degree. A second order of protection against Prager was issued. And then on January 11, 2002, Prager had broken that order of protection, too. From *The People of the State of New York v. Yaacov Prager*:

> Deponent is informed by Aron Hershkop that, at the above time and place, informant observed defendant seated in the front

passenger seat of an automobile and said automobile did then follow informant's vehicle through four right turns, on to Eastern Parkway, on to Albany Avenue, and on to President Street, and back on to Kingston Avenue, and back to above location, and informant did pull alongside curb and above mentioned automobile did then pull alongside curb behind informant's vehicle.

For Hershkop, the two cases were leverage. He had proved to the world that he could turn the other cheek, while Prager proved to the world that he could not.

# 9

A few days after the visit from De Luca, the first wave of parking cops showed up at Everything Automotive. Hershkop watched them approach through the smudged glass of the garage window. Well, De Luca had been good on his word, Hershkop thought. He'd warned you, he'd delivered his ultimatum, you turned it down, and now here they were, a pair of patrolmen, the yellow ticket books flapping showily from the pockets of their city-issued navy blue cargo pants, the utility belts sagging with plastic gadgetry. You couldn't always pick out a plainclothes detective, but you sure could always pick out a parking cop, even without all of the parking cop paraphernalia. Something in that off-kilter strut.

Two in the afternoon. Pretty soon, the last school bell would sound, and the streets would fill with high school kids, packs of them, singing and yelling and knocking one another around, but for now, this stretch of East New York was hushed, the only real sound outside the screech and whine of the police radios. The cops proceeded slowly, eyeballing the Shomrim scooters first and then swinging around to get a look at the back of the Shomrim command post, their eyebrows arching in amusement.

Unbeknownst to the cops, a few years back the Shomrim had owned an even bigger vehicle, forty feet long and as wide as a boat, but the thing had proved to be a hassle to drive around the narrow streets of Crown Heights. Hershkop had picked up the new van at a local police auction and spent the better part of a year getting it in shape, tuning up the battered engine, repainting the chipped exterior, festooning the thing with Shomrim stickers and decals of the official Shomrim shield. Originally, Hershkop had hoped that the command post could be used in traffic emergences or in grid searches for missing persons. The back room of the van was fitted out with a bunch of swivel chairs and some tables, as well as cupboards that the Shomrim guys had stuffed with CPR apparatus, maps of Brooklyn, spare uniforms, extra radios. You could run the operations of a modern army from back there.

But in the end, after all of that work, the command post had mostly just collected rust. Sure, the Shomrim took the vehicle out for special occasions—for parades or for bicycle registration drives—but it turned out that most of the Shomrim members were skittish about driving the truck, which was heavy and ponderous and prone to drifting into the corners, like a roller-coaster cart loose on the rails. Hershkop and his brother Gadi, who was a school bus driver, were now the only ones who gave the command post any exercise anymore.

Hershkop waited until one of the cops had his notepad out before he burst out of the garage, pulling up the hood of his sweatshirt as he walked, giving both of the uniforms his best thousand-yard stare. "Can I help you guys?"

"This your vehicle, sir?" the shorter cop asked.

"Uh-huh."

"You got a permit to park it here?"

"My shop's right over there," Hershkop said. "I've always kept vehicles out front. Kind of like a parking area." Which was essentially true. The area was mostly residential, apartment buildings and detached houses, and although much of the block was a no-parking zone, he'd never heard a complaint from his neighbors or from the NYPD.

"Well, I'm sorry, but you're going to have to find another place to put these things. The van, too."

"Why?"

"City regulations."

"How come you don't bother the Shmira guys? They've got their cars all over Eastern Parkway, and I know for a fact that you're not ticketing them."

The cop shrugged. "Look, I don't know about that. All I know is what I'm looking at right now. And these things are parked illegally. It's pretty simple. Move them, and we won't ticket."

"Now?"

"I'll give you 'til the end of the day." And smiling, the two uniforms hightailed it down East New York, strutting like prizefighters, pelvises pushed forward in victory. Hershkop didn't exhale until they'd rounded the corner of Albany, afraid that if he opened his mouth, even for a moment, he'd say something that he'd regret.

For as long as he could remember, the basement office on East New York, kitty-corner to the front door of Everything Automotive, had served as a kind of sanctuary for Hershkop. He loved the low-slung ceilings, the reassuring airlessness of the place, even the striated light, which crept in from the westward-facing windows and fell across the floor in long, jagged rungs. Hershkop's wife used the desk nearest to the entrance, but the rest of the office belonged to Hershkop and his buddies, who often huddled around the back desks, sharing stories, trading jokes, shooting the shit.

Whenever a visitor dropped by the Shomrim office, Hershkop would eagerly lead him to the collection of photographs that were stuck, gallery-style, to the back walls: The portrait of Gadi with Mayor Bloomberg. A picture of the Shomrim with Ray Kelly, everyone madly mugging for the camera. A photo of that time a fire truck—*a fire truck*—had slipped and slid into a crowded Crown Heights intersection, eventually ending up on its side like a wounded dinosaur, and the Shomrim had been there to help. The shot of four Shomrim guys dancing at a pal's wedding, arms interlocked, brows bright with sweat, heads thrown back in glee. Even a glossy photo of Hershkop and his youngest son, the kid wearing his own navy blue Shomrim jacket, fitted especially for his pint-sized frame. Relics from a brighter, happier time.

Proof that once the Shomrim were prized for their valor, beloved by their community. Hershkop trotted down the cement steps and pushed open the office door. His wife was at the front desk. She rolled her eyes and pointed at the phone receiver. He pushed a knot of radio belts off the nearest chair and kicked his legs up on the desk, thinking again about how the next few months were going to shape out, De Luca basically telegraphing his moves now like an aging boxer, no surprise left in his game at all. Hershkop figured he should be prepared for the worst. He leaned down and pulled open the file folder under the desk, then let his fingers roam over the colored tabs. Since 1999, he had been compiling documents on the Shmira and Shomrim feud, first in one metal cube near the door, then in a second file folder at the back of the office. He had hundreds of papers, thousands. More. They spilled across the dashboard of his Shomrim scooter, out of the cabinets in the Shomrim command post.

Of all of this documentation, Hershkop considered two papers to be of especial worth. The first was an open letter, dated January 2000 and penned by Mordechai Ettelson, the former executive director of the Crown Heights Jewish Community Council. The paper was essentially a proclamation of war, Hershkop believed—an attempt on the part of the JCC and the Vaad HaKohol, the elected council of *rabbonim*, to take a stand on the Shomrim and Shmira feud. It had been distributed in 1999, not long after the blood between the Hershkops and Prager went bad, and as far as Hershkop was concerned, the letter told you just about everything you needed to know about the quality of leadership in the community.

"To try to set the record straight," Ettelson had written at the top of the letter, "the Crown Heights Shmira is the only neighborhood patrol that operates under the authority and with the cooperation and support of the JCC and the Vaad HaKohol."

He continued,

Our thanks for your past and continued support of Shmira. The Crown Heights Shomrim is an independent group that had its origins in a political fight. . . . There is, unfortunately, a lot of tension between the old Shomrim coordinators and the present Shmira units. The Vaad refuses to be drawn into these politics and personal feuds; our focus has been, and will remain, simply on providing protection and services to the community.

When the Shomrim provided a service, we allowed them to continue to function. Now that all the units have left and rejoined
the Shmira, we welcome the opportunity to work together in a
united fashion for the community good.

A few lines later, Ettelson added the following:

The Vaad does not believe it is in the community's interest to
publicly attack individuals. The place to resolve differences is
before the Rabbonim, not on the streets. We request everyone
to once again strengthen their resolve to not let themselves be
distracted from our main task in these final moments before the
geula: to work together as one community with achdus.

Bullshit, of course, all of it bullshit, Hershkop thought. Ettelson
and his cronies on the JCC could put up a good front, rattle on
about *achdus*, or "togetherness," and *geula*, "deliverance"—a reference to the dawning of the Messianic age. Those guys could pretend
like they were above it all, that their role was divine, and that it was
the Shomrim who were responsible for all of the backbiting, but in
Hershkop's opinion, they were just as dirty as anyone, maybe dirtier.
They had been given the option to get behind the Shomrim, but
instead they had chosen the villains in the Shmira, and now they were
tacitly allowing a gang of criminals to patrol the neighborhood. Yes,
Ettelson's proclamation was despicable, it gave Hershkop a headache
just thinking about it, but he kept the letter and referred to it regularly. It was similar to the way some Democrats he knew watched Fox
News or listened to Rush Limbaugh—it got your pulse going, it reinvigorated your resolve.

For the same reason, Hershkop rarely went a week without paging
a thin, ragged paperback, published a few years ago by a Hasidic
organization in Israel. The book, which was written in a mixture of
Hebrew and English, told the story of his *zaide*, or grandfather—a
hero who had survived the travails of the *Shoah* and arrived in Crown
Heights not long after the war had ended, intent on participating in
the rebbe's messianic campaign. *Zaide* Hershkop was born in 1918;
he had been lucky enough to study in the village of Lyubavichi, in

Belarus, under the grand rabbis of the Lubavitch court. He had prayed on the same furrowed ground as Rabbi Zalman of Liadi; he had lived through the hard, dark years following World War I and survived the run-up to World War II; he had touched living history. At one point in his memoirs, he describes leaning out the window in Warsaw and watching a young rabbi ask a German soldier in which direction the market lay. The soldier had plunged his knife into the rabbi's gut and steered him in the right direction with the blade.

*Zaide* Hershkop had been drafted into the Red Army, but after a botched escape, he was instead sent to a labor camp in Siberia. *His* father, banished to Samarkand, was murdered for daring to stand up to an Uzbek bully in the bread line, but his mother and his sister survived the war, and the three of them were later reunited in Brooklyn. "A profound thinker, introverted, who spoke slowly in a sing-song tone opening people's hearts, gave his opinion and everyone listened, not a big speaker, never preached, yet shared his thoughts with others," read the introduction to the book, which had been penned by a rabbi named Gurkov. "People didn't realize he was giving guidance and so he influenced all those who heard him as if he was a new source of inspiration."

The book about his *zaide* gave Aron Hershkop plenty of inspiration. It allowed him to see himself as more than a simple Yid. It reminded of his proud lineage. Outsiders were often surprised to discover that Lubavitch society was essentially caste-based, with old-world Chabad aristocracy wielding the most power in Crown Heights and recent converts to Hasidism the least. The Hershkops were a powerful family, with deep roots in the beginnings of the Chabad movement. Aron was descended from brave, learned men, who had resisted at all costs—who had never let the fire escape from their breasts. Like the letter from Ettelson, Hershkop kept his grandfather's memoir close and handled its rough edges regularly; its property was talismanic.

The next morning they came for the command post. Hershkop was in the garage when it went down, stuck under the guts of an old four-door. He extricated himself slowly from under the car, brushed the grit off his ass, and picked up the Shomrim radio. The thing was practically burning up—everyone shouting at once.

"Alright, calm down," Hershkop said. "What's going on out there?" It was still morning. The problem was unlikely to be anything major, the really bad shit—the muggings and the assaults—almost always going down in the afternoon, when the streets were full, or at night, when the NYPD patrols slagged off, and no one was watching. It could be a car crash. Or a pedestrian hit up on Eastern Parkway. At least one *bochur* gets run over on Eastern Parkway every couple of years, Hershkop knew. Kids come from a farm in Israel and think that cars are just going to stop for them, and so they wade out into traffic, and by the time the Shomrim and Hatzolah get to the scene, it's just a body slumped on the asphalt.

"Aron, that you?" The kid was shouting into his handset.

"Yeah," Hershkop said, signaling for the mechanic in the back to turn down the radio, thinking the worst—maybe they *had* gone after his family, maybe this was Code Red, maybe his nightmares were coming true. Every nerve in his body was suddenly alive, his stomach dropping toward his feet like an elevator cut from the cables. He recognized the symptoms of panic—the way your brain is flitting everywhere and nowhere at once. He'd felt like this a few times in the past.

Once, when he was just a teenager, and he'd watched the riots sweep through Crown Heights from his perch on the apartment roof, seeing men he knew beaten with rocks and sticks, the windows of Jewish homes shattered, the fires spreading unabated. And again in 1994, when a Lebanese maniac named Rashid Baz had followed a van full of Lubavitch yeshiva students onto the Brooklyn Bridge, blasting away with a machine gun and a 9-millimeter Glock. Baz managed to hit four of the kids, including Ari Halberstam, who died a few days later in a New York hospital. Inside Baz's car, the police had found a shotgun, a .380-caliber semiautomatic pistol, a bulletproof vest, and a stack of anti-Semitic reading material. The guy was probably capable of something worse, and in a way the other students were lucky, but Hershkop had never forgotten driving out to the foot of the Brooklyn Bridge, seeing the ambulances, the trauma units, the SWAT squads, and thinking that all of the world had imploded in on itself.

"I just saw a cop leaving the 71st with one of those big black tow trucks," one of the guys said, the words coming so fast that Hershkop could barely identify the voice. "The truck is heading down Brooklyn Avenue. I repeat, the tow truck is heading toward you."

Hershkop sprinted across the street, his head tucked. The inside of the command post exhibited the usual clutter, a layer of dust a foot thick on the dashboard, someone's leather radio holster draped over the passenger seat. The smell of spoiled coffee creamer and wet paper. Hershkop produced a knot of keys from his pocket, jamming one and then another into the ignition, none of them fitting, his forehead needling with sweat. He heard the engine kick once and turn over with a dry, asthmatic cough, the whole chassis rattling, Hershkop feathering the gas with his steel-toed boot to move the process along. While he waited, he flicked the talk button on the Motorola. "Did you see who was driving?"

"No idea. It wasn't De Luca, that's all I know."

He looked up in time to see in the rearview mirror the looming black bulk of the NYPD truck. "Yeah, the tow truck is here," Hershkop said. "Can you guys hear me? The tow is on East New York and closing fast." Within a few seconds, Hershkop knew, the driver would be out of the tow truck, sizing up the front bumper of the command post, figuring out how to haul the thing away. Hershkop considered momentarily pleading with the cop, feigning ignorance— "please, sir, I had no idea, sir"—but he knew the guy, if he had half a bit of sense, would never buy it. De Luca had probably already raised the alarms at the 7-1, all of the uniforms clued in to what was at stake. "Fine," Hershkop said to himself, and as soon as the cop stepped down out of the tow truck, Hershkop dropped his toe onto the gas. The hulking van lurched forward in fits and starts, the fan belt squealing in protest, and Hershkop was gone, spinning the wheel hard at the corner of Kingston, the foot traffic on Empire Boulevard in sight.

"Guys, listen. I need a favor," he said into the radio.

All of Brooklyn opened up before him. He kept his right foot pressed almost to the floor, the truck shuddering and kicking, the speedometer hitting 25, 30, the flanks of the apartment complexes on Kingston becoming one hard gray blur.

When Hershkop was a kid, he had believed that he would never leave Crown Heights. Back then, eight blocks really was the end of the world. Although several relatives lived in Israel, Hershkop was unable to conceptualize how the rest of the city might be living, let alone the rest of the borough. Like a fifteenth-century cartographer, his great imagination, eventually petered out. Des Moines, Iowa; Washington, D.C.; Sacramento, California—these were names, not cities. Their residents might as well have been Martians. Hershkop understood, of course, that his worldview was a by-product of the rebbe's grand achievement. The rebbe had created and sustained a Jewish empire amid the clamor of the new world. He had built a shtetl, and it was a shtetl that no Jew wanted to leave.

Or it had been. These days, Hershkop wasn't so sure. His family was still here, his friends were still here, he didn't long to be anywhere else. At the same time, it was clear that something inconceivable was happening in Crown Heights. Something even more dangerous than the riots. Because if there was a silver lining in the clouds that gathered over Brooklyn in 1991, it was that shared feeling of *achdus*, of togetherness. In Lemrick Nelson Jr., the Jews of Crown Heights had been provided with a readily identifiable enemy; in Yankel Rosenbaum, they had a martyr. These days, any spat in Crown Heights was at least as likely to be between two Jews as between a Jew and a black man.

Hershkop passed an empty parking lot, where years ago some teenager had gotten rolled up in the automatic gate, and Hershkop had arrived just in time to pull him out, the kid's face by then purple, his forehead full of broken veins, the eyes big and yellow and halfway out of his head. That face, that kind of damage—you never forgot something like that. Hershkop shook his head, remembering the way the kid's mother had thanked him, treating him like some sort of hero, when really all Hershkop had done was manage to be in the right place at the right time, the kid just lucky, heroics having nothing to do with it, nothing at all.

"Uh, I think you got him on your tail again," the blast of static and radio noise nearly sending Hershkop out of his seat. He recognized the voice as belonging to a kid named Schneider, a Shomrim member about Lifshitz's age. A few blocks away from Eastern Parkway, the steady moan of the eastbound traffic already filling the cab of the command post, Hershkop caught a glimpse of the tow truck in the rearview mirror and, two car lengths behind the tow truck, the silver glint of Schneider's Maxima. They had a regular conga line working their way through Crown Heights.

"Listen, this is what I want you to do," Hershkop said, pulling the van to a halt at the red light, seeing surprise registered in the faces of the passersby. He might as well have been driving an Abrams tank down the boulevard. He waved back, put on his best Shabbos smile.

"What's up?"

"I want you to try to get in front of the tow truck. Cut him off if you have to, but he's too close behind me. I need some space." The tow truck driver, as if reading Hershkop's mind, had begun to edge up on the command post. The only thing Hershkop had to count on was the cop's sense of self-worth. In order to summon a few squad cars, the guy would be forced to admit that, no, he hadn't managed to tow the command post, because the command post had driven away, and now he was involved in a strange slow-motion chase through south Crown Heights, and hey, could anyone give me a hand here? Still, it was sure to happen sooner or later—the cop might be hesitant to admit he'd messed up, but he probably wasn't stupid—and Hershkop figured he had about ten minutes before he heard the first siren peal.

"Yeah, no problem," Schneider said. Hershkop pulled left onto President, a big wide boulevard, perfect for the kind of maneuvering he had in mind. He passed two brick mansions, and at the third, he jammed down on the gas, slapping the dashboard like a jockey urging on a reticent racehorse, praying that the command post had a little more pickup than the tow truck. Behind him, he saw the rack of lights atop the tow truck come alive, but the opening was there, and in came the Maxima, swerving hard toward the sidewalk on the south side of the street and then screeching back across the pavement, until Hershkop could see Schneider in the rearview mirror.

"Perfect," Hershkop said. "Now stall him. Give me a little space."

With his right hand, he flipped open his cell phone. Behind him, Schneider was creeping down President, the tow truck now riding his ass, Hershkop thinking he now had a minute, maybe less, before the cop realized he'd been had. "Gadi, you there?" Hershkop said into the phone. It was late morning, meaning that Gadi would have finished dropping off the last round of yeshiva students, and unless he was working a field trip today, which Hershkop didn't think he was, he was probably napping in the driver's seat of the school bus, dozing off until it was time to make the afternoon rounds.

"What's up?"

"They're trying to tow the command post. You in the lot?"

"Yep."

"I'm coming toward you."

Hershkop didn't wait for an answer. He snapped shut the cell phone and pulled the radio from his lap. "Adam," he said, "we're gonna circle going back toward the shop."

"10-4."

"Just give me a few car lengths."

"Okay."

At the next light, Hershkop peeled left, spinning the wheel hand over hand, seeing Schneider and then the tow truck, all three of them basically locked together now, for better or for worse. He barely touched the brakes on the downhill slope, letting the van gather speed naturally, hoping he wouldn't hit a light. He turned left off Brooklyn Avenue at East New York, bringing the chase full circle to where it had begun. The street was nearly empty. He saw a light on in the Shomrim dispatch office, and he saw his mechanic still standing out front of the shop, felt as if he'd left him there hours ago, but really it had been only ten minutes, less, everything sped up now. In the distance, two blocks east, he saw the sprawling cement lot Gadi used to park his school bus during off hours, and he saw Gadi standing in front of the bus, his profile recognizable even from quarter-mile off.

Hershkop picked up the phone again. Gadi answered after one ring. "I see you," he said.

"Slow him down," Hershkop hollered into the radio.

Schneider slammed on the brakes. The tow truck stopped. Hershkop didn't stop. He kept going, closing fast on the lot: 100 yards, 50 yards, 10 yards, and at the entrance to the lot, he grabbed the steering wheel hard, feeling the heavy vehicle tack hard onto one side of the chassis, nearly tipping over, Hershkop thinking what a sight that would be, what an end to the chase. But then the van bounced back up like a yo-yo. Hershkop nodded over at Gadi, who put the school bus in reverse, blocking any view of the command post.

"Schneider, where is he?"

"Behind me."

"Can he see me?"

"I can't even see you."

Hershkop vaulted down from the cab of the command post and joined Gadi at the fence. As they watched, the tow truck crawled toward them, pausing momentarily at the entrance of the lot, exhaust kicking up into the air in gentle, heavy puffs. The driver knew. He must know. It would take an idiot not to know. But then the tow truck was moving again, turning north up Troy, the driver barely visible through the tinted glass.

Hershkop turned to look at Gadi. He knew what was hanging over his big brother's head: multiple charges for assault, the possibility of jail time, the whole 749 fiasco enough to get him chased out of Crown Heights forever. But Gadi had remained strangely calm in recent months. Like Lifshitz, he seemed to believe that if the members of the Crown Heights Shomrim could keep level heads—if they could support one another—then no hurdle would be too high.

Gadi was the first person Aron called after De Luca had visited the shop. He had expected Gadi to go through the roof, to rage against the injustice of it all, and yes, Gadi had been furious with the actions of the NYPD, but he had borne the whole thing with an incredible forbearance, gripping Aron's shoulder, patting his back, promising him that they'd get through it together. It was a notably courageous stance, considering it was Gadi's ass that was on the line. If the 749 case went to court—and now that Aron had turned down De Luca's offer, a trial looked increasingly likely—it would be Gadi who would be in the hot seat. Aron would be a bystander, just another suit in the gallery.

"Thanks for that," Aron said.

"You got lucky. They're not going to make that mistake again."

Hershkop nodded. His older brother was right. The next time the city came for the Shomrim, someone was going to end up in jail.

# 10

Ben Lifshitz woke to the sound of the Motorola radio. He heard the screeching first in his dreams, and when he opened his eyes, he was almost surprised to find himself back amid the familiar shapes and shadows of his Crown Heights bedroom. He peered over at the alarm clock. Two in the morning. September 2008. Outside, on the horizon, the cityscape glowed a ghostly orange.

Lifshitz sat up on the edge of his bed, wondering if the shrieking had woken his parents or his brother in the next bedroom over. Unlike Ben, Menachem was your traditional old-school Chabadnik, his eyes set on a rabbinical ordination and then a posting to a Chabad house in some foreign city. Increasingly, of course, that kind of future was a pipe dream. Two decades ago, most young men in Crown Heights followed the same path: a few months of fund-raising in the community and then an assignment from the official office of the *shluchim*. Twenty years in the field, far from your friends and family, the only company a bunch of goyim, maybe if you were lucky a few secular Jews, and every day a battle to convince outsiders to see things your way.

The work was hard and draining, but for the rabbis who managed to open successful Chabad houses and attract a fair share of converts, there was glory aplenty. *Shluchim* returning to Crown Heights after a spell abroad were treated like kings—they had joined the Rebbe's Army, they had spread the rebbe's message. They had done their part to bring *Moshiach*.

These days, not only was it harder to obtain funding, what with the economy the way it was, but it was harder to find a city *not* already claimed by a *shaliach*. All of the major cities in the United States, for instance, were already spoken for, as were many of the European capitals. And you certainly didn't want to step on anyone's toes. There was still space in Asia or Russia, but the odds of success out there were much lower, and who wanted to live in the middle of nowhere anyway?

So now recent yeshiva graduates were increasingly hoping to sign on as a kind of under-*shaliach* at an established Chabad house and from there attract the attention of the Lubavitch leadership. The process was slower than it had once been and the promise of reward greatly diminished. Lifshitz understood his brother's motivations, but he was unable to share in his enthusiasm for a life lived abroad, the distances measured in miles and years. Wave good-bye to friends and family and board that plane and expect to be back in Brooklyn once a year, if you were lucky.

For Lifshitz, glory lay elsewhere. He had joined the Shomrim at seventeen, just months after he learned to drive. It was the fulfillment of a childhood dream, a day he remembered with fondness. His father, Yossi, had also been a member of a Crown Heights security patrol, and growing up, Ben had heard plenty of stories about the good old days. The thugs had run in fear from the Lubavitchers back then, scattering at the sound of the sirens. Yossi had worked alongside Israel Shemtov, the Red Baron. He'd chased robbers and rapists, thrown a few good punches. He had even told Ben that in the '80s, it wasn't uncommon for patrol members to police their own. They'd hear about a guy beating his wife, and they'd haul the guy into the back of the squad car, take him to a darkened basement, and work him over until he got the message.

If a few bones got broken, a few ribs cracked, well, what was there to say about that except that the evil were always punished. Ben appreciated the sentiment—sometimes, he understood, brutality was warranted—but he had always been less interested in fighting than in keeping the peace. *His* pride in being a member of the Shomrim was rooted in the warm nods and smiles he received from members of the community. He got the same rush from running down a purse snatcher that he did from changing a tire in the freezing cold.

And that, as far as Lifshitz was concerned, was the biggest difference between the Shmira and the Shomrim. The Shomrim were conscientious members of the community—they were fathers, brothers, husbands. The Shmira, on the other hand, in his opinion, were jokers, pranksters, minor-league thugs. Unfortunately, it was impossible to reason with thugs, and try as the Shomrim might to turn the other cheek, eventually the organization was always dragged back into the fight. After a while, the fight was all there was.

The radio screeched again. The sound this time was high and long, punctuated by grunts and moans. The serial jammer strikes again, Lifshitz thought. The symphony varied, from week to week. One evening, Lifshitz had opened his eyes and stared at the ceiling of his bedrooms and realized in astonishment that he was listening to some sort of fucking Christian hymn, the singer praising Jesus, the holy ghost, mother Mary, whatever the hell it was the Christians praised. More often, though, it was just a combination of static and a sound that resonated in your teeth—like nails on a chalkboard, like the tines of a fork dragged across an empty plate, like feedback from a broken amplifier.

Lifshitz stood up. It was going to be another long, sleepless night. He considered getting on his cell phone and calling up one of the Hershkops, but they might not be awake. Although it was standard procedure for most Shomrim members to keep their radios on at all times, in case a serious emergency developed, many of the guys had families, and they turned down the volume after a certain hour, in order not to disturb their kids. Lifshitz didn't have that problem. He was twenty-two, which was well nigh marriageable age in Lubavitch culture, but Lifshitz was intent on taking his time. No matchmaker yet.

On the bed, the Motorola was burping static. The kicker of this whole charade—the screeching, the Christian music—was that Lifshitz had a pretty good idea of who was jamming the radios, but until they had cold, concrete proof, there wasn't much he could do. The kid's name was Efraim Petrov. Probably twenty or twenty-one, a bit behind Lifshitz in school but close enough that their circles of friends overlapped. A few years ago, Petrov had signed on with the Crown Heights Shmira.

Whether a prospective recruit signed on with the Shmira or the Shomrim was often a matter of politics. Generally speaking, a moderate, old-school Chabadnik would join the Shomrim, and a messianist or a messianist-sympathizer would join the Shmira. Sometimes the calculus was even simpler: if you had a pal on the Shomrim, you might become a member of that organization, even if your uncle and aunt and all of your cousins were messianists. It was commonplace on Kingston Avenue to hear a Hasid refer to the "unholy alliance" between the Shmira and the messianists, and there was something to this: when there was a fight at the shul on 770 Eastern Parkway, the messianists would call in the Shmira to defend their interests, and the moderates would use the Shomrim as enforcers.

Still, in Petrov's case, it was probably just a matter of convenience, of a few friends on the Shmira getting the kid through the door, showing him the ropes, teaching him to hate the Shomrim. The Shmira boys passed this hatred from generation to generation, Lifshitz knew, instilling in each new member the belief that the Shomrim were there to be resisted, pilloried, ground into dust.

For a while, Petrov had been one of the quieter members of the Shmira, always there but never in your face, just another blue jacket and blue ball cap sauntering around Kingston. But then in June he'd found a job with a local gypsy cab company, doing late night and early runs up and down Eastern Parkway. A month later, the jamming commenced. To Lifshitz, it made sense that Petrov was the culprit.

Not only did the timing line up—the screeching commenced on nights that Petrov was on duty—but so did the method: whoever was fucking with the Shomrim radios was not just sitting in one place, because if he'd been sitting in one place, the Shomrim could easily have followed the signal to its source. No, the serial jammer was constantly moving around Crown Heights, looping through the back streets, circling Kingston, always in motion, always out of reach.

For kicks, Lifshitz picked up the radio, which had gone silent again. He pressed the talk button. "You there, Petrov? We're going to get you for this. We're going to get you, you hear that, Petrov?" No answer. A strange, gummy silence descended over the bedroom. Maybe the kid had picked up a fare. Lifshitz imagined him behind the wheel of the gypsy cab, steering with one hand, the other fondling the radio on the passenger seat. Short, blond, round little Petrov—an unlikely hack. Well, he'll go down sooner or later. "That's right, Petrov, you rat," Lifshitz said out loud. "It's over."

A couple of weeks earlier, Aron Hershkop had suggested that the Shomrim give Petrov a taste of his own medicine. He and Gadi and Lifshitz had set their Motorola radios to the channel used by the Shmira, just opened up, barraging Petrov with the most vile shit they could summon up. "Petrov, you were probably molested as a child, weren't you?" they'd say.

Or: "Petrov, is that Muslim rat Prager going to make you a lieutenant in his jihadist army? You going to make jihad, Petrov?"

Or: "Christian music, huh, Petrov? You must have been molested as a child."

Or: "Petrov, we know it's you. Your ship is sunk, Petrov."

Or: "Petrov, you're going to get it, you no good piece of shit, you and your Russian father."

Threats intended to get all the way under Petrov's skin, to shake him into submission. But Petrov had never responded. He had kept his cool. And now this. The night of a thousand shrieks.

Lifshitz was halfway across the room when the radio crackled to life again. "Hello?" someone was saying. "Hello?" The voice gave way to the sound of rock music, the tune at once familiar and distorted, Petrov probably wiggling his radio in front of the car speakers.

They needed a better plan. The Shomrim needed to shut Petrov up for good.


At 8 a.m. the next morning, Lifshitz grabbed his knapsack and booked on down Crown Street, the day mild, the city finally shaking off that oppressive late summer heat. At the corner of Brooklyn, Lifshitz turned left, deciding at the last minute that he'd do his work

today from the Shomrim dispatch office. Technically, Lifshitz could work anywhere. No office for him. No cubicles, no water cooler bullshit. He was lucky in that way. He made the bulk of his money from selling ads for CrownHeights.info—the crime scene and accident photography for the tabloids really only added up to pocket change, the excitement of it worth more than the actual cash—and you could sell ads from just about anywhere. You could sell ads while sitting on the couch in your pajamas, one hand on the mouse, the other on the TV remote.

Which is basically what Lifshitz had done when he founded the site a few years earlier. The dream at first had been to create a hub for Lubavitchers, a place where a *frum* Jew could come to keep track of developments in the community. Lifshitz plastered the top of the landing page with a photograph of the row houses of Crown Heights and settled on an Olde English ornate script for the mast, the design meant to suggest stateliness, trustworthiness. His timing was good. By 2006, the majority of Lubavitch households were online, and although the official Chabad website provided plenty of content, what people wanted was a site that tracked the stuff they really cared about—the bar and bat mitzvahs, the engagement announcements, the funerals, parking information, the latest gossip from Kingston Avenue. Lifshitz provided all of this. He posted dozens of news items a day, along with dispatches from Lubavitchers as far away as Australia. He encouraged a lively dialogue in the comments section under each article. He took photographs from parades, public events, conferences. He accepted opinion pieces from high-ranking Chabad officials.

And gradually, he adjusted the tone of the site to reflect his own politics. He plastered the Shomrim number on the left rail of the homepage, right next to the contact information for Hatzolah; he left off the number for the Shmira. When the messianists and the moderates clashed in the shul at 770 Eastern Parkway, he posted pictures of the damage allegedly done by the messianists. After the brawl at 749—a brawl that Lifshitz had been involved in—he was unequivocal in his denouncement of the *bochurim*. Over the years, Lifshitz had received more than one letter from prominent *rabbonim*, urging him to refrain from publicly commenting on community politics. He had pinned the letters in the Shomrim dispatch office, alongside the quote from Euripides, but he had never deigned to respond.

Lifshitz was from a new generation of Hasidim. He was a member of the Web age. He believed that Crown Heights had become too much of a ghetto. He believed that old line about sunlight being the best disinfectant. He reasoned that it was better to control the message than to sweep unsavory news into the corner. He understood that privacy in the twenty-first century was something of an illusion, and that the harder the *rabbonim* worked to obscure the inner workings of the Lubavitch community, the more curious outsiders would become. The site traffic soared. Lifshitz was soon receiving thousands of clicks a day, from ISP addresses around the globe. He raised ad rates and then raised them again. And local businesses paid. How could they not? Lifshitz had in essence answered their prayers: He had built a niche site read almost exclusively by Hasidim. It was targeted advertising at its best.

At twenty-two, Lifshitz was already a major power broker in the Crown Heights community—a regular Hasidic Hearst. He wasn't exactly raking it in hand over foot, but his only real expenses were server space and Web hosting fees, and he was living comfortably. More important, he enjoyed his work. He was a natural journalist. He had a feel for the story—for the things that people said they wanted to read about and the things they really wanted to read about.

Ten minutes later, Lifshitz pushed open the door of the Shomrim dispatch office and tiptoed to the back of the room. The desk was a mess. Paper everywhere. He planted his laptop on the only clear piece of real estate and spent the next hour answering e-mail. At 9:30, Aron ducked into the office to talk to his wife about a parts order, and Lifshitz flagged him down.

"Long night?" Aron said, pulling up a chair next to the desk.

"The jammer strikes again."

Lifshitz always acted a little skittish around Hershkop. It was less the age thing—they had almost a decade between them—than a fundamental difference in the way the two men saw the world. Aron was like Lifshitz's father: brawny, self-confident, strong-willed. A *sabra*. Lifshitz did his best to put up that kind of front, but at heart, he was more of a thinker than a fighter. And Aron, of all people, understood the distinction.

"So, what do you want to do about it?" Hershkop asked.

Lifshitz shrugged. "Well, I was thinking we might be able to use a little bit of outside help."

"Like a private detective?"

"Sort of. Actually, there are these guys down in south Brooklyn, down in Bay Ridge, and they do radio technician work. What if we hired them to trace the jammer? They have the right equipment—they could follow the noise right to Petrov's car. That way we'd know for sure. And if we knew for sure . . ."

"How much would something like that cost?" Hershkop peered down at Lifshitz.

"Couple grand, probably. Maybe less."

"All right. Let's do it."

"Really?"

"Why not?" Hershkop said and stood up. "We've got nothing to lose."


The techs took less than a week to catch up with Petrov. They might have worked even more quickly, but it turned out that Petrov had a good little game going—the kid was jamming the Shomrim radios only when he was in a high-radio-traffic area, around cabs and cop cars and ambulances. So the techs spent their first few nights on the job running circles all over Crown Heights, hearing the signal but unable to trace it definitively to one source. Luckily, Petrov had gotten sloppy. Or maybe he hadn't realized that he was being tracked. Either way, on a Thursday in September, when Lifshitz was at home, parked in front of his laptop listening to a Christian aria float out of the tinny speakers of the Motorola, the techs called in to say they'd tracked down their mark up in Prospect Heights, not far from the tip of Prospect Park.

"What's the car look like?" Lifshitz said.

"Maybe a Town Car?"

"That's the one," Lifshitz hooted. He would have to call Aron. It was only 10 p.m. He'd be up. After that, he could rouse a few other guys, try to head off Petrov near the plaza.

"Great. And you guys are sure?"

"Yeah. We're sure. It's coming from that car. But you'd better hurry—he's not going to stick around here forever." Lifshitz took down the plate number and barreled down the staircase with his radio in his hand. If he took the back streets and managed to avoid most of the lights, he could be at Grand Army Plaza in less than five minutes. He climbed into the bucket seat of his Nissan and drove fast, instinctively, traveling two blocks before he realized he hadn't even turned on the lights. The radio was blaring next to him, the sounds mostly feedback, normally the kind of thing that drove Lifshitz wild, but he found that he could stomach it now—the noise basically just the last cries of a dying animal. Passing out of the Jewish settlement, the apartment buildings going gray in this part of town, the front lawns dark and overgrown, Lifshitz got on his phone and dialed Aron's number.

"Yeah, we got him," Lifshitz said.

"Where?" Aron's voice suddenly alert.

"He's heading toward Grand Army Plaza. He's in a Town Car."

"On the way."

Out the passenger side window, Lifshitz saw the shadowy bulk of the Ebbets projects, sprawling over an entire city block. Half a decade earlier, those projects had been a playground for Hank Aaron and the rest of the Brooklyn Dodgers. And then in 1965, Walter O'Malley 1958 had yanked the Dodgers out of New York and sent them out to Los Angeles. O'Malley was looking for a bigger audience, but he might have also been convinced that white folks were no longer willing to visit this part of Brooklyn. Which was probably true. Back then, the neighborhood was going rough, the *alrightniks* hightailing it for the suburbs, the crime coming in, Bed-Stuy spilling over, the riots a few decades off, but the seeds were there, the neighborhood already seen as a front line in the race wars. This was way before Lifshitz's time, of course. It was even before his father's time, who had come to Crown Heights from Israel.

But like Aron Hershkop, Lifshitz was a great lover of the history of Brooklyn. It seemed to him that there was no other place in New York City—maybe no other place in America—that changed so much and so regularly. It was like that old joke about the weather in the Northeast: if you don't like the weather now, just hang on a couple of minutes. Lifshitz had heard family members complain about how bad Brooklyn had gotten in recent years, how the Lubavitchers were such pioneers, such stalwarts—they'd stayed put when all of the other whites had left. But Lifshitz took the long view. Take those projects, for instance. Yes, it was disappointing that a relic like Ebbets Field had been demolished. But before anyone got the idea to build Ebbets Field, that particular patch of Brooklyn had played host to a collection of huts and shanties known as Pigtown. It was said that you could smell Pigtown before you saw it. It was said you could smell Pigtown as far away as the island of Manhattan. It was said that when the rich Jews first settled on Eastern Parkway, they were forced to regularly beat back packs of savage goats, which every afternoon picked their way up the slope from Pigtown, intent on munching on some fresh *alrightnik* refuse. But Pigtown had given way to Ebbets Field, just as Ebbets Field had given way to the projects, and who was to say that it wouldn't come full circle again?

In fact, if you believed what they wrote in the real estate section of the *New York Times*, the grand old buildings off Eastern Parkway had recently become yuppie magnets. College students priced out of Park Slope, aging academics, struggling writers—even transplanted Manhattanites wanted a piece of the neighborhood. And would anyone tell *them* that the land underfoot had once been three feet deep with pig shit? Unlikely. Instead, the yuppies would continue their westward march, and pretty soon, the project house would be razed and replaced with a luxury apartment complex, one of those places with pool tables in the basement, a yoga room in the lobby, and a pebble "beach" on the roof. Brooklyn was perpetually trapped in a cycle of decay and renewal, and that was a pretty comforting thought—you could count on even the worst things going good, if only you could hang on long enough to see them change.

In the end, it all happened pretty quickly. Lifshitz came into the plaza from Eastern Parkway, straight west, seeing first the ghostly blue glow of the lights around the fountain and then the proud arch itself, slicing the fall sky in half. He paused at a red light. The trip out from

Crown Street had taken four minutes. Standing up a little in his seat, Lifshitz peered out into the plaza.

Two hundred years earlier, the area was a forest. Fifty years later, Frederick Law Olmstead showed up and started work on the parkway. The plaza was built after the boulevard was finished. It had been Olmstead's crowning touch—the ultimate flourish. The Grand Army Plaza, a monument to all of the soldiers of the Grand Army of the Republic, who had perished tamping down the Southern insurrection. In the early twentieth century, the last surviving Union veterans had been invited to march out from the plaza named in their honor and down Eastern Parkway. Black-and-white photographs from that day show a bunch of hobble-kneed geriatrics, one of the guys using his sword as a cane. When you thought about it, the Civil War wasn't so different from the feud between the Shomrim and the Shmira. A house, divided. Wasn't that what Lincoln had said? The difference here being that there was not much of a possibility of reunification. They'd been fighting for close to a decade, and they'd probably be fighting for a decade more, if punks like Petrov had anything to say about it. Lifshitz himself would be as old as that Union soldier before the Shomrim and the Shmira had laid the last of their grievances to rest.

The light went green, and Lifshitz let up on the brake. He spotted the black gypsy cab right away, lingering near the east end of the traffic circle, kicking up puffs of exhaust into the fall air. Lifshitz was pinned into the far left lane, close enough to the plaza to see the light playing off the gold statues on top of the arch.

"Can anyone hear me? I got Petrov," he said into the Motorola.

For several seconds he heard nothing but static. The other guys had probably turned their radios off, not wanting to hear any more Christian hymns. Lifshitz had his cell phone open when the speakers of the Motorola lit up. "Yeah, Ben, we see him. You see us?" It was Aron. Lifshitz poked his head out the window. He saw only traffic, the hard right angles of the cars and the trucks stuck here with him in the plaza.

"Look toward the park," Aron said. "Up toward Utica."

Behind him, someone was laying hard on the horn. The light had gone green. Coming around the southeast corner of Grand Army Plaza, Lifshitz caught sight again of the gypsy cab. He cut hard right across one lane, coming up just ten yards off the back of the cab. Eight yards, five yards, Petrov's round face and blond beard visible in the rearview. Lifshitz followed Petrov off the plaza and onto Utica and straight toward the two Shomrim scooters, which were parked in the right lane, their red-and-whites lighting up the asphalt.

To his credit, Petrov was smart enough not to go rabbit. He let himself be sandwiched in by the Shomrim scooters up in front and the Maxima in back, until the traffic died off, and the driver of the scooter on the left slammed on the brakes, and Aron Hershkop hopped out of the scooter on the right. Petrov got out last, his fingers raised toward the sky. Then Petrov was being pulled onto the sidewalk. "No hands," Lifshitz shouted. "No hands!"

It took Lifshitz a few seconds to get up next to Petrov, who had collapsed like a soggy pretzel, his knees and ankles crumpling under his torso, his mouth going a million miles a minute. As Lifshitz watched, a big fat tear slid out of Petrov's eye, slipped across the bridge of his nose, and dropped to the ground with a satisfying *splat*.

# 11

On Thursday, April 11, 1991, five days after the end of Passover, Menachem Mendel Schneerson traveled from his offices on Eastern Parkway to the Old Montefiore Cemetery in Queens, the resting place of his father-in-law, Yosef Yitzchak Schneersohn. Those were trying days for the rebbe. In 1988, Chaya Mushka, his wife of almost six decades—the woman who had accompanied Schneerson from the tumult of wartime Europe to the throne of the Lubavitch empire—had passed away at Cornell Medical Center in Manhattan. Schneerson, now eighty-eight years old and increasingly reliant on the support of his aides, had no immediate family remaining.

His mother and father were dead; one brother had been killed by the Nazis, and the other had died of natural causes in England, at the age of forty-three. Meanwhile, the library case had effectively soured his ties to the Gourary family. Schneerson remained constantly surrounded by his followers, but as Samuel Heilman and Menachem Friedman wrote in their biography of Schneerson, his followers "could not be his 'friends,' precisely because they were his Hasidim." Schneerson visited the grave of his predecessor, Yosef Yitzchak Schneersohn, "religiously and regularly":

But the responses he got from the dead man were all inside his own head and heart. Given this sort of personal isolation and solitude in the midst of the excitement of [his outreach work] and a growing coterie of people who nearly worshipped him and revered his every act, statement, or thought, what must have happened to his sense of proportion? To whom could he turn for counsel and advice? He claimed he was getting it from his late father-in-law, but what could be the nature of such communications? Could they have connected him to reality, or would they instead have reinforced his sense of being all alone in the world? Was he, moreover, becoming a person with so much power and influence that he was now too heavily anchored in his own vantage point and unable to see beyond it?

Perhaps unsurprisingly, given his own looming mortality, Schneerson had become in recent months fixated on the imminent arrival of the Messiah. Messianism—the belief that a flesh-and-blood descendant of David will redeem mankind, raise the dead, and return the Jews to the Holy Land—is part and parcel of ultra-Orthodox Judaism. Jerome Mintz has argued that it is "messianic tension" that gives direction to the Hasidic movement, and messianism is certainly an omnipresent part of Hasidic life, from morning prayers to evening davening. It is a goal, a touchstone, the reason to spread the *yiddishkeit*.

The question is not when the Messiah will arrive, but how he will arrive, and what one can do to help ensure his arrival. A Hasid does not wait for the Messiah passively, as one waits for the inevitable changing of the seasons. He or she waits actively, as one waits for a cross-town bus already spotted cresting the nearest hill. The Messianic age is considered to be imminent and indeed tangible—many Lubavitchers openly speculate about how they will be carried to Israel when the temple is rebuilt; some have been known to leave packed suitcases near the front door.

In his enduring optimism, a rebbe is no different from his Hasidim. He trusts fervently in the impending Messianic age and either secretly or openly hopes that he will be alive to see it. The motto of Yosef Yitzchak Schneersohn, the sixth Lubavitcher rebbe, had been *l'altar l'tshuvah, l'altar l'geula*, or "repentance immediately, redemption immediately." When Yosef Yitzchak Schneersohn died in 1950, without having brought *Moshiach*, his Hasidim were incredulous. Their leader had survived both the Russian Revolution and World War II; he had forecast the arrival of a redeemer; now he was dead and gone, and redemption remained out of reach. "A feeling of unease" was "gnawing at us," one Lubavitcher wrote in his diary at the time. "How could it be?" A year later, the bereft Hasidim of Crown Heights transferred their hopes to Menachem Mendel Schneerson.

Initially, Schneerson seemed to bridle at the sheer emotional weight of the load he was obliged to shoulder—in his early years, he referred back frequently to the teachings of Yosef Yitzhak, often as if his predecessor were still alive. But eventually, he warmed to his role. He became convinced that Yosef Yitzhak had paved the way for the Messiah, and that it would be left to him, a member of the seventh generation of the Chabad dynasty, to actually usher in the Messianic age.

Heilman and Friedman wrote that this conviction, which they nicely described as "a recurring leitmotif of the reign of Rabbi Menachem Mendel," was rooted in scripture: Just as there had been seven generations between the patriarch Abraham and Moses, Schneerson argued, it would take seven generations of Lubavitchers to welcome the Messiah. Schneerson structured his entire outreach campaign—from the "Mitzvah Campaign" to the work of the *shluchim* around the world—as means to this end. He saw himself as preparing the ground for the Messianic age. With every new Torah school, every murmured blessing, with every time a secular or nonaffiliated Jew tied on *tefillin*, the Messiah inched one step closer to earth.

Schneerson was not shy about discussing these divine aims. On the occasion of his seventieth birthday, for instance, he was asked by a reporter for the *New York Times* if he had any thoughts on a possible successor. "The Messiah will come and he will take all these troubles and doubts," Schneerson responded elliptically. "He could come while I am here. Why postpone his coming?"

In other words, there was little use in answering the question: the inevitable dawning of the Messianic age would obviate the need for an eighth Lubavitcher rebbe. Schneerson certainly had good reason to be optimistic. There were Chabad houses in every corner of the globe; the growing movement had won thousands of converts; the great politicians of the world regularly traveled to Eastern Parkway to pay homage at his doorstep; Schneerson's face appeared on bumper stickers in Israel, posters in South America, and the covers of news-magazines in the United States. Word of the Lubavitch campaign had traveled far and wide. The Hasidim had prepared the ground. It could be only a matter of years before the Messiah deigned to make himself known.

On August 2, 1990, Schneerson got the sign he was looking for: Saddam Hussein sent troops into Kuwait, directly threatening both Israel and the balance of power in the Middle East. The rebbe located a tract of the Midrash called the Yalkut Shim'oni, which prophesied that *Moshiach* would arrive only after a great war involving Israel and an Arab king. "The time for your redemption" has arrived, Schneerson said, quoting from the Yalkut Shim'oni. Israeli Lubavitchers and their relatives in Brooklyn worried that Hussein would make good on his threats to annihilate Israel; they asked whether they should flee the Holy Land. But Schneerson promised his Hasidim they would be safe. Months later, the U.S. Army swept through Iraq, Hussein capitulated, and Israel remained unbowed, if slightly battered. The rebbe was hailed as a seer.

At home in Crown Heights, the Jewish settlement rippled with messianic fervor. Heilman and Friedman reported that in the weeks before Purim and Passover of 1991, "every Sabbath was filled with talk about the impending arrival of the Redeemer." Lubavitch Hasidim, recalling the prophecy of the power of the "seventh generation," quickly connected the dots: Passover is a celebration of the original exodus from Egypt—"the archetype of the ultimate messianic redemption." Moses, seven generations distant from Abraham, had led the Jews to salvation, and now the rebbe, seven generations distant from Rabbi Schneur Zalman, would lead the Jews into the Messianic age.

And then: nothing.

The heavens did not part, the ragged dead did not crawl their way out of the earth to be re-anointed by the open sky, the Temple remained unbuilt. Lions did not lie with lambs. The Messiah tarried. In the shops of Kingston Avenue, in the parlors of the grand mansions of President Street, in the living rooms of the limestone row houses on Carroll and Union streets, the faithful prayed. The whole of the world seemed consumed by longing. The brash grew restless and wild; the practical did their best to resume their normal routines; the wisest counseled patience. If not this year, maybe the next. If not next year, the year after. The Chabad community held its breath.

No one blamed the rebbe for the delay. Such a thing was inconceivable—the leader of the Lubavitch Hasidim was considered to be infallible. If the Messianic age had not yet dawned—if the Jewish people had not traveled through the clouds to a new home in Jerusalem—it was no fault of the rebbe. It was just the way of things.

The rebbe, on the other hand, was free to speculate as to the nature of his failures, and on April 11, 1991, not long after his visit to the Old Montefiore Cemetery in Queens, he appeared to undergo a crisis of conscience. That night, once the evening prayers were finished— and as his aides scurried to rig up a microphone and speakers— Schneerson sat at his regular place at the back of the basement shul and confessed that all of his outreach work—the Chabad houses, the Mitzvah Tanks, the ceaseless davening, all of it—had led to nothing but *hevel verik*, or "futility." The Messiah, he said, was tarrying for one simple reason: Schneerson and his Hasidim had not tried hard enough. If they believed deeply, if they had *truly* spread the word of God, then the Messiah would have already arrived. "How can it be that until this moment," he sighed, "we have not been able to bring about the coming of the Messiah?"

And then he turned the tables on his Hasidim. He said he was speaking in public "because hopefully if I talk about it, maybe it will affect one, two, or three Jews who will be stubborn and will not agree to any substitutions other than *Moshiach*." He did not abdicate responsibility for the Chabad movement at large, but he did suggest that if *Moshiach* was ever to arrive, his followers would have to intensify their efforts:

What more can I do? I have done all I can to bring the Jewish people to truly demand and clamor for the redemption. Yet we are still in exile and, more importantly, an internal exile of distorted priorities. I leave it to you. It is not sufficient to mouth slogans. It is in your hands of each of you to bring the ultimate redemption with your actions. Through your study and observance of Torah you can bring about the peaceful world of Moshiach.

The following Saturday, Schneerson convened a full-scale *farbrengen* on the same topic. Again, he exhorted his Hasidim to rise to the occasion; again, he argued that the Jews remained in exile for a reason. This time, when the rebbe was finished speaking, a Hasid leaped to his feet with a suggestion: Wasn't it time, the man demanded, that the rebbe reveal *himself* as *Moshiach*? Seconds later, a second Lubavitcher asked Schneerson to "decree that the Messiah should come." The shul was consumed with titters, whispers, the low hum of singing. But the rebbe was adamant. "I know what my work is," he reportedly said. "Don't give me new assignments. I already said what work you have to do." In the secular press, Schneerson's words were greeted as proof that the rebbe had finally gotten real on the issue of messianism—that Lubavitch, in the formulation of the journalist Adam Mark, had adopted a new, pragmatist worldview.

The rebbe, Mark wrote in the *Jewish Week*, had delivered "the bluntest possible declaration that he has physical and mystical limitations and should not be 'bowed down to.'"


The idea that the rebbe could be the Messiah was not a particularly new one, nor—contrary to the "blunt" declaration issued by Schneerson—was it in any danger of being erased in 1991. In fact, the movement was growing, quietly and steadily. It is hard to identify the first strains of this messianism, whose adherents are now known in Crown Heights as *Mischistizn*, but it is likely that it existed as soon as Menachem Mendel took the reins of the Lubavitch movement. And why not? The Messiah is identified in scripture as a *tzaddik* hewn from flesh and bone, and to a Hasid, no one is more of a *tzaddik* than his own rebbe. Rabbi Yehuda Krinsky—once the rebbe's secretary and driver and now a major figure in the Chabad leadership—has repeatedly acknowledged this tautology, as have other high-ranking Lubavitch officials.

"Our sages teach us that the Messiah will be a human being who lives among us," Krinsky told a reporter for *Newsday* in 1988. "We believe that in every generation there is a person who has the qualifications to be the Messiah of the Jewish people. I don't know of anyone around now more suitable to fill the shoes of the Messiah than the Rebbe."

But there are levels to messianism—a sliding spectrum from a firm belief that the rebbe is the Messiah to the belief that the rebbe was merely a great man, with an exceptional ability to lead his people and a divinely ordained connection to God. There are also differences in how a Lubavitcher will act on his messianist beliefs. A moderate, for example, might tell an outsider that he doesn't know *who* the Messiah is—it could be anyone, and sure, it could be the rebbe, or it might not be, but listen, the rebbe is a great man, you understand? A messianist, on the other hand, believes it is his holy duty to act on his belief that the rebbe is *Moshiach*, the sooner to bring in the Messianic era. These levels—all of the colors of the spectrum—first bubbled into public view as early as the 1980s.

The journalist Sue Fishkoff has reported on some of the more noticeable early manifestations: A Lubavitcher who apparently rented a helicopter and scattered leaflets across the Israeli countryside, heralding the arrival of the redeemer. The children at Chabad summer camps, who took to singing a hymn with the words "our Rebbe, our Messiah." The *shaliach* in Israel who repeatedly told his congregants that *Moshiach* had already arrived. In April, not long after the rebbe had shouted down his messianist supporter at the *farbrengen*, David Nachshon, an Israeli Lubavitcher, penned a manifesto, urging the rebbe to reveal his true identity to the world. Nachshon obtained the signatures of a sizable contingent of Lubavitchers, and on May 25, he read the terms of the manifesto to the rebbe at the Chabad offices on Eastern Parkway. According to Heilman and Friedman, Nachshon and his supporters then burst into a spontaneous song-and-dance routine, while the rebbe waved his hands in time to the beat.

At other times, Schneerson pointedly sought to tamp down on messianist rhetoric. He threatened to walk out of 770 if his supporters did not stop singing *Yehi*, the messianist anthem; he chided the Hasidim who insisted on greeting him as *Moshiach*; he said hearing messianist talk was like being stabbed in the chest.

Many Lubavitchers argue now—as they argued in the 1980s and the '90s—that Schneerson denounced the messianist movement out of necessity. In private, they maintain, he condoned and even encouraged the *messianists*. There could be something to this: Schneerson had always been especially savvy about the image of Chabad, and he must have been well aware that many secular and especially Hasidic Jews saw the Lubavitch messianist strain as an abomination—a deliberate affront to Jews everywhere. "Who will be the next Rebbe when your Messiah Rebbe dies?" read a set of pamphlets distributed in Brooklyn in the '80s, as the *Mischistizn* gained traction. To critics of Lubavitch, the messianist movement was proof of what they had suspected all along: that Chabad was nothing but a cult of personality, centered around a charismatic and delusional leader.

They pointed to the infamous case of Shabtai Tzvi, a seventeenth-century rabbi born and schooled in the Russian town of Smyrna. In 1665, Shabtai Tzvi declared himself the Messiah and crisscrossed the Jewish world, attracting adherents and arousing what Elie Wiesel has called "indescribable enthusiasm and exultation." Thousands of Jews threw in their lot with Shabtai Tzvi and began preparing themselves for the coming of the Messianic age. Some sold all of their belongings; others set off by foot for the Holy Land, where they could have front-row seats to the redemption. But their faith was misplaced. Shabtai Tzvi was soon captured by the Turks, and in an attempt to save his own neck, he converted to Islam. He died in exile in Albania, not the first but—per Wiesel—certainly the "most prestigious of the false Messiahs."

The messianists in Crown Heights knew well the lessons learned from Shabtai Tzvi, and yet they remained undaunted. They were convinced that unlike the Jewry of yore, who had been so taken with the ministrations of a false prophet, *they* knew a *Moshiach* when they saw one. The boldest of the *Mischistizn* took to wearing yarmulkes stitched with script proclaiming the coming of Messiah and distributed messianist cassettes, posters, and faxes. They sang *Yehi* at every turn, putting particular emphasis on the words "king" and "Messiah." It was as if the harder they sang—the more ecstatically they prayed—the sooner *Moshiach* would come.

On Saturday, January 1992, a gaggle of Lubavitcher rabbis went so far as to convene a panel discussion, in which they arrived at what they described as concrete proof of their rebbe's role in the redemption. They announced their findings via worldwide satellite feed; they hoped that by "crowning" a king, Schneerson would be quicker to reveal himself to the world.

They pointed to new portents: the dissolution of the Soviet Union, the ascension of the *shaliach* Berel Lazar to chief rabbi of all of Moscow, a multinational nuclear disarmament treaty that seemed to ensure the universal peace promised in scripture. They declared the Hebrew year 5752 the "year of blessings in everything" and issued a legal document officially identifying Schneerson as *Moshiach*. The messianic fire had never burned more fiercely. Deliverance had never seemed closer at hand.

And then: nothing.


At 3 p.m. on March 2, 1992, a month and a half before his ninetieth birthday, Menachem Mendel Schneerson again arrived at Montefiore Cemetery, in the company of his driver and trusted aide Yehuda Krinsky. In the year since he had instructed his Hasidim that redemption now lay in their hands, Schneerson had visited the grave of his father-in-law dozens of times, often staying for hours at a time. There must have been much on his mind: the future of the outreach movement that he had helped build, the growing messianist faction, the aftermath of the race riots that had nearly torn Crown Heights apart. On most days, Krinsky would escort Schneerson as far as the door of the small enclosure, the *ohel*, built over the grave, and then pull the door shut behind him, leaving the rebbe to his prayers. Krinsky told Samuel Heilman that the rebbe typically entered the *ohel* around 3 p.m. and emerged well before sunset, in order to attend the afternoon prayers back at 770.

But on this day, the rebbe remained at the grave until 5:40, five minutes after the last rays of the winter sun had slipped over the horizon. Worried, Krinsky made his way to the door of the *ohel* and rapped hard with his fist. There was no answer. Krinsky pushed his way into the enclosure and found Schneerson slumped on the grave-yard floor, his eyes closed. He had suffered a stroke. Krinsky immediately called Hatzolah, the Hasidic ambulance service, but Hatzolah was slow in coming—Krinsky remembers that there was a problem with a bad battery—and then there was a debate over whether the rebbe, the king of the Lubavitch empire, should be taken to a secular hospital. "A stricken Messiah does not go to a hospital," Heilman and Friedman wrote, "there to follow the orders of physicians and nurses, stripped of his clothes and his dignity."

Instead, Schneerson was ferried out from the *ohel*, through the knotted early evening traffic, and toward his room at 770 Eastern Parkway, where he would remain for weeks, paralyzed and quiet, surrounded by courtiers and doctors. Like Yosef Yitzhak, Menachem Mendel had not written a will. Eschatological concerns prevailed: Both Schneersons had planned on surviving to greet *Moshiach*. What use would a scrap of paper be when the redemption came? But Menachem Mendel was not only a religious leader. He was also the leader of a sprawling religious movement, which stretched to all corners of the globe. In recent years, he had begun to delegate some of the day-to-day community matters to his underlings, but until his stroke, the buck had stopped with the rebbe. Who would now take the reins of the community? A courtly drama began to play out at 770, out of view of the Hasidim of Crown Heights, plenty of whom saw the stroke as no special impediment to the arrival of *Moshiach*.

Was it not possible that Schneerson was only testing the faith of his Hasidim? "The rebbe is now in a state of concealment," a Lubavitcher said at the time. "The Jews could not see Moses on Mount Sinai and thought he was dead. They built a golden calf and had a vision of him lying dead on a bier, whereas he was in fact alive and in a state of concealment." So that was that: the rebbe would soon emerge from his self-imposed state, like a man shaking his arms out of a winter coat, and lead them to the Temple. More petitions were issued, more declarations distributed. For a people who had until recently been absolutely certain that *Moshiach* was ascendant, it must have been impossible to understand that

Schneerson would in fact never recover from this first stroke. The Chabad leadership did little to help. Krinsky announced that the prognosis of the rebbe was good and joked that Schneerson was "not keen on this enforced hiatus."

Behind the scenes, the mood was much more panicked. The stroke had permanently disabled Schneerson, who was to remain in a wheelchair for the rest of his life. His more optimistic aides believed that Schneerson had near full command of his faculties; others understood the extent of the damage left by the stroke. The Lubavitch spokesman Zalman Shmotkin told Sue Fishkoff that the rebbe had expressive aphasia and "was physically unable to communicate his needs and wishes." In the absence of a definitive pronouncement from the rebbe, a tug-of-war broke out among the highest-ranking advisers. On one side was Krinsky, who eventually came to lead the moderate faction of the Lubavitch movement. Krinsky never disavowed the possibility that the rebbe was the *Moshiach*, but he declared that his priorities were the *shluchim* in the field and the future of Chabad. On the other side of the aisle was the Lubavitch official Leib Groner, whose politics were thought to align with those of the messianists.

On Rosh Hashanah of 1992, the rebbe made his first poststroke visit to 770. It swiftly became clear, Heilman and Friedman wrote, that Schneerson was "no longer a leader; he could only watch in silence. It was left to his handlers to inform the world what he was thinking." During the next few months, a bizarre charade regularly played out on the dais of the shul at 770. According to at least one observer, Groner and Krinsky would often grapple over which direction the rebbe's wheelchair should be pointed—toward the messianists or toward the moderates—as if Schneerson were a marionette and they his puppet masters.

Still, the faith of the Jews of Crown Heights remained unshaken. Many Lubavitchers purchased so-called Moshiach Beepers, so they could be notified when the rebbe was to make an appearance at 770. In late 1992, David Remnick of the *New Yorker* joined hundreds of Hasidim as they sprinted from their homes to the basement shul, where a curtain was lifted, exposing the rebbe, "his head bobbing gently." The assembled Hasidim, "overcome with pleasure and spirit," broke into song, harmonizing to the familiar and circuitous strains of *Yehi*. Remnick continued,

> At first, the singing was relatively soft, but then, as the Rebbe began to make small irregular nodding motions, up and down, side to side, he sent the crowd into a pandemonium. "It means he hears us! It's his way of singing with us!" one of the young men next to me exclaimed. The floor rumbled as the volume of the singing increased. Then the Rebbe, as if he sensed the hysteria, made a barely distinguishable gesture with his left hand, and one of his aides closed the curtain.

And then: nothing.

The messianists grew impatient. In February 1993, Rabbi Shmuel Butman, the self-declared leader of a group called the International Campaign to Bring Moshiach, invited the press to a "coronation" ceremony at 770 Eastern Parkway. Finally, Butman said, the rebbe was ready to reveal himself to the world. A satellite feed was provided; the rebbe made his appearance on stage; eventually, he was wheeled back to his chambers. "Tonight was like every other night," Krinsky later told disappointed reporters. "The rebbe just wanted to be with his people."

From 1992 to 1994, the condition of the rebbe grew increasingly grim. He was hospitalized first for gall bladder surgery and then for cataract surgery, and then on March 8, he suffered a series of seizures. He was taken to Beth Israel Medical Center in Manhattan, where he eventually slipped into a deep coma. The NYPD maintained around-the-clock presence at Beth Israel; news media from around the world reported daily from the street outside. In the hallways of the hospital, Lubavitcher Hasidim milled anxiously, praying and singing and occasionally even fighting with one another for a chance to visit with the rebbe. (Aron Hershkop and Yanky Prager were among the Hasidim arrested for brawling at Beth Israel.) Many continued to believe that even the coma was nothing but a hiccup—a necessary stepping-stone on the path to redemption. But on June 12, the rebbe died. His body was taken to Crown Heights, where it was washed and wrapped in fine linen; later, the funeral procession wended its way slowly down

Eastern Parkway, toward the same cemetery where Josef Yitzchak Schneersohn had been interred.

Remarkably, the messianist movement did not peter out on the rebbe's death. Sue Fishkoff reported that even as news spread throughout Brooklyn of the passing of the leader of Lubavitch, some Hasidim "danced and sang with tambourines, in the desperate hope that, even now, their Rebbe would summon his superhuman will and rise from the grave to usher in the Messianic Age." As Fishkoff noted, normative Judaism holds that the Messiah will be a mortal man, and that he will be anointed during his lifetime. But for True Believers, death is no impediment to the ascension of a true Messiah. They point out that the soul of a *tzaddik* remains close to his buried body for years, decades, even centuries. This posturing is often written off by outsiders as a simple denial of death; at worst, it was seen as bearing a distinct resemblance to early Christianity.

"If [Lubavitchers] believe the Rebbe could have been *Moshiach*, fine, I agree," Dr. Norman Lamm, the president of Yeshiva University, told Fishkoff in the 1990s.

> Many people could have been the *Moshiach*, and he had a far better chance than most. But to say he's the *Moshiach* after he died? The whole polemic we've had with Christianity for two thousand years is that we say a *Moshiach* who did not accomplish world peace, who did not accomplish the redemption of Israel and the world, is not *Moshiach*. And here we're told that [the Rebbe] can be. If that's the case, why were we so reluctant to accept Jesus?

In the years directly following the rebbe's passing, the Lubavitch community was thrown into a deep existential crisis. Reporters and scholars flocked to Crown Heights to observe how the messianist struggle would play out. Would the messianist faction win out, forever tarnishing the reputation of Chabad? Or would the moderates grasp the reins of the movement and appoint an eighth Lubavitcher rebbe? The squabble was widely identified in the secular press as a battle between pragmatists and extremists—between the Hasidim who believed that a dead man had not actually died and the Hasidim who believed that the power of Chabad had always lain in the *rabbonim* in the field. And indeed there was evidence to be found of a pitched conflict.

The International Campaign to Bring Moshiach, for example, continued to churn out propaganda from the Chabad headquarters, often on official Chabad letterhead, prompting numerous injunctions from Krinsky and the moderates. In early 1996, Butman arranged for a billboard to be erected near the George Washington Bridge, proclaiming the rebbe—now dead eighteen months—the *Moshiach*; Butman also organized a second coronation ceremony, this time at the New York Hilton, promising that reporters would soon experience "the greatest event in the history of mankind." The magazine *Beis Moshiach*, or House of Messiah, went into circulation, along with a Web site of the same name.

Meanwhile, the moderates labored to outflank the messianists, issuing their own publications and videos and stressing above all the very human achievements of the rebbe, evident in the network of Chabad houses that stretched from New York City to Bombay to Melbourne and beyond. In 1998, the Central Committee of Chabad-Lubavitch Rabbis in the United States and Canada, fed up with the antics of Butman and his supporters, publicly spoke out against messianist activities. "Conjecture as to the possible identity of Moshiach is not part of the basic tenet of Judaism," the committee announced in a statement distributed to the secular press, adding that "the preoccupation with identifying the Rebbe as *Moshiach* is clearly contrary to the Rebbe's wishes."

For several years, as the power struggle between moderates and *Mischistizn* consumed the offices at 770 Eastern Parkway, it looked as if the Lubavitch movement might be ripped apart—divided into two competing factions, each jostling for the right to spread the message of Chabad Judaism. But today, a decade and a half after the passing of the rebbe, the situation in Crown Heights has lapsed into something more closely resembling a protracted cold war. Yellow flags still flap proudly over many of the houses off Kingston Avenue; boys and men still wear *Moshiach* pins and yarmulkes. Intermarriage between messianist and moderate families is rare; so is friendship between a fervent messianist and an avowed moderate. And most Lubavitchers agree that a successor to Menachem Mendel Schneerson will never be named—a viewpoint that seems, on the face of it, to be an implicit endorsement of messianist politics.

But moderates couch the end of the Lubavitch dynasty in practical terms: The rebbe had no children and thus left no direct heirs to the throne. Moreover, they argue, Schneerson was so successful in his endeavors—so beloved by the Jewish world at large—that the appointment of an eighth Lubavitcher rebbe would be an unsatisfying coda to the achievements of the seventh. They maintain that the messianist debate is just a matter of noise; they say the real evidence of the rebbe's afterlife is the fire that burns in the heart of every *shaliach* in the field. "He taught us all to be rebbes, in our own way," one twenty-something Lubavitch rabbi maintains. This rabbi, like many young Lubavitchers in Crown Heights today, refuses to discuss whether believes the rebbe was *Moshiach*. To him, it is beside the point; one could argue for days about the identity of the Redeemer, but it would not bring him any closer to earth. The work is the thing—for now, the rebbe lives in his message.

Not everyone, of course, is able to hold forth with such equivocation. There remain plenty of fervent, outspoken messianists in contemporary Crown Heights—men and women who not only believe that the rebbe is the Messiah and that he will soon return to earth to redeem them, but that it is their sacred duty to spread the word of the coming of *Moshiach*. Many of these *Mischistizn* are young Israelis, with only a fleeting memory of the actual rebbe. They may have met Schneerson when they were very young; others were born after his death. They come to Brooklyn in their late teens or early twenties and rarely wander far from their domicile at 749 Eastern Parkway or the shul across the street. Absent a concrete connection to the rebbe the man, these *Mischistizn* worship the rebbe the legend. They sleep in bedrooms festooned with literally dozens of photographs of the rebbe, distribute stickers and fliers bearing the messianist slogans, and speak of Schneerson with unchecked ardency.

The Israeli *Mischistizn*—often referred to as the *Tzfatis*, after the town of Safed, in the north of Israel, which many of these boys call home—are supported in part by a small contingent of Crown

Heights natives. Together, the Crown Heights messianists and the *Tzfatis* have claimed the basement shul at 770 as their stronghold. On Friday evenings, the floor fills with *Mischistizn*, who will often spend hours singing *Yehi* and dancing under an upraised yellow flag; occasionally, they will direct their voices toward the dais, as if the rebbe were still there, peering back at them from his chair. To some moderates, this is considered the ultimate heresy—a desecration of the rebbe's memory—and during the last few years, Agudas Chassidei Chabad, which owns 770 and the surrounding offices, has filed several lawsuits in secular court, seeking to wrest away control of the shul from messianist supporters. On December 27, 2007, a judge ruled that Agudas had "possession" of the basement—a finding that while advantageous to Agudas in spirit has proved exceptionally hard to enforce.

On Friday nights, the senior Chabad leadership tends to remain upstairs, near the former offices of the rebbe, while downstairs the *Mischistizn* are allowed to run free. Occasionally, this standoff has given way to real violence, most spectacularly in 2006, when the police were called to 770 to break up a full-scale riot between moderate *shluchim* and *Mischistizn*. But by and large, most moderates seem to have tacitly agreed to worship elsewhere, usually at the smaller shuls that dot the side streets and the boulevards of Crown Heights.

On a personal level, the attitude of moderate Lubavitchers toward the messianists varies greatly. Some Brooklyn natives are notably solicitous of these True Believers and attribute the messianist ideal to youth or naivete. They point out that many of the *Mischistizn* are recent converts to Lubavitch, and that it is only natural that their fervor burns especially brightly. One moderate Lubavitcher—let's call him Ari—said that when he was a child, he held beliefs very similar to those of the messianists, but that he grew out of them and learned to appreciate the rebbe for his earthy accomplishments. Ari predicted that similarly, the vast majority of *Mischistizn* will eventually become moderates, just as a fiery young liberal will often slip toward conservatism in his or her old age.

Others are inclined to read the situation more darkly. "They have taken a great rebbe and made a small *Moshiach*," as one popular moderate saying goes. To the "antimessianists," the *Mischistizn* are not a passive threat—they are an active menace and a serious problem for sane-minded Lubavitchers everywhere. It is important here to again stress that messianist beliefs fall on a very wide spectrum, which encompasses the outspoken messianists, the passive messianists, the passive moderates, the outspoken antimessianists, and every stripe in between. All may or may not believe that the rebbe is *Moshiach*; their differences lie in whether anyone has the right to say that Schneerson was the Redeemer. Antimessianists worry that the *Mischistizn*, and especially the *Mischistizn* living in the dormitory at 749 Eastern Parkway, could worm their way further into the Chabad infrastructure, eventually coming to dominate the movement at large. This would be a disaster for many reasons, chief among them that a secular Jew—prime convert material for a *shaliach*—is liable to be very turned off indeed by the idea that a goodly portion of his would-be brethren believe the Messiah has already been identified, and that he will soon be rising from a graveyard in Queens.


On Kingston Avenue, it is not uncommon to hear the *Mischistizn* identified, usually in whispers or murmured asides, as the "Taliban"—they are seen as nothing less than terrorists, eager to spread a fundamentalist doctrine. They are ridiculed for their personal hygiene, for scraggly beards and body odor, for their relative poverty. They are said to breed like rabbits, to live on top of one another, to be greedy and conniving. "They are not like us," one antimessianist explained. "They are stupid people—they live in their own filth." And indeed, as this comment indicates, much of the struggle between messianists and antimessianists is class-based. Lubavitch is inherently a caste culture, with old-world Chabadnik families, whose roots in the movement extend back centuries, considered to be the equivalent of Brahmins. Hanging on the bottom rung of this society are recent converts from abroad—and bottom-most of all are the young *Mischistizn* from Israel, who arrive each year in droves and live on as little as a few hundred dollars a month, their lives consisting of prayer, study, and the yellow flag.

There are a couple of supreme ironies at play here. The first is that the attitude of the antimessianists toward the messianists is in fact a near mirror image of the attitude of many secular Jews toward Hasidim. In *Holy Days*, the journalist Lis Harris wrote that several of her Jewish acquaintances held opinions of Hasidic culture that "might have been drawn from the lexicon of classic anti-Semitism: 'They're really dirty. Have you seen how they keep their homes?' 'No one is pushier.' 'I hate their standoffishness.' 'Why do they think they're better than everyone else?' 'They're certainly unhealthy—you can tell just by looking at them.'" And so on. Each one of these statements—all of them "mistaken," Harris noted—could just as easily have been uttered by a Lubavitcher during an antimessianist tirade. For the antimessianists, the *Mischistizn* are "other" and must be distinguished at all times from the Lubavitch community as a whole.

The second irony is that the current position of the *Mischistizn*—the fact that they are able to hold any sway at all in Crown Heights—is in some ways a by-product of the success of the rebbe's mission. Schneerson always made it a point to send his best and brightest into the field; he handpicked *shluchim* for various important posts and looked especially for Lubavitchers who had calm and even temperaments and a deep knowledge of Chabad theology. To be a *shaliach* was considered the highest of callings, and during the '80s and the '90s, hundreds of talented and charismatic Lubavitchers set off from Crown Heights to open Chabad houses around the globe. Most—although certainly not exclusively—hailed from established and moderate Chabad families. Their work required constant and unflagging diligence, and they found time to return to Crown Heights only rarely, usually around the high holidays or for the annual conference of the *shluchim*. In their place, Crown Heights filled with the ranks of the very men and women they had converted—men and women who were often on a very different political wavelength.

After the rebbe died, in 1994, it quickly became apparent that the balance of power no longer lay in Crown Heights. Instead, it lay abroad, with the *shluchim* in the field. Krinsky and other former

Schneerson aides have done their best to maintain the momentum of the Chabad movement, but the messianist debate, combined with the absence of a rebbe, has wreaked havoc in the Lubavitch community.

The word one hears most often these days in Crown Heights is "vacuum." There is a vacuum of leadership at the main Lubavitch shul at 770 Eastern Parkway. There is a vacuum of leadership on the Jewish Community Council, the organization that helps run the neighborhood. There is a vacuum of leadership at the local rabbinical court. And in the vacuum of Crown Heights, it is incumbent on every Lubavitcher to make his or her own destiny.

# 12

Her first instinct had been to decline, politely. The request had
arrived back in November 2008, not long before Thanksgiving,
when Joyce David was sitting in her office at 16 Court Street in
Brooklyn, thirty-six floors up by elevator, peering out the window
over the river and toward the jagged metal maw of Manhattan. On
a clear afternoon, you could see almost as far as the Bronx, but today
the clouds had rolled in early, and everything after Midtown was sunk
into a uniform mass of gray and black.

From below came the granulated burp of the buses working
their way through the knot of streets that surrounded the tower at
16 Court—Clinton and then Pierrepont and then Cadman Plaza,
past the parched greenery of Columbus Park, and finally north in
the direction of the high stone arches of the Brooklyn Bridge. Thirty
years ago, when David had first enrolled in law school, downtown
Brooklyn had seemed like a kind of maze—she had been startled
by its sheer franticness, the way at noon the streets filled with bail
bondsmen and lawyers in frayed suits and fidgety undercover cops
taking a break from testimony, everyone walking and talking at once,
and not a spare piece of cement in sight. But eventually the area
had become as familiar as home, the courthouses and the law offices

arrayed around Borough Hall no different to her than her own living room.

David turned back to her computer and scanned the e-mail again. The message had come from the administrator of the 18B assigned counsel service, which matched local lawyers with clients unable to afford representation. Under the statutes of 18B, any indigent resident of New York, charged with a crime and disqualified from Legal Aid representation, is provided with, for minimal cost, an attorney screened and certified by the city of New York. Unlike the Legal Aid squad, the 18B team is made up of trial case veterans, who traffic primarily in private work and pick up the occasional 18B for the money or for the thrill. For David, 18B work was all about the thrill. The cases that she might never have gotten a look at otherwise. The stories she might never have heard.

This one fit the bill. The defendant was Chaim Hershkop, a Brooklyn resident accused of gang assault. According to the e-mail, Hershkop's codefendants included his younger brother, Yehuda, and his older brother, Gedalia, along with three other young men from the Crown Heights neighborhood of Brooklyn—all of them members of a Lubavitch private security patrol. The Hershkop file had originally belonged to a veteran Brooklyn attorney named Carl Becker, but Becker had recently fallen ill; now the assigned counsel administrator needed a replacement before the thing hit the courtroom.

David knew that she probably should ignore the request. She should pull on her jacket, ride the stuffy lift down to the ground floor, wrestle with the afternoon traffic, return to her empty apartment in Brooklyn Heights, and do some legwork on a case that would actually pay the rent. Assigned counsel work was a crapshoot—you were just as liable to end up with a trial that bled on for weeks and left you with nothing but empty pockets and a sense of lost time. Meanwhile, even if David did take the case, she would have to be on her best behavior—with six defense attorneys, most decisions would have to be made as a team. Not such an easy thing when you were used to steering courtroom strategy.

But the case had at least one saving grace: it was obviously mired in Jewish politics. And Jewish politics were in Joyce David's blood.

• • •

She had been born in Brooklyn, into a family of Orthodox rabbis. When David was still a child, her father found a job as a cantor at a Conservative synagogue in Wilkes-Barre, Pennsylvania, and moved his family west. Among David's oldest childhood memories was the sound of his honeyed baritone floating over the heads of the congregation—and underneath the song, the sibilant lisp of prayer book pages turned in concert. She wasn't always an especially happy kid. Even back then, she'd been short and overweight, and she often joked that in Wilkes-Barre, she felt like a round peg in a square hole. When she was fourteen, her father sent her back to Brooklyn, to study at the yeshiva in Flatbush, partly because he was worried that if she stayed in the cornfields of Pennsylvania, she might end up marrying a goy farmer.

New York, raucous, big, and seemingly boundless, was more suited to David's personality. She moved in with her grandparents, into a house near the intersection of Beverley Road and Coney Island Avenue in a nice residential neighborhood. Later, she would say that everything that ever happened in her life happened in that house. Downstairs, her grandparents maintained a synagogue and a catering hall; upstairs, the mood was subdued and ordered. David and her female cousins were forbidden to talk at the dinner table and were reminded at all times to conduct themselves like ladies. What a woman had to say was *schtuss*, or "bullshit," her grandfather told David. But David knew that it was really her grandmother who had always run the show, and after David finished studying at the yeshiva, she decided she would have what her Bubbe never did—a chance to shoot off her mouth.

It took some time. At first, David enrolled at New York University. Her major was physics, which in many ways wasn't such a departure for a yeshiva kid—both science and Talmudic scripture traffic primarily in questions of where one world ends and the next begins. Questions of divisions and boundaries and barriers, and always, more questions than answers. But physics turned out to be a more subterranean business than David had anticipated—she could not imagine a life bound to a dimly lit classroom, the only noise the squeak of chalk—so she abandoned physics, switched to journalism, and took a minor in film. She figured she'd be a hard-charging investigative reporter. Either that, or she'd pack off for the Himalayas and write elegiac poetry between sips of hot Nepalese tea. And then toward the end of her stint at NYU, she found herself married—to a Jewish man, as her father had wished—and pregnant. Before graduation, she had a baby girl. After graduation, she had a son.

For more than two years, she stayed at home with her two children. The dreams of a newsroom career began to fade, as did the health of her marriage. She obtained a divorce. And then one afternoon, she had her epiphany. This was in her Brooklyn home, while her son was in her lap and her daughter was playing on the floor and the television set was tuned to *Sesame Street*. Usually, David treated the program like background noise, just more blissful chatter, but on this occasion, one of the skits caught her attention. On the screen, Big Bird was frantically explaining to the other residents of his neighborhood that Mr. Snuffleupagus really existed—that the creature wasn't just a figment of his imagination. Big Bird was having a really hard go of it. Some of the other characters were laughing. David found herself growing agitated. "What's wrong with you people!" she shouted. Her son gazed up at her; her daughter paused on her way across the rug; David tried her best to smile.

God, she thought. I've got to get out of the house.

That afternoon, she made up her mind to enroll in law school.

She graduated from Brooklyn Law in 1977 and found a job at the Legal Aid Society. She routinely did the kind of work that might cause a refined corporate lawyer to vomit down the front of his three-hundred-dollar tie. It was the '70s, and the murder rates in New York were soaring. But David reveled in the challenge.

"I enjoy going into tough neighborhoods, into the netherworld," she once told a reporter. Her cases were offering her what she'd pined after back in Flatbush—the chance to think for a living, to put her chutzpah and her big mouth to work. Moreover, even though the Legal Aid Society would never make her rich, she finally had her financial independence. She could afford to feed and clothe her children on her own—to send them to a well-regarded local yeshiva day-care program—and if she had to toil seven days a week to do it, well, that was how it went.

In 1983, David left Legal Aid and went into private practice. She quickly came to be regarded as something of a glory hound. She took on high-profile clients like Van Anthony Hull, the twenty-nine-year-old college student who went on a shooting spree at Brooklyn Technical College. She defended alleged cop killers, famous football players, and one of two brothers accused of murdering a respected Long Island physician. She broke barriers. She became the first woman president of the Kings County Criminal Bar Association. She served, variously, as vice president of the New York State Association of Criminal Defense Lawyers, a member of the board of the New York State Defenders Association, and chair of the Brooklyn Women's Political Caucus. She appeared frequently on *Court TV*, where she was a bracing and memorable presence—the obstreperous Jewish attorney from Brooklyn, her hair cut short, her eyes moving quickly behind her oversize glasses.

In 1986, David wrote a book called *What You Should Know If You're Accused of a Crime*, which she intended as a primer on criminal law, from arrest to booking to prearraignment interview to arraignment and beyond. She kept the prose simple and direct and the tone friendly, as if she were chatting with a new client in the visitors' room of a prison. But she did not condescend to her readers—she was firm but empathetic. "People exposed to the Criminal Justice System for the first time often feel like they're in a foreign country with strange rules, procedures, and language," she wrote. "The Criminal Justice System, just like the rest of life, is not always fair. That doesn't mean we give up, it just means we try harder."

*What You Should Know* comprised thirty-odd pages, most of it filled with advice on navigating that "foreign country." David covered the intricacies of the attorney-client relationship:

> You're not helping yourself if you think your lawyer will do a better job if she thinks you're innocent. It's not a good lawyer/client relationship if you don't trust her enough to be truthful.

The psychological realities of a trial:

> It's upsetting having criminal charges hanging over your head.
> Lawyers who are sensitive to their clients' feelings often act as
> psychologists and social workers as well as lawyers. Maybe that's
> why we're also called counselors.

And when to hire a distaff litigator:

> In certain cases it might be especially advantageous to be repre-
> sented by a woman lawyer—especially if you're accused of com-
> mitting a crime against a woman.

The balance of the book, humbly bound with heavy blue paper and
glue, consisted of biographical information and a card, which David
encouraged her readers to cut out and hand to police officers or prosecutors in the case of arrest. "I do not wish to answer any questions
without speaking to an attorney first," the card read. "I do not consent
to a search of my home, my car or my person. I do not consent to
being in a line-up or a show-up. I will not waive any of my constitu-
tional rights."

Within just a few years of publication, the book had become one
of the sought-after volumes in the libraries of the New York correc-
tions system, and on Rikers Island, home to some of the most violent
offenders in the state, copies are still regularly passed back and forth
among inmates.


More than once, a visitor had commented on the old-timey feel of
Joyce David's office—the smoked glass on the door, the elegant orna-
mental flourishes near the windows, the broad desk like something
out of an old Bogart flick. But the place was showing its wear. The
tiled floor was crumpled up at the corners, exposing the cheap wood
and vinyl underneath, and water damage had painted the ceiling in
trippy yellow patterns—a constantly changing Rorschach test.

On the far wall of the room, David had hung up several courtroom
portraits, representing the arc of her career to date. The palette of the

portraits was distinctly muted, full of pastels that made David look as if she were wrapped in gauze from head to foot. But she liked the art—kept the portraits prominently displayed, looked them over once in a while when she was feeling down. It was evidence of how far she'd come since that house on Beverly Road and Coney Island Avenue.

There was David alongside the accused stalker Diane Schaefer and then again alongside Bassam Reyati, an accomplice to the Brooklyn Bridge shooter. David's defense of Reyati, she remembered, had driven the tabloids wild. "ORTHODOX JEW FOR THE DEFENSE IN BRIDGE SHOOT," read the headline in the *Daily News*—as if it was unthinkable that a Jew, and especially one from a family full of rabbis, would deign to defend an Arab. "In order to protect my rights, I have to be prepared to protect other people's rights, too," David had said at the time.

She meant it, of course, but let's face it—the Reyati case had also been an opportunity to play investigative journalist. To dig in deep. To conduct some urban anthropology. After a few long moments, David opened up the e-mail program again and typed out a response to the 18B administrator, offering to take the Hershkop assignment.

Until the trial got under way, David communicated with Chaim Hershkop mostly by e-mail. She met with him in person first, of course, and got a good feeling from the kid. He was much smaller than his brother Gadi, in stature and in height, and his thick beard was several hues lighter, but he had the same soft eyes, the same elastic demeanor. He would be a natural on the stand, she thought, if it came to that. But for the most part, they chatted electronically, which was okay by David. She preferred to have written, rather than oral, communications with her clients; it cut down on the possibility of serious miscommunication, which could come back to bite them both later.

Like many people who grew up in Brooklyn, David had a pretty good grip on the world of Chabad. Her father and her grandfather had regularly mingled with the Lubavitch community, and she often attended services at a Chabad synagogue in Brooklyn Heights. She found the rabbi there to be not only smart and capable, but also exceptionally kind, and when her father died, she had donated one of the family Torahs to the Brooklyn Heights congregation. On Fridays, she even invited a pair of yeshiva students from Crown Heights to talk to her about theology—she regarded this as both necessary and vivifying, an extension of the theological training she had received back in Flatbush. Sometimes, David and her young visitors—neither of whom were, as far as she could tell, messianists—found themselves discussing religious politics.

David had originally come in contact with messianists during the Brooklyn Bridge case—the father of one of the victims was a member of the rebbe's inner circle—and she had a good handle on the stakes. Chabad was a global empire, and its leadership had been greatly eroded since the death of the rebbe; the only way to understand the messianist divide was by realizing that it reflected a fight about the direction of the movement. The fact that there were so many messianists in Crown Heights was unsurprising. Chabad had always attracted a varied crowd—in the 1960s and the '70s, it was the hippies, and in the '80s, it was New Agers from the suburbs. When you make outreach a priority, as the rebbe had—when you throw open your doors to everyone—you couldn't be surprised when a few kooks showed up at the party.

Those kooks, of course, did not make the ultimate message of Chabad any less powerful. But David understood how deeply upsetting messianism might be to a committed moderate. Her father had always told her that she should never take scripture too literally. It wasn't that Talmudic or biblical lore was made up, he said, but that it was allegory—a way for people to get their heads around the eternal and elusive truths. Fundamentalism had scared her father, and it scared her. To David, a chair was a chair, and a table was a table. "Look," she had told the two Lubavitch boys one afternoon. "If the Messiah had already arrived, things would probably be a little different. They'd probably be better. Don't you think?" They had nodded happily but noncommittally. Before she agreed to represent Chaim Hershkop, David had assumed that most Lubavitchers were similarly equivocal on the messianist stuff—or at least uninterested in fighting a full-scale battle about the Messiah.

She soon learned how wrong she'd been. In the months before the trial, Chaim Hershkop sent her dozens of e-mails, some forwarded from Ben Lifshitz, all of them containing evidence of a deep schism in the Lubavitch community. The very fact that the case had reached this point at all was bad enough—it indicated a failure at the level of the *Beis Din*, which should have settled the conflict months ago—but there also seemed to be a sustained effort by several parties in the Lubavitcher settlement to destroy the Shomrim. Of these parties, the most prominent was the lawyer and Shmira member Paul Huebner. Chaim had explained to David that once, the Shomrim had been known as the better of the two anticrime patrols in Crown Heights; until recently, it was the Shmira that had been known as the trouble-makers, the shit-stirrers.

That had begun to change in 2007. Huebner, probably with the help of the other Shmira guys, had zeroed in on the assault as a way to put the Shomrim out of business and had spent the last few months denigrating the Hershkops at every turn. Part of this animosity was rooted in wrangling over a children's camp that the Hershkop family had once owned and that several Shmira supporters had attempted to take over—lawsuits and countersuits had been flung back and forth with surprising alacrity for years—and part of it was a simple power struggle. Crown Heights was a relatively small place, and there was room for only one patrol. As David understood it, things had come to a head after the assault of Andrew Charles, when the NYPD had approached both groups, starting with the Shomrim, and asked them to reach some sort of bargain. The Shomrim had refused, citing the criminal records of several Shmira members, and the Shmira, seeing nothing to lose, had happily agreed.

In the spring of 2009, a contingent of Shmira members had sub-mitted to background checks and undergone training with the NYPD. They were given space in the squad room at the 71st Precinct House, keys to several city vehicles—including some smart little hybrid cars, with racks of flashing lights on top—caps and uniforms, and badges. They became full-fledged members of something called the Civilian Observation Patrol, or COP; they reported to the community affairs desk at the 7-1. For the NYPD, the COP program was a stroke of genius. It allowed the police to keep a tight rein on the Shmira without making the Shmira members feel as if their rights were being infringed. And it worked, for a little while. Then the *Daily News*, probably relying on a tip from someone in the Shomrim—although none of the Shomrim would ever admit it—reported that several of the gentlemen working for the COP program had a history with the police.

Yanky Prager, for instance, the leader of Shmira and now a member of COP, had been charged with threatening to torch Aron Hershkop's house. And then there was Leib Skoblo, a giant of a guy, with a baby face and a perfectly rounded gut. Back in the 1990s, Skoblo, who also worked as an auxiliary officer in Brooklyn, had apparently been collared for punching a black teenage girl in the face.

The NYPD was meant to be carefully vetting each COP candidate—how had Skoblo and Prager slipped through the cracks? Publicly, the police remained mostly mum, acknowledging that background checks were part of the application procedure for COP but refusing to discuss specific admission criteria. The Shomrim, meanwhile, suspected—and not implausibly—that the city was so desperate to get a handle on the feud that it was willing to overlook the foibles of the criminals in the Shmira. But the Shomrim had bigger things to worry about.

In early 2009, a Brooklyn grand jury had returned a litany of charges against the six Shomrim members involved in the 749 assault, including gang assault in the second degree and assault in the second degree. Hershkop and his fellow defendants faced serious jail time. To make matters worse, on June 10, 2009, Levi Huebner had filed a multimillion-dollar lawsuit against the Shomrim. The plaintiffs in the suit were Yaakov Shatz, Gavriel Braunstein, Moshe Gurfinkel, and Schneur Rotem—the same four men identified as victims in the criminal case. According to Huebner, the members of the Shomrim—"Crown Heights Safety Patrol, Inc."—had "assaulted and battered the Plaintiffs without any provocation or justification on the part of the Plaintiffs." From the suit (all sic):

31. Shomrim Patrol was negligent in failing to provide a safe environment for Plaintiffs, in allowing Plaintiffs to be assaulted and battered, and in allowing a dangerous and violent persons to be agents, servants, employees and/or members which created a danger to the Plaintiffs.

32. As a result of the negligence by Shomrim Patrol, Plaintiffs were severely injured and damaged, rendered sick, sore, lame and disabled,
sustained severe nervous shock and mental anguish, great physical
pain and emotional upset, some of which injuries are permanent in
nature and duration.

33. As a result of the negligence by Shomrim Patrol, Plaintiffs suffered
and in the future will be permanently caused to suffer pain, incon-
venience and other effects of such injuries.

And on it went. Huebner was asking for $4 million in compensa-
tory damages and an additional $12 million in punitive dam-
ages from each defendant—an absolutely ludicrous sum, given the
financial circumstances of most of the members of the Shomrim.
But Huebner was no fool. He had filed the suit not only against
the individual members named in the criminal case, but against
the Shomrim organization as a whole, and everyone knew that the
Shomrim organization was run in part on the fiscal largesse of Aron
Hershkop. If a Brooklyn jury did somehow return a guilty verdict in
the criminal case—or if any of the Shomrim members allocuted to
any of the charges—Huebner might have a shot at making the lawsuit stick. And if the lawsuit stuck, Hershkop would have to cough
up some cash.

On pro-Shomrim blogs, a conspiracy was sketched out: Huebner,
along with the help of cops such as Officer Brian Duffy and Brooklyn
district attorney Charles Hynes, was intent on ridding Crown Heights
of the Shomrim, who had so arrogantly refused the offer of the
NYPD. Of course, in order to accept that explanation, one would
have to believe that the police and the Brooklyn DA operated in perfect concert—that city lawyers and city cops were complementary
parts of one exceptionally well-oiled machine.

Nothing, David knew, could be further from the truth. Yes, the
police and the prosecutors had the same aim: to put criminals in
prison. But their means varied widely, and there was often friction
between these two wings of the criminal justice system. There were
no smoky, poorly lit poker rooms where powerful men hashed out
deals; this was not a detective novel. A man such as Charles Hynes did
not approve sweeping charges against a group of defendants—likely

leading to a long trial that would suck up time, resources, money, and even political goodwill—just because a cop or two had had their feelings hurt.

No. The likely answer was the most obvious one. For decades, the city had struggled to tamp down on the activity of the Hasidic anti-crime patrols in Crown Heights. By going after the Shomrim, the Brooklyn DA could make a simple point: gang violence is not tolerated in New York City, no matter whether the perpetrators are black, white, Hispanic, or Hasidic. But as David would say often in coming months, in this particular race, the prosecutors had picked the wrong horse.

They made a motley crew, the six of them—all weathered Brooklyn court hands, brought together under one roof for one of the strangest cases of their careers. Among the bunch were two privately hired attorneys: Tedd Blecher, a mustachioed attorney in his fifties, with frantic, uncombed hair and a fondness for baggy suits, had been hired to represent Ben Lifshitz. Gadi Hershkop, for his part, had obtained the services of Israel Fried, a smart young litigator who had started out in the Brooklyn DA's office and now handled plenty of cases involving the Lubavitch community. An interesting contrast, Izzy and Blecher—one snappily attired and brash, the other slow-moving and a little unkempt but deceptively caustic.

The rest of the defense team was 18B. There was David, the oldest and most experienced attorney in the courtroom, representing Chaim Hershkop, and then there was Mitchell Salaway, exceptionally tall and lanky, always fiddling with the thin metal chain that connected his wallet to his belt. (In 2010, Salaway would be named by the *New York Post* as one of twenty-one attorneys in New York City who had somehow pocketed more than $156,000 a year on assigned counsel work alone.) A reserved, well-coiffed lawyer named Steven Williams—whom David knew by reputation—had been assigned to Pinson, and Susan Mitchell, whose office was located not far from David's, on Court Street, was representing Slatter.

As the trial date drew closer, the defense team met several times as a group. The video was the thing, they agreed—it was the video that would hang their clients, or it was the video that had the power to get them off the hook. David had watched the footage shot by Beliniski several times and had become convinced that even though the prosecution had introduced the evidence, the defense could make it work in their favor. Sure, there were plenty of red-faced Shomrim members to be seen—plenty of grimacing and jostling and shouting—but the fact was that at no point did anything occur on tape that might be construed, however generously, as gang assault. In fact, the opposite was true: a reasonable member of the jury would likely watch the video and see that it was the Shomrim who were surrounded by *bochurim*. They would see Ben Lifshitz, screaming out for his glasses; they would see skinny Yehuda Hershkop, standing on a bed, leaning away from the fray, as if he was worried that he was about to get smacked.

Yes, the video would work for all of them and especially for David, whose client was alleged to have committed his part of the gang assault after the video camera was turned off. "In this day and age," she'd said, "if they don't have you on tape, it didn't happen, right?" And the rest of the team had nodded. Of course, they hadn't thought the case would ever get that far. In the months before the Shomrim case hit the docket at Brooklyn Supreme Court, the DA had repeatedly offered the defendants a deal: misdemeanor assault instead of felony gang assault, a sentence of probation, and maybe some anger-management classes. Save us both some time, they said, which made sense to David. A plea would save Chaim Hershkop the hassle of taking off work, save him the possibility of getting tossed in jail for a year or two, save him the trouble of seeing his name—and the name of his family—dragged through the secular press.

But it had been impossible. Hershkop had refused. They all had. On a practical level, if the Shomrim members took the deal, they would leave themselves more vulnerable to the civil lawsuit. Huebner didn't necessarily need a plea or a guilty verdict to win that suit— the burden of proof was very different in civil court than it was in criminal—but if the judge required the Shomrim guys to allocute before the plea was accepted, Huebner could certainly enter that allocution as evidence in the civil suit.

Yet more than the civil lawsuit, which was a long shot anyway, was the not insubstantial matter of pride. Once the trial had

concluded—once a verdict had been rendered, one way or another—
Chaim Hershkop would have to return to Crown Heights, and he
wanted to be able to return a vindicated man. He wanted full absolu-
tion—it would not be enough to tell friends and family that he had
"only" been saddled with a minor assault rap. In fact, in some ways,
Hershkop believed that it would be better to go to prison with his head
held high than it would be to utter a false confession for something he
never did. No, he didn't want the deal, thank you very much. He would
leave his fate in the hands of a jury and God.

And so on Wednesday, October 28, 2009, in a room on the second
floor of the Brooklyn Supreme Court, jury selection began in the
case of *The People of New York v. Schneur Pinson, Benjamin Lifshitz,
Nechemia Slatter, Chaim Hershkop, Yehuda Hershkop, and Gedalia
Schneur Hershkop*.

It would be two long months before a verdict was read.

# 13

On the morning of November 2, 2009, Aron Hershkop stood under the eaves of the Brooklyn Supreme Court on Jay Street, his hands jammed in his pockets. He had exchanged his grease-stained Carhartts and tattered Shomrim jacket for a fine linen suit, a dress shirt opened two buttons at the neck, and a pair of loafers, so meticulously shined that the toes appeared almost reflective. Save the velvet yarmulke, Hershkop blended in well here—he might have been mistaken, in his gruff demeanor or sartorial gravitas, for any of the hundreds of lawyers and paralegals who passed daily across the burnished tiles of the courthouse lobby.

Through the glass, a long line of spectators, witnesses, and defendants were working their way toward three metal detectors. Each machine was manned by two or three court cops, their guns riding high on their hips, their uniforms finely creased and immaculately cuffed. Overhead, in the corner of the lobby, a flat-screen television spat out instructions in a variety of languages, accompanied by brightly rendered images and graphics: no guns, no drugs, no recording equipment.

As Hershkop passed through the doors, a cop marched a cuffed guy past security, the cop and his perp dressed more or less the same—Starter jackets, ratty jeans, big fat ugly basketball sneakers. The difference being that one of them had a gun. One of them was going to his Staten Island home, with its immaculately manicured lawn and short fence and his kids and his wife, and the other was going to be sleeping on a metal pallet, tugging at a moth-eaten blanket that barely covered his toes. Hershkop wondered how long his brothers and friends would last in lockup. He gave Gadi a few weeks, maybe months, but the rest? Dicey. Six Yids in yarmulkes and thick beards. Might as well plaster targets to their backs.

For months now, long before the grand jury came down with its indictment—long before the civil lawsuit was served—Hershkop had attempted to use every ounce of his considerable political sway to get Huebner to back off. He had spoken to members of the Jewish Community Council, pleaded with cops and liaisons with City Hall, requested audiences with the most senior of the Chabad *rabbonim*, and thus far, he had gotten mostly lip service. Sure, moderates regarded the messianists of 749 as a nuisance at best, and yes, they agreed that Huebner's involvement in the criminal trial was disgraceful, but what could be done? Huebner was his own man, they told Hershkop. He would get his comeuppance, in this world or another. Be patient.

Hershkop thought of the computer printout that Ben Lifshitz had hung over his computer desk: "When a good man is hurt, all who would be called good must suffer with him." But Euripides hadn't understood Hasidic culture, how messed up things could get, how two-faced people could be. He made suffering sound noble. In Hershkop's experience, it was not noble. It was excruciating—a dirty business.

So in the end, he had begged Rabbi Moshe Bogomilsky, a longtime family friend and a powerful figure in the Lubavitch community, to take action. Owlish, plump, garrulous old Bogomilsky. If anyone could draw attention to the Shomrim cause, it would be him. In late October, days before jury selection got under way, Bogomilsky had issued an open letter to all of Crown Heights, asking that each dutiful Jew contribute to a *Pidyon Shevuyim* fund—literally, from the Hebrew, "the ransoming of the captives." In ancient days, *Pidyon Shevuyim* was often collected if a Jew had been unfairly imprisoned by a goyish authority. And when you thought about it, the trial of the Shomrim was really no different. Huebner had been the catalyst, but it was the secular authorities who had pressed the case, ratcheted up the charges and the stakes—put the men of the Shomrim in the same league as gangbangers and thugs.

"Torah rule dictates that Jewish people should bring their disputes, arguments and grievances against a fellow Jew to a *Beis Din*," Bogomilsky had written. "Going to the civil court system is a heinous iniquity and a blatant contemptuous behavior against Torah."

He continued,

> Unfortunately, due to the laxity of some in this regard, a group of people are now in court defending themselves against a possible seven year incarceration and a lawsuit of 150 million dollars, G-d forbid. These men are family heads who have altruistically given much time for the enhancement of the security and wellbeing of the Crown Heights neighborhood. While there are good chances that they will be vindicated, nevertheless, large sums of money have already been expended for their defense and much more is immediately needed. . . . May we speedily witness the elevating of the Torah banner and the ultimate redemption.

He signed the letter, "With profuse advance thanks and blessings to merit Divine rewards, Sincerely yours, Rabbi Moshe Bogomilsky." The Shomrim, in turn, had created a site to collect *Pidyon Shevuyim* funds. Visitors were encouraged to select from a range of donation amounts, from $10 to $300; they could use PayPal and submit a payment by credit card or call the Shomrim hotline, and a member would be dispatched to pick up any donations. "For over 15 years," read copy posted to the site, "the Shomrim, under its current leadership, has been gladly helping the Crown Heights community—from assisting a crime victim in filing a police report, to helping someone with a flat tire—without ever once asking for anything in return. Unfortunately, the situation has changed and six of our volunteers are facing serious criminal charges stemming from an incident in which they were called for assistance."

The site was a limited success. Collections had come in from across Brooklyn—from the Borough Park and Williamsburg communities, from Flatbush and farther south. And the money would certainly help offset some of the fees levied by Fried and Blecher, the two privately hired attorneys involved in the trial.

But Hershkop understood that the real cost of the trial would be felt in the quotidian—Gadi, for instance, wouldn't be able to drive the school bus every day. Ben would be able to man CrownHeights .info only in his spare time. And supporters like Aron Hershkop, who planned to trek out to Jay Street for every hour of the trial, would be forced to leave their businesses in the hands of subordinates. No mere *Pidyon Shevuyim* fund could cover all of that. The Shomrim would need to raise thousands, tens of thousands, maybe more.

Hershkop had already sat through long hours of the kind of clerical wrangling that proceeds every criminal trial and then the jury selection, and not a single Jew had been picked, unless you counted the alternate. Parked on that hard wooden bench, Hershkop had immediately sensed the enormity of what his friends and brothers were about to be put through. Not just the prison time hanging over their heads, although there was certainly that, too—he had no particular urge to sit with his three brothers in the visitors' room, to hug in plain view of a bunch of snickering guards—but the time involved in the undertaking, the strange pressures of being constantly on a stage.

Already, the press had taken an active interest in the trial. Hershkop had seen one guy from the *Post* and a tall, bespectacled, forty-something guy he would later identify as Scott Shifrel, a veteran reporter on the courts desk of the *Daily News*. Hershkop gave both of them even odds of making the Shomrim look like jackasses—even odds that the boys would come off as heroes. You never knew with the press. They were drawn like magnets to the Lubavitch community, and half of the time they actually dashed off something worth reading. In this situation, a secular reporter might be able to tell the rest of New York something about the rift in the Lubavitch kingdom—a rift that most outsiders failed to recognize.

Hershkop joined the throng—some whites and Hispanics but mostly blacks, the teenagers happily jostling against one another, intentionally ignoring the stern glare of the court cops—waiting to pass through the metal detectors. Near the front of the line, the sounds from the street—the screech of tires, the blare of horns, the creak of rusty bicycle chains, the slap of dress shoes on concrete, the hiss of the steam escaping from under the loose manhole covers—faded and then disappeared altogether. Hershkop dropped his wallet and keys into a scarred gray plastic cup, took off his belt, and, when the detector remained quiet, he collected his belongings and gave a purse-lipped smile to the unsmiling cop manning the machine.

The courthouse was essentially a narrow, sharp tower, which rocketed out of the pavement at the corner of Jay and Johnson streets, up and over the skyline of downtown Brooklyn. Several televisions in the lobby flashed the last names of the myriad defendants on the docket today, along with a room number and a presiding judge—defendants lucky enough to draw a courtroom on the top floors could expect to hear their ears pop at least a few times a day. Hershkop passed the screens and jogged up the stairs, toward the second-floor landing. He was late. Today, the prosecution would deliver its opening statement, followed by the defense, and if time permitted, the first witness would be called.

Hershkop bounced onto the second-floor landing and nearly collided with Ben Lifshitz and his attorney, Tedd Blecher, who were locked head to head, Blecher doing the talking, his thick hands moving swiftly, signing out some sort of tactic like a quarterback in a huddle. Behind Blecher, on a row of fake leather chairs, sat Hershkop's brother Chaim, muttering in Yiddish into his cell phone. The strong strip lights overhead made Chaim's skin look chapped, glassy. To the left, the lobby spilled off toward Ceremonial Courtroom 2, where the trial was being held. Hershkop waved to his brother, who raised one eyebrow in recognition. He passed the court cop stationed at the door—a young guy, uniformed and visibly bored, his eyes on the sports section of the *Post*—and pulled open one heavy wooden door. The chamber bore a closer resemblance to a laboratory than to the kind of courtrooms featured on TV. There was no dark wood paneling here—no green-lidded desk lamps, no antique ornamentation, no enormous canvas of blindfolded Lady Justice, fiddling studiously with her overloaded scales.

Just a few beveled metal letters glued to the far wall: "In God We Trust."

Some spectators turned to watch Hershkop enter. He spotted Schleimy Klein, his combed and flattened red hair looking even more red than usual, and his father and his uncle and a few of the younger Shomrim guys, one of whom had been ballsy enough to leave his Shomrim jacket, logo-side up, draped across the bench. Gadi, straight-backed and smiling, was parked at the defendant's table, scribbling something in a notebook, while Israel Fried talked into his right ear. The judge had not yet entered the courtroom, and the jury box was empty. Weiss and David Steingard had not yet made their way to the prosecutor's table and sat instead on a second-row bench, Weiss taking some notes, Steingard fiddling with his BlackBerry. Hershkop tried to catch their eyes, but it was useless—they knew enough to ignore the distractions.

In front of the judge's bench, the court clerk was talking to the court reporter, a tall, curly-haired woman who appeared to be in her thirties. Long legs, tall heels, sharp suit. "It's like, you know, I'm Italian, right?" the woman was whispering. "I'm also Catholic, but me and my husband don't identify ourselves as Catholic. No, we say we're Italian, right? But if you're Jewish, it's different. You probably don't say you're Italian, even if you're Italian Jewish—you just say you're Jewish. Weird, right?" The court clerk nodded sagely.

Hershkop found a seat next to Klein and took his friend by the shoulder. They sat like that for a moment. The courtroom hummed around them. Voices rose, fell, dropped into a circuitous murmur. The bailiff, an aging guy with a heavy hard paunch and a head full of wild white hair, walked down the center aisle, looking for cell phones. "Keep those things off," he said to a kid sitting behind Hershkop. Eventually, Lifshitz and Blecher reentered the courtroom and found their seats, amid a great shuffling of paper. Hershkop closed his eyes. When he reopened them, Klein was tugging at the crook of his elbow, people were jumping to their feet, and the judge, the Honorable Albert Tomei, was climbing up onto the bench, the hem of his robes trailing regally behind him.

A courtroom scene, observed in passing: A man and a woman share a bench near the back of the gallery. The man is a well-known and well-respected Lubavitch rabbi. For convenience, let's call him Rabbi G. Rabbi G is dressed in a gray jacket and gray slacks, the jacket a slightly different shade of gray than the pants; clearly, the two items were purchased separately and paired in the half-light. The knees on the slacks of the pants are shiny. The cuffs extend too far. The shoes are bad. The rabbi leans forward. He raises his glasses and removes the gunk. He is listening to the woman. The woman is Devorah Lifshitz, the mother of Benjamin Lifshitz.

She is dressed in ultra-Orthodox haute couture: High-heeled boots that extend nearly to her knees. A fine black skirt, free of lint and dust. A well-tailored jacket, buttoned nearly to the neck. Gold and silver jewelry on the neck, the ears, peeking out from under the sleeves of the jacket. An expensive brown wig, centered perfectly on the head, nearly undistinguishable as a wig, even under this harsh industrial lighting.

". . . and then his glasses were knocked off," she says. "And those animals, they stepped on the glasses. And my son goes looking for the glasses, and he's digging around on the floor, trying to get them to stop, but no one can hear him. You'll see all this on the video. Just wait."

Rabbi G nods.

"So my question is, you know, how can this be assault?"

"Right."

"I mean, it's like you get robbed and the cops come and the cops slap the cuffs on you and let the criminal go. That's what—"

"Sure."

"Am I wrong?"

"No."

"Thank you. Thank you for saying that."

They are quiet. After a moment, the rabbi leans forward again. "What's the best-case scenario here?" he asks.

"Well, of course, best-case scenario is a not guilty verdict. For all of them. Did you know they're facing fifteen years in prison for this? They need vindication. Prove to the world that they did nothing wrong."

"And what's the worst-case scenario?"

Devorah Lifshitz raises one arm and drops the hand at the wrist—a gesture of resignation and despair. "I don't even want to think about it," she says. The rabbi opens his mouth to respond, but the judge peers right at Rabbi G, slams down his gavel, and court is called to order.


As far as David Steingard was concerned, Tomei was the right man for the Shomrim case, which already seemed on the brink of spinning out of control. Tomei was a career Brooklynite—his family was from Brooklyn, he had attended college and law school in Brooklyn, and he had served more than three decades on a Brooklyn bench, both as a Civil Court judge and as a Supreme Court justice. He had a reputation as something of a funnyman—his niece was the actress Marisa Tomei, and apparently the judge himself had dabbled in some amateur comedy work—but he also prided himself on having a severe allergy to bullshit.

In 2006, during a particularly convoluted murder trial over which Tomei presided, the *Times* had run a long story about the judge, highlighting his gruff, efficient courtroom manner. "[Tomei] has a desire to get to the proverbial jugular vein of what the case is about," a prominent lawyer explained to the *Times*. "He's there to do a day's work. He would not be happy, as a no-nonsense judge, with lawyers who posture." Well, there were certainly plenty of posturing lawyers in Ceremonial Courtroom 1 of the Brooklyn Supreme Court. And already there were enough procedural convolutions to stretch this trial out for weeks, months.

Late on Sunday night, Steingard and Weiss received word that Levi Huebner and a handful of *bochurim* had been called to an evening session of the Crown Heights *Beis Din*. The *rabbonim* apparently warned Huebner and the state witnesses that testifying against a fellow Jew was a grave sin; the witnesses were encouraged to drop the civil lawsuit and even consider refusing to testify in the criminal trial. According to some of the Hasidim on hand for the hearing, the *bochurim* had agreed to the terms set out by the *Beis Din*. That was a major problem. Why the *rabbonim* had taken so long to rule on the issue, Steingard didn't know—presumably, there were politics involved—and frankly, he didn't care. What he did know was that no one should be messing around with his witnesses. So that morning, he had requested a quick conference with the judge and announced that he was mulling over witness-tampering charges against the *Beis Din*. It wasn't such an outlandish idea, from a legal standpoint: no one, not even a Lubavitch rabbi, was allowed to tell a witness what he could or couldn't say on the stand.

The judge had listened to the allegations, nodded gravely, suggested some alternatives, and in the end, Steingard and Weiss had settled with the threat of tampering charges and a stern warning from Tomei, who had warned both the witnesses and the defendants that under no circumstances were they to discuss the case with—or take instructions from—anyone outside the courtroom at 320 Jay Street.

Now Steingard stood and watched Tomei whisper a few words to the court clerk, Tomei blocking the mic with the palm of his hand. Steingard had never seen a courtroom this clamorous. Just three days in, and the judge had already warned the spectators four times about the noise level, once coming close to really losing it, his cheeks bright red, his teeth bared, every instruction punctuated by a slam of his fist on his desk. The outbursts usually stopped the chattering for approximately five minutes, at which point one spectator would whisper something to his neighbor, and then everyone would be talking again, typing out love notes and messages on their BlackBerrys, iPhones, Nokias, the eaves of the room filled with beeps and bloops and the dry skittering of unpocketed handsets across the hard wood of the gallery pews. The bailiff, an older gentleman, presumably unaccustomed to babysitting a bunch of rambunctious Hasids, had taken to wandering up and down the aisle, sometimes jabbing one long gnarled finger at the audience and other times tiptoeing toward his target and physically wresting the offending gadget from the hands of an incredulous spectator.

Hey, what did the bailiff expect? Lubavitchers like to talk.

Steingard turned to look at Weiss, who was leaning back in his chair, flipping through a pile of loose-leaf yellow paper. They had long ago decided that Steingard, the more weathered of the two prosecutors, would give the all-important summations, but it was Weiss who would be the first one out there onstage, in front of a bunch of glaring defendants, an impatient judge, and a gallery of seething Hasidim. On the first day of the trial, during the lunch break, when they were shooting the shit in the lobby of the courthouse, Steingard and Weiss had been approached by a short, pear-shaped Lubavitcher. The woman was clad in a long jeans skirt and a blond wig, and her face was pancaked with orange makeup. "You two," she frothed, "you ought be ashamed of yourselves. How could you!" She turned away and stormed back the way she'd come, her sharp heels tapping out a staccato drumbeat on the floor.

It was a lightbulb moment for Steingard, that little speech saying so much about the mind-set of the defendants and their supporters. These people somehow had it in their heads that not only did an assistant district attorney choose the cases he prosecuted, but that he had some sort of personal stake in how they turned out. As if moral rectitude—and not the balance of evidence and the facts on hand— was the governing factor in any trial. As if a prosecutor was a rabbi and not an instrument of the American justice system. Since the interaction with the Lubavitcher woman, Steingard had decided that it was in his best interest to keep his head down. But passing the Shomrim kids in the lobby or on the way to the john, he was not above shooting them his best shit-eating grin and even whistling a little bit, a high-pitched ditty, something amorphous and repetitive— whistling until he saw their faces burst into a map of raised purple veins and then giving them his back, as if nothing had happened, nothing at all.

Weiss got up there around 10:30 a.m. The jury watched him maneuver his way from behind the desk, and Steingard watched the jury. Among the members was an older black guy who always looked like he was asleep, a pair of white women, a Hispanic man, a black woman. Not a bad representation of Brooklyn itself, when you thought about it. Weiss coughed, collected himself, walked up to the jury box, and began. "'Get that camera. Turn off that camera,'" he said. The jury member in the front row of the box looked confused. Weiss continued, helpfully,

Those were the words that the defendant, Gedalia, Gadi, Hershkop said so we would not be able to see what happened next. And what did happen next were the fractured orbital eye socket, a fractured finger, broken tooth, and multiple contusions and bruising all over the bodies of four people.

His opening gambit thus revealed, Weiss could loosen up, move fluidly back and across the floor of the courtroom, one hand in his pocket—probably more affectation than real relaxation—the other his signal hand, the fingers wrapped around a pen as if it were a baton. In many ways, Steingard knew, any opening statement was no different from the first few lines of a play—it was the moment when the members of the jury decided whether they liked you and, more important, whether they were going to follow you through intermission and into the final act. So you worked them the way an actor worked an audience. You didn't talk over them. You talked to them. Whenever possible, you worked without your notes, because an overreliance on your notes could indicate that you didn't respect the audience enough to learn your lines. You made eye contact.

Or you kept your eyes trained approximately two feet above their heads. Either way, you were facing the jury, you were giving the jury your attention, and those guys behind you? The defendants? Forget them. Listen to my story. Watch my hands. Watch my eyes. Concentrate. If they believe you, they will believe your story. If they believe your story, you will have won. This is what they don't teach you in law school; this is what good lawyers have always intuitively known; all of this Weiss understood.

Of course, the gang assault case against the Shomrim was chock full of its own peculiar exigencies. If Weiss went out too soft—got too mired in politics and religious matters—he ran the risk of losing the jury. If he went too hard, he'd look like he was castigating a crew of community servants. He had to strike the right balance: thoughtful but firm, patient but commanding. The Shomrim, Weiss told the jury, "have walkie-talkies. They look and they dress in a manner very similar to the police department. And they also drive around in vehicles with the decals of this organization that have lights and sirens." He paused, letting his lungs fill with air, the dramatic silence enough to cause Steingard, who knew the speech already, to lean forward in his chair.

"However," Weiss said, "even though these members of the Shomrim patrol have the trappings of authority, they are not the police. They do not have carte blanche to do whatever they want. And they certainly cannot abuse whatever authority they do have." Steingard looked to the right rail of the courtroom. The defense team was seated in one long row, engaged to various degrees in Weiss's performance. Fried was spinning a notebook on the table; Steven Williams had his eyes on the judge; Blecher was taking notes.

Before the trial started, Steingard had never met Williams or Blecher, who was really a civil attorney, with not a lot of trial experience—he'd been roped in to represent Lifshitz in the gang assault case and then all of the Shomrim in the civil suit pressed by Huebner. The rest of the team Steingard knew well, either by reputation—in the case of Joyce David—or because they had crossed paths on prior cases. It was a formidable group of litigators. But Steingard was counting on the sheer unwieldiness of the case the defense attorneys had been handed: six defendants with varying degrees of involvement in the crime, a veritable library of documentation, the language barriers, the politics.

"You're going to hear testimony about what the dispute was about," Weiss announced, peeking up for a moment at the judge. "I am going to tell you that it was a silly argument between two roommates. It was an argument over a bed and a person wanting to stay there for the weekend and his other roommate did not want to. That's it. That's what the fight was about." At that last line, Chaim Hershkop twisted noticeably in his chair.

Weiss pressed on. "These are two roommates who didn't really get along because of certain beliefs," he said. "They belong to different sects of the Lubavitch community, and they follow certain different customs. Even though they all study together in the yeshiva, they have some of these differences." Steingard nodded. So far, so good. Before the trial started, he and Weiss had agreed that they'd walk a delicate line when it came to religious politics—they would acknowledge that Wilhelm was a moderate and Gurfinkel a messianist, and they would admit that the two roommates had long been at loggerheads.

But they would stress that religious factionalism had less to do with this whole mess than did simple testosterone. They would work their hardest to peel back the mumbo-jumbo, the bullshit, the quackery, and strip the case to its core—a gang, the victims of the gang, and some broken bones.

"Now," Weiss said, "defense counsel may try to confuse you and talk about a larger issue—"

Joyce David leaned forward. "Objection," she said.

Williams stood up. "Objection," he said.

"Sustained," Tomei said.

"—what I will say is on trial before you are six defendants," Weiss continued. "And what they're on trial for is the attacks on Elkon Gurfinkel, Yaakov Shatz, Gavriel Braunstein, and Schneur Rotem."

The remainder of the opening followed a familiar rhythm. Weiss described the dormitory, leaving out the unbroken squalor of the place. He admitted that there had been an argument but maintained that the argument had been settled. He pointed out that by 9 p.m., things were quiet enough that Shuki Gur—the unofficial resident assistant of 749—felt comfortable returning to his own bed. "It was on his way back to his room," Weiss said, "that the events that would leave four students to end up in the hospital that night began. Because at that moment, a few members of the Shomrim gang—"

"Objection to the term *gang*," David said.

Tomei studied David, as if he were seeing her for the first time. "Objection sustained," he said.

"—in full uniform entered the room," Weiss said.

He did not use the word *gang* again in his opening statement. Instead, he took a subtler tack, eschewing limpid and commonplace verbs for the language of war, soldiering, police work. He stressed that the defendants had not just entered the room but "burst" into it; he described the altercation as a "full-blown melee"; he explained that choke holds and uppercuts and drop-kicks and sucker punches were used; he said that Hershkop and Lifshitz and company worked their way through the room in tag-team fashion, one guy picking up where his buddy had left off. The judge may not allow me to call the Shomrim a gang, Weiss seemed to be saying. But it doesn't take a sociologist to know what gang violence looks like.

Weiss took special note of the gloves worn by Gadi Hershkop:

The witnesses will tell you and they will describe that when they were being hit, the force from the hand and the gloves felt unusual, that they felt that there something hard inside the gloves and that was their impression. It felt exceptionally hard and heavy and appeared to be much larger and looked different than a normal black leather glove. You will be able to see up close on the video how large that glove looks when Gadi is punching Gurfinkel.

Again, Weiss said everything by not saying it directly. He did not actually know whether Gadi Hershkop had used sap gloves on the night in question or even whether Gadi Hershkop owned sap gloves, but he could build from the recollections of the alleged victims a plausible case that a weapon was used. This was important for two reasons: On the one hand, the mere insinuation that the defendant owned the kind of gloves favored by Mafia men and street brawlers might be enough to turn a jury against Hershkop. On the other, if Weiss could show that the eldest Hershkop brother had used anything more than his bare fists, he would meet the burden for aggravated assault—a felony crime that would likely earn Gadi Hershkop at least a few months behind bars.

Weiss concluded on a bravura note, his feet working faster on the tile floor, the hesitation gone from his voice, the members of the jury swiveling their heads in concert to watch him pass. "Neighborhood patrol groups are supposed to help out and protect the people of the community," he said.

They only have authority as the community allows it and wants it. On December 29, 2007, those defendants crossed that line and abused their powers. At the end of this case, I am going to come back and ask you, after you had an opportunity to hear all the witnesses in this case and to understand what the defendants did that night, I will ask you to hold these defendants responsible.

Weiss stopped pacing. He stood in front of the jury box. He locked both hands behind his waist. The fabric of his jacket strained against his chest. "Thank you," he said with a smile. In the back of the room, someone coughed.

The defense delivered its opening methodically and—considering the complexity of the case—relatively quickly. Blecher, for his part, told the jury that the Shomrim were "like Boy Scouts," outmatched and overpowered by an angry mob. Fried told the jury that the evidence in no way matched the description David Weiss had just offered of the alleged crime. Williams told the jury he found the whole matter confounding.

And Joyce David let the jury in on a dirty little secret: the trial, from top to bottom, was the unfortunate by-product of a long vendetta between the Shmira and Shomrim patrols, with a little bit of Hasidic religious factionalism tossed in to boot. Levi Huebner, a lawyer for the Shmira, "orchestrated this case," David said, speaking in cocktail party patter, as if she were dishing dirt on the guy across the room. Huebner "played the DA's office; he played the police," she added.

Oh, and then there was the small matter of the civil lawsuit, which David said gave Paul Huebner about 144 million reasons to want the six defendants tossed in prison.

# 14

Q: What is your occupation?

A: I am a rabbi in Colombia.

Q: What does that mean?

A: The rabbi of the Lubavitch sect goes all around the world to make sure that all the people and especially the Jews add as much goodness and kindness. So my job is in Colombia to be in a little town next to the beach making sure—

The Court: You have to speak a little louder into the mic. Repeat what you just said.

A: My job is to be in Colombia to make sure that all the Jews, not only Jews, all people who might be there, add as much goodness and kindness to help bring the redemption as soon as possible.

Thus began the testimony of Shuki Gur, a former resident of the yeshiva dormitory at 749 Eastern Parkway and the first witness called by the prosecution. From her seat on the right side of the courtroom, Joyce David watched Gur with curiosity. He was of middling height, with a thick black beard, sleepy, overfull eyes, and a relatively good command of English. Gur had been one of the first *bochurim* in Room 107 on December 29, 2007, and Steingard and Weiss

187

were clearly hoping that Gur could help outline the chronology of the brawl, place it in context. But Gur seemed to possess something close to disregard for the court, as if earthly matters—and especially a two-year-old brawl—were beneath him. He fiddled with the yellow pin on his lapel and adjusted his oversize black yarmulke, which bore in looping cursive script the motto of the messianist faction. He studied the ceiling.

Behind David, in the gallery, the members of the audience were swaying restlessly, side to side, back and forth, on the slippery hard wooden pews. Few were clad in full Hasidic dress regalia—many had stopped into the courtroom on their way to work or between shifts at a local shop or garage, the soft skin in the folds of their knuckles still caked with dirt—and David had seen a couple of boys wander in wearing jeans and T-shirts and frayed sneakers. These were friends of her clients, she knew, pals from yeshiva or grade-school buddies or cousins and in-laws.

They shared with the Hershkop brothers the same freewheeling crudity; they swore with abandon, jostled one another around by the shoulders like jocks in a locker room, told jokes filthy enough to make your earlobes burn. Yet David had found that she was comfortable around her client and his friends. There was something familiar about them—worldly, secular, bumptious. She had an especial fondness for Ben Lifshitz, who had drummed up plenty of actionable information on the *bochurim* and Huebner and even pulled from Facebook a picture of one of the *bochurim* standing in front of an oversize yellow messianist flag, holding in his hand a sharp and shiny machete. That photo she had tried to introduce as evidence—an indicator as to the vicious mind-set of the alleged victims—but the judge had simply shaken his head.

"Can you describe their uniforms?" Steingard asked Gur.

"They look very much like police uniforms, but their badge is different," Gur said. "It says on it 'Shomrim,' and it has a picture of 770, the building." When there was no objection, Gur continued. He explained that the Shomrim worked out of a garage on East New York; that the organization had walkie-talkies and carts with flashing lights on top; that the members often poked their noses where they didn't belong.

"And are there other branches outside of Crown Heights?" Steingard asked. Again, David studied the jury. Steingard was doing this for them: separating the actions and the reputations of the Shomrim patrols in other neighborhoods from the allegedly debased Shomrim patrol in Crown Heights. He had their attention.

"Yes," Gur said.

"Are these branches independent or work together?"

"They are independent. Each one works alone, but—"

"I am going to object," David said. "There's been no foundation laid that this witness is an expert on the Shomrim organization. All this is hearsay."

"Objection is sustained," Tomei said.

Steingard nodded and changed tack. He led Gur carefully through the buildup to the brawl: his decision to try to mediate the dispute in Room 107, his realization that the dispute was already resolved. Gur had been well trained. His answers were succinct. His demeanor was relaxed. He framed himself as the unofficial king of 749—the guy who could have defused the situation had he been given the chance. In fact, he said, before the Shomrim arrived, "the atmosphere in the room was calming down." After the Shomrim arrived, things started to get bad. He said that he was particularly struck by the vehemence of one Benjamin Lifshitz, who repeatedly asked Gur to kiss his ass.

"What did he say?" Steingard asked.

"He said, 'Kiss my ass.' Three times."

"Do you see Benjamin—"

Tomei interrupted, and for a moment, the testimony veered close to farce. "Did he say, 'Kiss my ass three times,' or did he say, 'Kiss my ass'"? Tomei asked.

"He said three times, 'Kiss my ass,'" Gur said.

"Three times. Okay. In one sentence."

David felt a sudden fondness for the people around her—for her fellow defense attorneys, for the court reporters, struggling to keep up with the flood of strange Yiddish and Hebrew names, for the judge, for the rambunctious audience members, even for Steingard and Weiss, two good lawyers saddled with a case that was quickly ballooning out of proportion. They were all like cast members in a B-movie, David thought. Every morning, they all sailed through those doors, and everyone had his or her part to play, and you stuck to your part, and if you won, it was good, and if you lost, at least you had given it your all, and at the end of the trial, you all walked to a nearby bar and had a drink.

Steingard circled Gur, his hands jammed emphatically in his pockets. Steingard asked that Gur identify Lifshitz. Gur complied; Lifshitz sat down. Looking at Lifshitz and then at Steingard and then finally letting his eyes rest on the jury box—not on the actual jury members, but on the polished wood of the enclosure—Gur claimed that he had repeatedly asked Yossi Frankel to leave the room.

But Yossi Frankel had refused, and shortly thereafter, the rest of the Shomrim had barreled into Room 107, and the alleged assault had commenced. He remembered that the Shomrim had "taken up posts" around the room, and that when the real police had arrived, the six members had moved toward the door, as if they'd just been in 749 to take in the scenery—as if they were just taking a stroll.

And then a moment of near calamity, for both prosecution and defense: Shuki Gur was discussing the video captured by Beliniski. He told the jury that when the Shomrim had begun demanding the camera, Beliniski had popped out the tape and surreptitiously handed it off to a couple of friends, so that a record would remain of the assault. Tomei asked Gur to identify the men who had taken possession of the tape. Gur refused.

"I don't want to say their names because they might do something to them," Gur said, the first "they" being his friends, and the second "they" being the Shomrim. All six defense attorneys jumped to their feet.

"Objection, your honor," David said.

"Objection sustained."

"Move to strike," Susan Mitchell said.

"Ask for mistrial," Williams said.

"Join in that request," Blecher said.

"Denied," Tomei said. He turned to the jury. "Ladies and gentlemen, disregard the last statement, alright? There's no bearing on the guilt or nonguilt of either of the defendants." Later that afternoon, after the jury had been dismissed, the defense team asked Tomei to take another look at the implications of what Gur had said.

"The impression left on the jurors," David said, was that there was reason to fear the Shomrim. "That they have acted out in the past. That's totally improper here." Williams again asked for a mistrial. He was joined by Mitchell and then Blecher and then Salaway and then David.

"You all join," Tomei snapped. "Separately and jointly, the application is denied. Anything else?" The trial was adjourned until the following Wednesday. The defendants filed out of the courtroom, followed by their lawyers.

David, walking next to Hershkop, her briefcase filled almost to the bursting point with papers and highlighters and pens, felt energized. Although the judge had denied their motion, she was certain that he had understood the reason for the vehemence of the defense objections—and also that he had begun to see the flimsiness of the case being presented by the people, which essentially amounted to hearsay and a video. And as far as she could tell, there wasn't much on the video at all.

# 15

In early November, a flier began circulating among the Lubavitcher Hasidim of Crown Heights. Copies were jammed into mailboxes and the curved metal gates of the yards on President and Union; they were slipped under locked doors and placed in the lobby of 770; they were passed wordlessly—but with a smile—among the yeshiva students; some editions, angrily discarded and bearing the stamp of a muddied boot print, fluttered north and south with the wind or up into the trees off Eastern Parkway, the branches now rendered skeletal and sharp by the early fall chill.

"In their arrogance, the Hershkops and gang believe they are above the law," the note on the top of the flier began. "They continue to threaten and intimidate the Bochurim and their families, in defiance of the court's order, in a calculated attempt to have the charges dropped."

The first two pages bore headshots of Ben Lifshitz and Aron Hershkop and a still image from the video captured by Beliniski on the evening of December 29, 2007. The photograph showed Gadi Hershkop reaching forward, his faced screwed up into a snarl. There was also a photocopy of a court order of protection taken out by Gurfinkel, who alleged that Lifshitz had repeatedly threatened his

193

well-being; Lifshitz had been ordered by a Brooklyn judge to stay away from Gurfinkel until the trial was concluded.

Everyone had a different opinion about who was behind the flier. Officially, it was billed as an open letter from the *bochurim* to their fellow Lubavitchers, and although the flier contained a litany of grammatical mistakes, the English was passable and at least decipherable; save Gur, few of the *bochurim* wrote much English at all.

Some believed that the flier was the work of the Shmira. They pointed out that Yossi Stern had a buddy who owned a copy shop and said that they had seen Shmira members walking around Crown Heights with stacks of the fliers, handing them out like candy. The Shmira did not disavow responsibility for the flier, but neither did they stand behind it. Others thought the letter had been written by members of the community council or maybe even by the Shmira lawyer, Levi Huebner.

"Despite the intimidation," the flier read, "the Hershkops and Shomrim gang were given many opportunities by lawyers, community activists, including Dov Hikind"—a New York assemblyman with deep and long-standing ties to the Hasidim of Crown Heights—"directors of Hatzolah, the Vaad Hakohol, business people and professionals from our community, and even members of their own families, pleading with them to settle." The flier described the terms of a deal allegedly offered to the Shomrim patrol:

1.  A written apology to each of the victims.
2.  Remove their hate-filled websites from the Internet.
3.  Issue a letter to the community in which they promise to cease from any further fighting, refrain from contact with any of the Bochurim, and to abide by the above-mentioned conditions.

The letter continued,

> By committing to these simple steps the Bochurim believe that the Shomrim would cease in attacking or harassing them or dispensing any further vile lies and hate on the Internet. This offer was flatly turned down by the Coordinators of Shomrim. As quoted by the gang leader of Shomrim, Aron "Leli" Hershkop, "we will never apologize. They must apologize."

Even after these offers, the intimidation by the Hershkops and gang continued. "I'm gonna kill you," a Shomrim gang member threatened one of the Bochurim. Emails were sent to parents of the Bochurim, telling them how they will never see their sons alive again. Contrary to Hershkop's claims, this is not a political fight, nor a Shmira-Shomrim showdown, this is a case of gang assault. The charges are being brought against the Shomrim members by the District Attorney.

In Ceremonial Courtroom 2, on the second floor of Brooklyn Supreme Court, the flier was handed incredulously from Gadi Hershkop back to his brother Aron in the gallery, forward again to Slatter and Pinson, then across to Chaim Hershkop, and finally over to Ben Lifshitz, who took one look at the first page and crumpled the flier up in his fist, his knuckles going white with the effort. He felt a little sick.

On Wednesday morning, David Steingard requested that the lights be dimmed. Word had gotten around Crown Heights that the video evidence would be shown today, and the gallery was fuller than usual. Steingard spotted a couple of reporters he knew and at least one whom he didn't, along with a group of young married women—presumably wives or sisters of the defendants—seated in the back row, their arms crossed tightly across their chests. To his left, Weiss was fiddling with a couple of files on the laptop. Steingard studied the gallery. One kid, a slim, bug-eyed Lubavitcher, no more than twenty-two years old and dressed in cargo pants and a torn blue sweater, met Steingard's gaze and then returned his attention to the ceiling.

Steingard often amused himself during breaks in the proceedings by imagining which of these guys was behind the blog "Who is Shmira?" In recent weeks, the site had taken to posting pictures of both Weiss and Steingard, usually headlined by a barrage of colorful pejoratives. Weiss, for his part, was able to shrug off that kind of stuff. He told Steingard he thought the blog was hilarious—stupid fan fiction from a bunch of thugs, but certainly nothing worth getting litigious over.

Steingard wasn't so sure. He worried about his wife, about his family; he worried that someone would see his name on the blog, do some cursory research on the Web, and track him down. At any rate, the blog was almost certainly run by one of the defendants, and he figured his best shot at shutting down the site would be putting the Shomrim Six—as they had taken to calling themselves—in the nice cozy confines of a prison cell.

The lights fell. Steingard stood up and walked to the right wall, where a now still image of the fight was projected. Gur sat patiently on the stand, wrapping the strands of his beard around his thumb. Seen in these proportions, Room 107 actually looked fairly spacious and the men of the Shomrim and the *bochurim* like giants. But no matter what magnification you viewed the video at—or what speed—it still appeared to be a kaleidoscopic mélange of fists, elbows, shoes, glasses, black fedoras.

Steingard led Gur through the video carefully, making sure his witnesses said aloud the names of each of the alleged assailants. He drew blood at least once. He brought up a picture of Gadi Hershkop, his body pointed in Gurfinkel's direction, and he asked Gur to describe what happened. Gur said Gadi had punched the *bochur* square in the face, and that the kid had fallen to the ground.

Tomei interjected, apparently unsatisfied with the precise tack of Steingard's questions. "Can you see there is an arm that is depicted?" Tomei asked.

"This one?" Gur pointed.

"Yeah. In the screen. Is that connected to Gadi or not?"

"Yeah."

"Let the record reflect it is Gadi's—it looks like Gadi's—well, there is an arm with a glove, and it is extending straight out, and the witness has testified that it is Gadi's arm," Tomei said. "Alright."

That was a win, no matter which way you sliced it, Steingard thought: his witness had pretty conclusively linked Gadi Hershkop to some sort of assault, and there was video evidence to back up the testimony. Still, the hill remained steep: Gur had really nailed only Gadi. There were five more defendants facing gang assault, and unlike Gadi, those five guys had done the bulk of their fighting off camera.

In the early afternoon, Steingard turned his witness over to the defense. At first, the cross went relatively smoothly. Gur remained collected; he smiled; he joked about apparent aberrations in his prior testimony; he made sure to peer over occasionally at the jury box and extend a reassuring nod.

And then Blecher wandered up toward the stand, his hands behind his back. Steingard, watching him go, could sense by this forced nonchalance that Blecher was about to play his major trump card. "Now, if I may," Blecher said, "with the leave of the court, could the witness please stand up and face the jury?"

Gur stood.

"You have on your lapel a pin, sir?"

Steingard was out of his seat before Blecher had finished with his question. "Objection!" Steingard said, and to his left, he heard Weiss echo the objection, their voices carrying up into the eaves of the courtroom. Silence. Tomei looked at Gur, then at Steingard and Weiss, and then at Blecher, who had a "What, me? No way!" expression plastered across his mug. Steingard was thinking, The balls on this guy, to do it this way. The regular rustle of the voices in the courtroom rose one octave and then another, some of the women actually talking now, not just whispering, the bailiff zipping across one aisle and then another, his hands held in front of him, the gesture more pleading than anything else.

"Quiet!" Tomei exploded. "I don't want any talking in the courtroom. Now or ever." He motioned for the prosecution and defense teams to approach. Steingard found himself standing next to Blecher, who had worked up a hell of a sweat, the beads collecting in the frazzled strands of hair over his ear, his eyes bright and triumphant. Everyone began talking at once. David, Blecher, Weiss, Steingard—they were all talking now, talking over one another, the prosecution upset about the intrusion of community politics on a gang assault case, the defense thrilled that finally they'd have a chance to show the jury what had actually transpired, the judge looking as if he were poised somewhere between another outburst and a fit of giggles, his lips drawn tight across his face in one flat horizontal line.

"Ladies and gentlemen," he told the jury. "Remain in your seats. We will step outside. Do not discuss this case amongst yourselves or with anyone else." He stepped down from the bench and walked out the back of the courtroom, followed by a small parade of staff—court reporter, court clerk, attorneys, all of them with their heads bowed. "Let's go," Tomei said, once they were out of view of the jury and safely into the hallway.

Steingard went first. He pointed out that during a previous session, Blecher had agreed not to broach the topic of messianism; by asking Gur to stand and show his pin, he was not only breaking his word, but he was confusing the jury. "The questioning on the pins and hats and the writings are all heading toward this issue of messianic divisions, which he clearly intends to address," Steingard said. "I have no idea, in good faith, how that evidence is going to come out. He is going to bring out ancient rifts in the community. There's no evidence in this case, no evidence in this case that this particular incident had anything to do with these messianic divisions—"

"That," Blecher said, interrupting Steingard, "is absolutely untrue, your honor." Blecher pointed out that Wilhelm had effectively been forced to vacate Room 107 because he was not a messianist, and his fellow dorm mates were. "They all wear these badges, yellow badges, on their hats or lapels," Blecher said. "They wear yarmulkes. They all basically were sticking together. Basically, you could see it in the dormitory. They have these signs up. It is a strong indication that if you're not a believer in that sect, you're not welcome here. That was precisely what was happening. That is the reason that there was this fight, Your Honor. It always goes back to them ejecting a student who wasn't a member of that sect."

They batted the issue back and forth like this for another minute or so, Steingard holding fast to his objection, Blecher maintaining that nobody would be in court right now if there hadn't been a schism in Crown Heights, the judge's hands half-raised, his cheeks puffed, eyebrows raised—he looked to Steingard like a teacher sorting out a schoolyard brannigan.

"This will do nothing," Steingard said, "but cloud the jury's ability—"

"No!" Blecher muttered.

"—to look at the evidence and apply the charges in this case."

"No," Blecher said again. "It is just not part of the truth. It is not, you know—"

Steingard held up both palms toward Blecher. "You don't have to convince me. Stop."

Tomei cleared his throat. "Let me ask you something," he said. "How does this belief that this mêlée arose because of two sects having different beliefs—"

"Because they don't permit people in that dormitory who don't share that belief," Blecher said.

"If there was just one person," Tomei said after a moment, "maybe that would be relevant. We got a great number of people that are involved in this, and as I said before, some who may have assaulted, may have assaulted others, and the majority not assaulting anyone—"

"But I think—," Blecher tried again, the fight nearly out of him, his shoulders slumping.

"—all right?" Tomei barked, silencing Blecher. "But the difference is in what may have been the precipitating factor here. I think it is a collateral issue which will distract the jury and has nothing to do with the assault, all right? I am going to deny—" He corrected himself. "I am going to sustain the motion."

"Thank you, Judge," Steingard said.

"That is it," Tomei said. But that wasn't it—not quite.

Joyce David stepped forward. "I need to put in my two cents," she said.

Tomei sighed.

"This also may have to do with the credibility of the witness," David said, "because my understanding is that the group that believes that Rabbi Schneerson is the Messiah and that the Messiah already came believed they can do anything that they want to the people who don't believe the same way. They can lie. They can hurt them."

Behind David, Blecher was nodding fervently, his head practically bobbing on his shoulders. "Because look, this witness is put up there as a rabbinical student, as a rabbi," David continued. "This gives him—sort of bolsters his credibility because somehow he is a man, you know, of God. But if, in fact, their beliefs allow them to break these kinds of rules, then it may go to the credibility of the witness—because otherwise, if I were on the jury, I would think he is a rabbi, he is not going to lie under oath."

"I will instruct the jury that the status of the particular witness has no bearing on his credibility," Tomei said. "He is to be treated like any other witness, and they are to take that into consideration." Tomei thanked David and then pointed toward the door.

"Your honor," Blecher said, "respectfully, you have my—"

But it was too late. The five defense attorneys and the two prosecutors and the court reporter and the judge were already filing back into the courtroom to face the jury, and Blecher, bowing his head, followed suit.

# 16

In recent days, Joyce David had begun to worry that the trial of the Shomrim Six, which had originally looked as if it would wrap up by early November, might end up spilling into the new year. The back-door wrangling over the messianist politics—whether it was vital to the case or ancillary, and David was of the opinion that it was certainly vital—had consumed both prosecution and defense and taken away from time that should have been used for testimony. Meanwhile, because of Shabbos laws, most of the witnesses and all of the defendants had to be back in Crown Heights early on Friday, which meant that even on a good week—and there had been plenty of bad weeks, full of their own distractions and digressions—they were all spending only four days in court.

Already, the jurors were getting restless. One had a bad cold and had pleaded with the judge to be dismissed. A second was pregnant and due within a few weeks. A third had lost her position at a local television network.

David sympathized. Months earlier, she had planned a big vacation to San Francisco, where her daughter and her grandchildren lived. It would be her first real break in more than a year—a time to relax, to sleep off the tensions of the job. Now it seemed possible that she would not make this vacation at all. She scanned her notes: at least three more witnesses left to go and then summations, and after summations, jury deliberations, and after jury deliberations, sentencing. She pictured herself celebrating the holidays in the sterile environs of Ceremonial Courtroom 2, a glass of lukewarm champagne in hand.

At the front of the chamber, Izzy Fried, the defense attorney hired by Gadi Hershkop, was grilling Yaakov Shatz. Shatz—the same *bochur* who had evaded the Shomrim by throwing himself out the window of Room 107 and crawling along the air shaft to safety. The kid had a small frame, baby face, cartoonishly round eyes. To his credit, he was putting up a hell of a fight, doing his best to keep his answers to two words or less and refusing to be drawn out.

Because Shatz spoke only Yiddish and Hebrew, an octogenarian translator had been brought on board, but the translator employed a decidedly Victorian form of English—for instance, he insisted on referring to the yeshiva students as "lads"—and Fried was regularly forced to ask for a clarification. The translator was a real throwback. Earlier that morning, the guy had blithely strolled into the courtroom half an hour late, doffed his hat to Tomei, and blamed his tardiness on the sluggish speed of the courthouse elevators. "They move like the Atlantic Ocean!" he said, delivering the line in the lilting intonation of a Borscht Belt comedian. The judge had not been amused.

"You took it upon yourself to ask Frankel to leave the room," Fried was saying to Shatz. The translator leaned forward. Fried repeated the question: Had Shatz asked the Shomrim member Yossi Frankel to vacate the premises?

Shatz smirked. "Yes," he said. "One of those who asked him was me."

David watched Fried approach the stand, his hands locked behind his back, his jacket open to the waist. Fried was perhaps the most natural trial litigator in the courtroom. He was fast, aggressive, theatrical. He communicated with his eyebrows, raising one to the jury when a witness stumbled, and raising the other to his fellow attorneys when he was hammering home a point. He clearly delighted in the circus atmosphere of a major criminal trial—in the opportunity it provided to showboat, to play to the crowd. He carried business cards bearing a terse three-word tagline: "Your best defense." As in, Your best defense is a good offense. "I always say, 'If you can't wow 'em with words, you wow 'em with evidence,'" Fried had recently explained to the rest of the defense team. "'Can't wow 'em with evidence, wow 'em with words.' And this trial doesn't have much of either. The facts don't seem to line up." In Fried's reckoning, the trial of the Shomrim Six would come down to whom the jury believed. Would they trust the steadfast community men of the Crown Heights Shomrim Rescue Patrol? Or would they trust the shifty *bochurim* of 749 Eastern Parkway? From the start of proceedings, Fried had concentrated on slashing the testimony of the *bochurim* to ribbons. He wrestled with prosecution witnesses over even the smallest inconsistency, the theory being that when you added up all of those small inconsistencies, they started to look a whole lot like a very big conspiracy.

"I'm asking you about yourself," Fried barked at Shatz. "And, again, I'm going to ask you to please pay attention to my questions and limit your answers to my questions. I asked if you asked Frankel to leave."

"Yes." Shatz looked uneasy.

"Okay, thank you," Fried said and practically leaped back to the defense team's table. He opened up a manila folder and fished out a stapled stack of documents. "And you testified that you asked Frankel to leave at the moment he entered the room?"

". . . No," Shatz said. He shrugged.

"That's not what you testified to?"

"It's possible that he came in, I don't know if it was the second he entered or half a minute later."

"Your Honor," Fried said, waving the stack of documents, "I'm going to reference the witness's testimony on direct examination. It's page 389."

Tomei swiveled in his chair and flicked the stem of the mic in the direction of his mouth. "Ladies and gentlemen," he said, "at this time, defense counsel is seeking to impeach the credibility of this witness by showing that at an earlier time, that is, when the witness answered questions on direct, he made a statement that's inconsistent with his present in-court cross-examination. Ladies and gentlemen, it's up to you to determine whether it is inconsistent, number one, and number two, if it is, to what extent it impeaches his credibility. It's not being offered for its truth." He motioned at Fried, a kind of half bow. "Go ahead," Tomei said.

Fried read aloud from Shatz's prior testimony. "'Question: At what point did you ask him to leave? Answer: At the moment he entered.'" A squawk went up from the gallery. David smiled. It was a small point, a quibble, really—the matter of when, exactly, Shatz had asked Frankel to leave. And yet it went to a larger point: Yaakov Shatz couldn't keep his story straight. Yaakov Shatz said one thing to the prosecutors and another to the defense team. Yaakov Shatz couldn't be trusted. In David's experience, this was the kind of thing no jury was likely to forget.

Shatz was still grinning, but there were less teeth in that grin, David thought—the insolence had been scrubbed off. Fried stepped up the pace of his questioning, needling the kid from every possible angle:

Q: And that's because you believe that Shomrim members don't belong inside the yeshiva. Correct?

A: No.

Q: Well, isn't that what you said on direct exam?

A: No.

Q: Your Honor, I'm going to again read from Mr. Shatz's direct testimony.

The Court: Give me a page and a line.

Mr. Fried: Page 389, line 17.

The Court: Page what?

Mr. Fried: Page 389, line 16.

The Court: Same instruction applies here. Go ahead.

Q: Mr. Shatz, do you recall being asked the following question and giving the subsequent answer: "Question: At the moment he entered, you asked him to leave. Why did you ask him to leave? Answer: Because he doesn't belong in the building and I know him as part of the Shomrim group."

A: Correct.

Q: And that's why you asked him to leave; correct?
A: Correct.

The further Fried got into the cross, the more confused Shatz became. He coughed and sneezed. He closed his eyes and opened them wide. He fiddled with the lapels of his jacket. While the *bochur* watched, Fried produced a copy of a lawsuit—the same lawsuit that alleged the Shomrim had "severely injured and damaged" Shatz and his friends. The same lawsuit that listed among the ailments of the *bochurim* "severe nervous shock and mental anguish, great physical pain and emotional upset." The same lawsuit that demanded $4 million in compensatory damages from the Crown Heights Shomrim, along with an additional $12 million in punitive damages from each defendant. The same lawsuit that was organized by Paul Huebner, a member of the Crown Heights Shmira.

Presumably, Shatz, being a party to the lawsuit, should understand its particulars. But it quickly became clear that Shatz didn't understand the lawsuit at all. "I'm not suing him," Shatz said of the Shomrim member Schneur Pinson, although he was suing Schneur Pinson, along with the rest of the Shomrim, and for millions of dollars. Shatz was falling into the trap, David thought to herself, and he seemed to know it.

After a few more minutes of testimony, Fried asked for the lights to be dimmed. The video appeared again on the wall.

"Mr. Shatz, did you just see yourself grab one of the Pinson brothers?" Fried asked, referring to the two Shomrim members.

Shatz waited for the translator and then shook his head. "I don't recall," he said.

"Well, you just watched it on the screen," Fried said.

The interpreter grabbed his beard with one fist. "What?"

Fried raised one eyebrow. "You just watched it on the video."

". . . Okay," Shatz said.

"You were pushing him?"

"I don't recall."

"Well, you're behind Mr. Pinson, correct?"

"Yes."

"And he's not even facing you?"

"Yes."

Fried nodded back toward the defense table. Blecher pressed a key on a laptop, and again the noises of the dormitory at 749 Eastern Parkway filled the room. On the screen, Shatz had Pinson by the arm. Blecher paused the video. "Mr. Shatz," Fried said. "That's you again, isn't it?"

"Yes."

"Whose hand are you grabbing?"

"Pinson."

"Mr. Pinson is not even interacting with you, is he?"

"I don't know."

"Well, none of the Shomrim are interacting with you in frame 17:27."

"I don't recall that."

Fried sauntered over to the wall where the image was projected. The video played again. Fried signaled. The video stopped. Frame 17:45. Now Shatz was standing next to Gadi Hershkop, who was surrounded on all sides by black hats and jackets—a snarl of *bochurim*, all arms and fingers and fists. "This is my client," Fried said and pointed to Hershkop. "And he had just choked you, allegedly, seconds before this frame?"

"I don't know."

"But you're standing a foot away from him?"

Shatz conferred with the translator. "About," he said.

"You weren't afraid that he was going to assault you again?"

"I was afraid."

"It doesn't look like you're afraid, does it?"

"Okay . . ." Shatz retreated into his raised shoulders.

"You didn't leave the room?"

"No."

"And he's not fighting with you in this frame, is he?"

"No."

"And you have no visible injuries, do you?"

"No, I don't see any injuries here." Shatz paused. "Near the neck," he added.

"Well, not enough to get you out of the room, right?"

"I didn't want to get out of the room."

Fried walked straight up to the stand. He was eye to eye with Shatz. "Why should you, right?" Fried asked. "You wanted to fight."

"Objection!" Steingard said.

The objection was overruled.

# 17

Compared to the other *bochurim*, Schneur Rotem was a relatively docile witness. He allowed himself to be steered, first by the prosecutors, who asked him to describe the scene inside Room 107 of the dormitory at 749 Eastern Parkway, and then by the defense team, which proceeded to rip his story to shreds.

Through it all, he remained calm. He told David Steingard that he had not hit anyone on the night in question—no, sir, he wouldn't think of it. He recalled that the police had quickly cleared the room, and that he, Schneur Rotem, had hid in the bathroom, emerging only once he was sure that the coast was clear. He remembered walking toward his friends. He remembered being tossed to the ground and beaten furiously with hands and feet, and he remembered narrowly avoiding being beaten with the butt end of a fire extinguisher.

And he remembered it vividly and explicated his memories clearly and even looked at one point toward the jury and nodded and smiled. This was the kid in the picture produced by Lifshitz—the guy wielding that machete, standing proudly in front of a flapping yellow flag—but on the stand, he might as well have been Bambi.

• • •

Steingard finished with the direct examination around eleven. Rotem picked his ass off the chair, as if he were finished for the day, but Tomei gave him a sidelong glare, and Rotem was back in his seat within half a second flat, acquiescent again.

Because Rotem had fingered Chaim Hershkop as one of his assailants—"I saw immediately Chaim Hershkop bend down and lifting [the fire extinguisher] up above the head in a form that he was going to throw it on me," he had said—Joyce David would be responsible for much of the cross examination.

Much was at stake. David believed that by now a felony gang assault conviction was out of the question—she and Fried and the rest of the defense team had helped see to that. But a litany of misdemeanor charges remained in play, and David knew that her client would consider even a misdemeanor conviction to be a major defeat. For the defendants, after all, this trial wasn't just about a simple brawl. It was about the good name of the Crown Heights Shomrim. It was about whether the Shomrim belonged in Brooklyn. It was about justice, secular and cosmic.

A conviction would provide ammunition to the NYPD and the Crown Heights Shmira, which clearly wanted the Shomrim shut down for good, and to Paul Huebner, who would continue to press the lawsuit against the organization long after the conclusion of the criminal trial. An acquittal would be further proof of the God-given right of the Shomrim to protect the kingdom of Crown Heights.

This was no time to take her foot off the gas.

Still, David played the cross extremely loose at first. She let Rotem give a little spiel about his seniority at 749, his years abroad. She kept a warm smile on her face. She talked to Rotem as if he were an old friend. She laughed when he said something funny. Then she began easing Schneur Rotem back toward the brawl.

"Now isn't it a fact," she said, "that students who were dressed like you, with a special flag pin and special writing on your yarmulke, were fighting with students who didn't wear the flag pin and the special yarmulke?"

Rotem looked stricken, his eyes going milky and soft. "No," he said, faintly enough that the judge had to tilt his ear toward the stand.

David's plan was simple: Having proved that the *bochurim* were unreliable witnesses, she would now turn the tables on the witnesses. She would repeatedly and explicitly identify Rotem as a hard-line messianist, disconnected from earthly realities. She would make the jury see Rotem as her clients saw him—as a *mosser*, or "rat," with a special enmity toward the Crown Heights Shomrim. Because, as Izzy Fried had pointed out earlier, the fracas at 749 Eastern Parkway wasn't assault. No, sir. It was an ambush, plain and simple. It was a rowdy group of students, high on their own fanatical beliefs, who had pounced on the Shomrim.

"Isn't it a fact," David said, edging closer to Rotem, "that there's a group of students in the dorm who are part of a different group of Lubavitch Hasidim and dressed like yourself, who disagree passionately with the students in the other group, who don't believe the same way you do?"

"Objection, Judge," Steingard said.

"I'll let him answer," Tomei said.

"Could you repeat the question?" the translator asked, and David did.

"I don't go into the beliefs of anybody," Rotem answered, finding his footing again. "I believe what I believe."

"That's not my question."

"Okay . . ."

"Aren't there arguments between you, who believe the way you believe, and those people in the student population who don't believe the way you believe?"

Rotem wasn't stupid. He saw where David was headed. "There could be thoughtful disagreement," he said.

"Isn't it a fact that the disagreements have gotten quite passionate?"

"No."

She let that one sit. "No?" she said. "There have never been incidents of this split between the two factions?" David smiled. No matter what race or creed or gender, a witness always got the same panicked look when he or she was on the ropes—an animalistic kind of terror, like a squirrel about to be demolished by a cross-town bus. The DA had taught Rotem well, and the *bochur* was a good student, but he had not been prepared for this. He cast a frantic look toward the prosecutors.

"Objection," Steingard said.

"Sustained," Tomei nodded. "He said no."

"I shouldn't have to be bound by his answer, Your Honor."

Rotem raised a finger to the ceiling, and everyone—Steingard, David, and Tomei—pivoted in his direction. "Can I go to the bathroom?" Rotem asked. One of the defendants groaned. David shrugged. Tomei called a two-hour lunch recess, and the jury filed out of the courtroom.

Between late November and early December 2009, CrownHeights. info, the Lubavitch news site operated by the Shomrim member Ben Lifshitz, posted two editorials on the 749 case. Both received a flood of angry comments from the CrownHeights.info readership. The first op-ed was attributed to "A Crown Heights Mother." This mother, whose name was likely known only to Lifshitz, wrote that she had not stepped foot in a criminal courtroom since the '90s, when Lemrick Nelson was acquitted of murder.

"I haven't been interested in watching another criminal trial since," the mother wrote. "However, yesterday I went to show support once more for Jews, this time six of them." She continued,

> The issue is six young Lubavitchers are facing jail. You don't know what goes through the jury's heads but at least if you go you can help the defendants by showing the jury we care about them; they are always there for us. Now it's our turn to be there for them. At the end of the day, private security patrols are on trial. Who knows what the consequences could be?

The second editorial was submitted by Rabbi Shea Hecht, the chairman of the National Committee for the Furtherance of Jewish Education. Hecht, who hosted a radio show devoted to Jewish issues and who had been vociferous in his criticism of the government response to the riots, made it clear in his editorial what side he took.

Like "The Crown Heights Mother," Hecht pleaded for his fellow Lubavitchers to support the Shomrim Six.

"I have sat through well beyond my fair share of court proceedings," he wrote, "and I'm very familiar with the way things play out. A man takes the stand and believes that he has control, that he can tell his story the way it needs to be told. The absurd song and dance that is taking place at 320 Jay Street is evidence of just how naïve that belief is. Every word, every motion that takes place in court is masterfully controlled by the attorneys. After all, that is their art." Hecht hinted that more was at risk here than the welfare of the defendants. There was also the matter of how the Chabad movement might be damaged by the tenor of the trial:

> [O]ur way of life has been debased in court. The court transcripts are busting with references by the judge and the attorneys to "lapel pins" and "yarmulkes with writing." The Lubavitcher Chassidim, the Rebbe, Crown Heights, the imminent coming of Moshiach, 770. . . . Everything that means anything to us is today represented in Supreme Court through a "yellow flag" prism. Our associations, motivations and whether or not six fellow Chassidim will sit in prison will be determined according to the writing on our yarmulkes.

More than fifty remarks quickly piled up in a comments section under the editorial, most of them exuberant. "Overjoyed," one commenter wrote, "that Rabbi Hecht did it again, [and] appalled that this had to be written!"

Rotem spent the break cooped up in one of the two small conference rooms off the second-floor landing. On her way to the ladies' room, Joyce David passed the window of the room and caught a glimpse of the kid slouched forward over the table, gripping in one hand a faded leather prayer book. Behind David, on the second-floor landing, the Shomrim boys milled happily. Aron Hershkop joked in Yiddish with his brother Gadi; the room filled with overloud laughter. In recent days, David and the rest of the defense attorneys had done their best to encourage the six defendants not to get too excited. The jury was an unpredictable animal. Things could still go pear shaped. Privately, though, David felt the same giddy optimism. Rotem would topple like a Jenga tower, if only she could find the right block to pull.

Near the end of the recess, David passed Blecher. He was carrying a bag full of tuna fish sandwiches from the cafeteria down on Jay Street—food for the defendants, whose kosher diet basically ruled out any standard deli counter fare. Blecher nodded to David. In the back pew of the courtroom, a journalist was scribbling in an open notepad—no surprise there.

David knew that many of the reporters who had cycled through the courtroom were hoping for some sort of big confrontation between Huebner and the Shomrim Six, which would, of course, give a very public face to the Shomrim and Shmira feud. David, back in October, had floated that very idea among her fellow defense lawyers. Why not call Huebner to the stand? It might be fun to have a shot at the guy. Get him up there and break him down. But in the end, the defense team had decided that Huebner was too unpredictable. They could make their case without him.

At 2:30 p.m., the jury was again summoned. Joyce David, from her perch at the front of the courtroom, turned to watch the bailiff escort Rotem through the doors. Rotem held his head up proudly. In his wake, a great hiss arose, and unlike Shatz, who had not favored the men and the women in the gallery with so much as a fleeting glance, Rotem was happy to indulge his audience—he drew the corners of his face into a great smirk and slowed his strut, coming within a few inches of the defendants. He took his seat with painstaking care, and as David gathered her papers and approached the stand, she saw that Schneur Rotem—this impertinent, machete-wielding *bochur*—was grinning, as if the Messiah himself had dropped down into the courtroom.

David wasted no time on preliminaries.

"Isn't it a fact," she said, "that you and your friends have destroyed property in the community?" An objection was extended by Steingard and sustained by Tomei, so David switched course.

"Isn't it a fact that the other group refers to you as the Taliban?"

"Objection!" Steingard said.

David shot out the cuffs of her jacket. That last question, she could see, had rattled Rotem. *The Taliban.* Well, that would rattle anybody. "Have you ever carried a weapon?" David asked. She could feel a new kind of energy in the courtroom, something very different from the heightened nervousness that had marked the first few days of the trial. She had Rotem on the run.

Steingard was back on his feet, almost shouting now. "Objection," he said. Tomei frowned at David. "Sustained," he said.

"On the night in question," David continued, "did you have a weapon with you?"

"No."

"Isn't it a fact that you own a machete?"

"Objection!" It was Weiss this time.

"Your honor, I'm going to ask for a sidebar again," David said.

"Good," Tomei shot back. "Denied."

"Can I have one?"

"No."

"Did you have anything to drink that day at all?" David asked Rotem.

"If I had the possibility?"

"Did you have anything to drink that day?"

"What are you talking about?" Tomei interjected. "Alcoholic beverages?"

"I'm not interested in Diet Coke," David snapped back. Tomei examined her over the top of his glasses. She dropped her head to one shoulder in apology.

The translator murmured to Rotem in Yiddish.

"No," Rotem replied. "I didn't drink that day."

"You didn't have any wine?"

"I made certification over the wine, yes."

"Did you have wine at the Havdalah ceremony later in the day?"

The translator frowned. Oh boy, David thought. Here we go. "Did you have wine where?" the old man asked.

"Havdalah," David said.

"Hatzolah?"

David waited until the laughter in the gallery had settled into a low titter.

"Not Hatzolah," she said. Not the volunteer ambulance service. "Havdalah. Ceremony between the Sabbath and the non-Sabbath?"

The ceremony, she felt like shouting, that you presumably partici-pate in every Saturday. The ceremony where you drink wine. She was hoping the jury was picking up on all of this. She cast one look in the direction of the box and then focused again on Rotem. "No," Rotem was saying, "I didn't drink."

The denial came out as a kind of squeak—a knot of rapid-fire Hebrew. The kid was wobbling again. David returned to her papers, letting Rotem stew. Haltingly, she began to lead him through the scene in the hallway outside of 107. She trod carefully at first, softly challenging some of Rotem's recollections—how, for instance, did he know who was hitting him if he lost his glasses?—and waiting for him to trip up. A successful cross was like a tight game of poker. You kept the cards close to your chest, and when your luck was suddenly good, you went all in.

Around three fifteen in the afternoon, David got the opening she was looking for. Rotem was explaining the fetal position he had assumed on the hallway floor. He gave a little demonstration with his hands, curling his forearms up over his head, until his face was no longer visible.

"And you tried to protect yourself, right?" David asked.

"In a passive way."

"Are you saying you're a passive person?"

Rotem turned to the translator. The translator replied in Hebrew. Rotem spoke again, this time more forcefully. "What is the meaning of *passive*?"

"You said yourself you just protected yourself in a passive way."

"Correct."

"That was your word."

"Correct."

"So I'm asking you if you're a passive person."

"Yes."

"You never would use your fist to defend yourself, would you?"

"I try not to," Rotem said.

Long after the lights were dimmed in Ceremonial Courtroom 2, and the defendants had returned to their homes in Crown Heights, Joyce David would remember Rotem's response—those four mono-syllabic words—as the tipping point of the entire trial. The single moment when momentum shifted irrevocably to the side of the Shomrim Six. The moment it became clear that the prosecution would be lucky as hell to come away from the whole mess with a single lonely conviction.

"Have you ever used your fist to defend yourself?" David asked. She knew the objection was coming before Steingard was out of his chair. David could sense how furious the judge was, and yet she was so close—she couldn't let up now.

"Have you ever carried a machete?" she asked.

"Objection!" Steingard said.

"Sustained," Tomei said. "I don't want to remind you again. Don't bring that up again." David looked at Rotem. His mouth was agape. David sat down. She produced a stack of grand jury testimony. She ran Rotem through his account: from the hallway to the street out-side 749 and from the street into the Hatzolah ambulance. So there he was, poor, passive Rotem, lying down in the ambulance, talking to the EMTs.

"Isn't it a fact," David said, "that you told them that you were involved in a fist fight?"

"I was in the place," Rotem replied. "I received blows."

David shook her head. "Didn't you tell them you were involved in a fist fight?"

"It's possible. I don't remember what I said."

"Isn't it a fact that you complained of pain to your left hand from the fight?"

"Yes, I complained about pain in my left hand."

David waded forward. "Now later on," she said, "you spoke to the doctors as well." She looked at her notes. "In the hospital, at Kings County Hospital. Right?"

"Correct."

"Isn't it a fact that you told them that you were in a fight?"

"I don't remember the words that I said exactly."

"Your Honor," David said, "at this time I would like to offer the certified hospital records into evidence, especially the portions to be used for prior inconsistent statements." The evidence was duly introduced. "At this time," David continued, "I want to read from the document in evidence, specifically the ambulance call report." She held up the document. "'Patient states he was involved in a fist fight,'" she read. "'Patient complains of pain in left hand from fight. Patient denies any other injuries or pain.' Later, from further medical records: 'Patient was in a fight.'" *Patient was in a fight.* Not: *Patient was beaten up.* If Schneur Rotem was really the victim of assault, then why would he have told doctors he was in a fight? Why would he feel pain in his hand? The courtroom was silent.

"Did you see Levi Huebner at the hospital?" David asked.

"I believe that, yes."

"Do you know who called him?"

"No."

"Did you know him at that time?"

"I knew who he was."

"Was he an important person in your community?"

"It's possible to say so."

"He walks around like he is an important guy?" That one elicited a hearty chuckle from somewhere near the back of the room. The judge rapped the gavel.

"Objection," David Weiss said.

"I'll allow it," Tomei said.

"A big shot?" David asked, a hint of a smile extending across her cheeks.

"Objection," Weiss said.

"Overruled," Tomei said.

"It's possible to say that he walks with particular clothes." More laughs.

"It's the clothes that make the man?" David offered, thinking to herself that the translator couldn't even interpret the oldest aphorism in the book. Steingard objected.

"Sorry." David grinned. "I withdraw it."

"Did you know he was an attorney?" David asked. Levi Huebner may not have initially told Brian Duffy that he was a lawyer, but the *bochurim* certainly knew it—they knew the politics at play, they knew every last detail of the Shomrim and Shmira feud, and they knew exactly what it meant that Huebner wanted to represent them.

Of course, by pursuing this line of questioning, David was running the risk of muddying the waters. The jury, faced with an overload of information about religious factionalism in Crown Heights, might be distracted from equally germane matters, like the fact that Yaakov Shatz couldn't keep his story straight. Like the fact that Shuki Gur couldn't conclusively demonstrate that the Shomrim had assaulted him. Like the fact that Schneur Rotem had apparently told doctors he was involved in a fist fight.

Rotem nodded. Yes, he knew Levi Huebner was an attorney.

"When did you next see Huebner after he was in the hospital with you guys?" David asked.

"On Sunday."

"That is the very next day, right?" No mistaking the import of that particular visit. By Sunday morning, less than twenty-four hours after the incident at 749 had gone down, Levi Huebner was at the homes of the alleged victims.

"Yes," Rotem said faintly.

"By the way," David said, "the hospital put a cast on your hand, right?"

"Correct," Rotem murmured.

"And they told you which area you had a little break, right?"

"Yes . . ."

"Did they ask you if you got that injury by punching someone?"

He stammered in Hebrew, the translator struggling to keep up with him. "I don't recall such a—I don't recall," came the translation.

"You don't recall them telling you that this is called a boxer's fracture?"

"Objection!" Steingard shouted, but Tomei was waving him off.

"I'll allow it," Tomei said.

"Didn't the doctors tell you that you had a boxer's fracture?" she asked.

The boxer's fracture, the brawler's fracture, the barroom fracture—the nickname for the injury varied from one ER to the next. A break at the knuckle of the pinkie finger, where the bones of the hand are the weakest, a break typically caused by hitting an extremely hard object with a closed fist. The kind of wound suffered by amateur street fighters. The kind of wound that Rotem had received.

Schneur Rotem, once alleged victim and now apparent assailant.


David had only one item left on her agenda, and that was to connect the dots—to reiterate the importance of the relationship between Huebner, a Shmira member, and the yeshiva students. To make clear that the fracas at 749 Eastern Parkway was not an isolated event but part of a long-standing feud between two competing vigilante patrols. To wrap everything up in a neat little bow and hand-deliver it to the members of the jury.

"Now when did you first discuss Mr. Huebner filing a lawsuit for you?" David asked Rotem.

"I don't recall the date," Rotem said.

"Was it your idea or his idea?"

"It was the idea of four of us, the four wounded ones."

"You all decided to talk to Mr. Huebner about filing a lawsuit for you?"

"It was forces that were forming."

*Forces that were forming.* David couldn't have put it more poetically herself.

"Isn't it a fact you have a big motive to lie in this case?" David continued.

"Objection, Judge," Steingard said.

"If he understands the question, go on and answer it," Tomei said.

"Again," Rotem said. "Come again."

"Isn't it a fact that you believe in your mind that if these people are convicted, that you will get a lot of money?"

"Objection."

"Overruled."

"No," Rotem said.

"Didn't Mr. Huebner tell you that?" David asked.

Rotem shook his head balefully. "No," he said.

But the damage had been done.

# 18

On December 2, 2009, the People rested. It had been almost two years since the brawl at 749 Eastern Parkway and exactly a month since David Weiss delivered his opening statement. A long month—as long as most of the attorneys in the courtroom could remember. A longer two years. Joyce David glanced at Chaim Hershkop, who had his arms crossed hard over his chest. She knew that Chaim, even more than his brother Gadi, had allowed the trial to consume him, and now, with the prospect of a final verdict only days away, he had grown wan and serious, as if the fate of the world itself hung in the balance. Well, in many ways, of course, it did.

"Ladies and gentlemen," Judge Tomei said, turning toward the jury, "at this time we're going to adjourn to tomorrow morning. Do not discuss the case amongst yourselves or with anyone else. Do not visit the scene where these crimes allegedly occurred. Have no contact with the parties involved, and have a very good evening." Slowly, the members of the jury rose to their feet and filed out of the courtroom, their heads bowed. The door closed behind them with a muffled thump.

In *What You Should Know if You're Accused of a Crime*, her insider's guide to the criminal justice system, David had explained that the burden of proof in any trial rests entirely on the shoulders of the prosecution. The defense "does not have to prove anything," she wrote. "The jury is supposed to decide, based on what the prosecution presents, if they're convinced of your guilt *beyond a reasonable doubt.*"

As far as David was concerned, in the trial of the Shomrim Six, the People had established no such thing. During the last few days, as the trial had wound to a close, the members of the defense team had discussed asking the judge to dismiss the bulk of the charges against the Shomrim. After all, the defendants hadn't been indicted on just one count. They'd been indicted on hundreds, and few of them seemed likely to stick.

Chaim Hershkop, for instance, currently faced charges of menacing; assault with intent to cause physical injury; attempted assault with intent to cause injury; two counts of criminal possession of a weapon (one of the weapons being a fire extinguisher, and the other being a pair of sap gloves); and gang assault in the second degree.

This last charge—the most serious of the bunch—carried with it the possibility of several years in a federal prison. To David, it was almost laughable. The People were miles away from proving that any of the Shomrim boys—let alone Chaim Hershkop—had caused serious physical injury to anyone, in concert or not.

*No* [margin note]

Now, with the jury gone for the day, Joyce David climbed to her feet, and over a steadily growing symphony of mutters from the gallery, asked that almost the entire case against her client be thrown straight out the window. She argued that the *bochurim* had failed to conclusively link her client to the crime. She pointed out that Schneur Rotem had not been asked directly to identify Chaim Hershkop in court. She maintained that there was no proof her client had hefted a fire extinguisher or strapped on sap gloves.

"Even if you take the evidence in the light most favorable to the People, you may be left with a menacing," David added. She peered down at the table. "I'm going to ask you to dismiss Count 11, Count 12, Count 13, 14, 15 . . ." She paused. "Sixteen and 17 seem sort of redundant. And, actually, Schneur Rotem never indicated that he felt he was in imminent danger or imminent physical injury."

Tomei looked down at David. The silence extended for one second, two, three.

"All right, is that your motion?" Tomei said, finally.

"Thank you," David said and took her seat again.

On the other side of the courtroom, David Steingard frowned. He understood that the next few minutes—much more than the deliberations of the jury or the reading of the final verdict—would determine the fate of the trial. With a rap of his gavel, Judge Albert Tomei could effectively nullify the case that the People had spent thousands of dollars and gallons of elbow grease to assemble. He could prevent the jury from weighing hundreds of charges against the defendants— he could whittle the number of charges on the table down to a couple of measly misdemeanor assault raps. He could deliver a win to the Crown Heights Shomrim and a major loss to the Crown Heights Shmira.

Steingard watched as each member of the defense team took his or her turn petitioning the judge. Every petition adhered to the same simple rubric laid out by David: The burden of proof had not been met. There were yawning gaps in the testimony of the witnesses. The evidence presented by the People was deficient. Through it all, Tomei sat stone-faced. Steingard knew that the judge, too, was frustrated with the pace of the trial—frustrated with the antics of the court-appointed translator, frustrated with the cagey witnesses, frustrated with the histrionics of the eight attorneys in the courtroom and the eight accompanying egos.

But to his great credit, Tomei had not allowed his irritation to get in the way of his work. He had remained calm and businesslike, even allowing himself the odd joke here and there, probably in order to keep his own sanity. Now he produced a stack of indictment sheets, and with the help of the court clerk, he set about answering the petitions of the defense attorneys.

It was quick work.

One by one, the attorneys stood up and delivered a little speech, along with a list of proposed dismissals. And count by count—the list of charges seemed to drag on into infinity—the judge issued his official reply. The answers were greeted at the defense table with silence. The six defendants sat one row farther back, wearing tight puckered smiles. Susan Mitchell, the attorney for Nechemia Slatter, took the floor after David; after Mitchell, the floor was ceded to Steven Williams, the attorney for Schneur Pinson. The final lawyer to stand was Israel Fried. "Mr. Fried?" Tomei intoned.

"Yep," Fried nodded.

"Gedalia," Tomei said.

"Yes. He's in every single count, your Honor, so we saved the best for last. I'm going to move to have the first count dismissed. Any count that had a mention of a weapon and the weapon being a sap glove."

"So count 1 will be dismissed against him. And count 3," Tomei agreed. "Now, number 4 is with regard to Elkon Gurfinkel. That's the sap glove. That's dismissed."

"Number 4 is dismissed," the court clerk echoed.

"What else?" Tomei asked.

"Count 5," Fried said.

"Count 5 is the sap glove. Yes, 5," Tomei pointed to the clerk.

"Five is dismissed," the clerk said.

"Count 6 . . ." Tomei stopped himself. "No, 7. Six is assault in the third degree. That's okay. It's in."

"Seven is out. Eight should be out—it's also sap gloves."

"Eight and 10 are out," Tomei said.

"So 7, 8, and 10 are out?"

"Yes," the judge said. "And 11 is out and 14 is out."

Steingard studied his notepad. A year later, having left his post at the office of the DA for the greener and more lucrative shores of private practice, he would recall that he had known more or less what was coming. That he had prepared himself for it. But at the time, sitting under the bright lights of Ceremonial Courtroom 2 and listening to the judge dismiss one charge after another, he was chagrined. Startled at the speed at which the prosecution's case had been dismantled.

By the time the six defense attorneys had finished petitioning the judge—by the time Israel Fried returned to his chair—the vast majority of the charges against the defendants had been dismissed. Only a few piddling misdemeanor counts remained. Steingard exchanged a glance with David Weiss.

No one was going to prison.

The trial was effectively over.

The courtroom burst into noise.


In the end, the jury took only a few hours to reach a verdict. This was on December 9, a week after the defense rested and three days before the first day of Chanukah—a holiday, appropriately enough, commemorating the victory of Judah and his rebel Maccabee army. The courtroom gallery was full, and as the jury filed back into the courtroom, the audience members shifted anxiously on the wooden pews, straining to get a better look at the judge. Maybe there was something to be read on Tomei's face.

Some hint—some augury of the news to come. But there was nothing.

The morning before, Ben Lifshitz had published a piece on CrownHeights.info, urging community members to show some last-minute support as the trial neared its conclusion. By his estimate, the Shomrim Six had spent upward of $200,000 on their own defense, a sum only somewhat offset by the $25,000 in *Pidyon Shvuyim* donations.

Meanwhile, few of the defendants had been able to work during the last six weeks, and some had families to look after. The trial had been a tremendous drain—financially and emotionally—and Lifshitz, for one, was looking forward to its conclusion. He listened as Tomei issued his instructions to the jury. The court clerk motioned with his hands, and the six defense attorneys rose, followed by the six defendants.

The foreman read each finding slowly. Next to Lifshitz, Chaim Hershkop was drawing deliberate, steady breaths. Lifshitz bowed his head. He knew his mother and father and brother had all traveled to downtown Brooklyn to hear the verdict, and he took strength from their presence. Although the bulk of the charges of the Shomrim Six had been dismissed, dozens still remained, and it took the better part of ten minutes before the foreman was finished. Only then did Lifshitz allow himself to really exhale. Only then did Lifshitz allow himself to hear the backslapping from the gallery—a symphony of hoots and hollers and the rustling of clothing as the members of the audience dashed out into the lobby to wait for the defendants.

After weeks of testimony, the jury had found five of the Shomrim Six innocent of all charges. There was only one conviction.

Exactly a year later, the Shomrim met at the house of one of their supporters to count their blessings and remember the heavy toll the trial had incurred. They drank, they ate, they told war stories. They marveled that the jury—composed of men and women who knew next to nothing of life in the Lubavitch kingdom—had managed to see through the deceptions of the *bochurim*. That they had cut through the posturing and the business of the lawsuit and reached a just and fair decision. The verdict, Ben Lifshitz would write on CrownHeights .info, was a vindication from a "vicious blood libel"—it was nothing less than true "salvation."

He quoted a few lines from a song often sung at Chabad *farbrengens*: "G-d has redeemed my soul in peace. . . . Men of blood and swindle, may their days be halved."

# Epilogue

In early February 2010, Gadi Hershkop was sentenced for his role in the fracas at 749 Eastern Parkway. The rap was misdemeanor assault, a far cry from the felony gang assault charges the DA had originally pursued, but a serious crime nonetheless, and one that still carried the possibility of a substantial fine. Unlike the trial, which had been held in the cavernous Ceremonial Courtroom 2, the sentencing was staged in a small chamber near the top of the Supreme Court building, twenty floors up by elevator.

Proceedings were set to begin at 10 a.m., but the Lubavitchers in attendance were by now used to the elastic way things worked at 320 Jay Street, and they took their time finding their seats. Aron Hershkop, dressed in his best beige suit, watched them arrive—Steingard and Weiss, both of them looking a little bored; the requisite gaggle of rumpled journalists, some of them clutching white notepads to their chests; his brother Chaim with his wife and a friend; Benny Lifshitz and Nechemia Slatter and the rest of the Shomrim kids, clumped happily together in the back pew of this truncated little gallery.

And then around 10:15 a.m., Gadi himself appeared, following Izzy Fried toward the front of the courtroom, smiling back at his supporters. One more court session, Aron Hershkop thought, and then it would be over. Fifteen more minutes, and life would return to normal. The previous week, after the verdict had been read, Hershkop had joined the rest of the Shomrim boys on the pavement outside the courthouse, half expecting a show of exuberance. Instead, they'd clung to one another like survivors of some distant shipwreck, battered by the length of the trial, which had comprised twenty days of arguments and testimony—something like two months in real-world time. "It was all one big waste of time," Slatter told a reporter for the *Daily News*, before he and his fellow defendants said their good-byes and wandered south down Jay Street, under the heavy winter sky.

They'd left it to the lawyers to put on the real show. "It's the district attorney's money," Joyce David told one reporter. "A lot of resources for nothing."

And Izzy Fried, when asked what kind of sentence his client was likely to face, merely shrugged. "Community service? He's already doing community service: he's Shomrim."

Initially, the six Shomrim members involved in the brawl had taken a break from street work. Not because they were intimidated or worried about another police crackdown, but because they were tired—because they wanted to catch up on sleep, family time, work. And also—yes, of course—because the trial had validated their worst fears about the community. Rabbi Shea Hecht had written his op-ed, and there had been a few letters of support, but where was the outpouring of grief and anguish for these six boys who had been hung out to dry by their fellow Jews? The only answer must be that the community was in some way complicit. The community had turned the other cheek. These mothers and fathers and friends who had leaned so heavily on the Shomrim when their tires went flat, when they were mugged, when their homes were broken into, had all but vanished as soon as the Shomrim had been arrested.

Ben Lifshitz and some of the other younger, unmarried Shomrim guys had started floating the idea of leaving Crown Heights for good once the civil case had been settled—maybe moving farther south into Brooklyn, maybe as far as New Jersey. Anywhere but here in the Heights, where the air was poisoned. "For me, Crown Heights is like a murder scene," Lifshitz had said. "You think of all the shit that has happened in the community, all the blood that has been spilled, all the violence, all the riots. Yeah, right, some parts of Crown Heights are beautiful, and yes, my family is here, and yes, my friends are here, but me? I'm tired of the chalk outlines."

In recent weeks, however, Gadi, Chaim, and even Lifshitz had started to answer a few calls. They'd turned their radios back on. Proudly donned the blue Shomrim jackets. Canvassed Kingston, Carroll, Union in their Shomrim scooters. It was hard to stay away from the job, it turned out. And hey, was there a better *fuck you* to the haters?

A friend had told Hershkop that Huebner had been pleased with the verdict, but Hershkop thought that was nonsense—just another deception. Huebner might be telling people that the trial had gone his way, but it took only one peek at the trial transcripts to see that the *bochurim* had been gutted on the stand.

The sentencing itself was a blessedly swift affair. David Weiss pointed out that Gadi had committed a serious crime, a violent crime; he recommended probation. He sat down. Fried stood up. Poetically and languidly, he recounted Gedalia Hershkop's many contributions to the community and the city of Brooklyn—Gadi was a father, a school bus driver, the kind of man who did everything for others and nothing for himself. Through it all, Gadi stood silently by Fried's side. Fried concluded with a plea for leniency. The judge looked down at Gadi. Did the guilty party have anything to say for himself? Gadi shook his head. He did not.

"Fine," Tomei said, and rapping the gavel once against the bench, issued his sentence: three years' probation, and within ninety days, Gadi would have to enroll in anger-management classes or else face additional charges. It felt like a balloon had been loudly deflated, and everyone in the courtroom was just stuck sitting there, sucking air.

The judge wandered off. Aron Hershkop stood up. He watched the audience filter through the double doors in more or less the order they had arrived—Lifshitz first, the morning *Post* tucked into the back pocket of his slacks, Chaim and his wife, the reporters, Gadi and Fried. On the way out into the lobby, Hershkop found himself behind Steingard and Weiss.

"It's exactly what we offered them in the beginning," Steingard was saying. "Could have saved themselves some trouble. . . ." Hershkop shook his head. The guy didn't get it, never would. Yes, the Shomrim Six had been offered—in exchange for a plea to misdemeanor assault—a sentence of anger-management classes and a few years of probation. But the DA had always failed to see that there was shame in accepting that deal. Something akin to groveling.

Outside the courtroom, a handful of Shomrim boys crowded around Gadi, jostling with one another to get hold of his shoulders, his arms, his hands. Steingard and Weiss looked on in amusement. The knot of limbs now rotated and whirled, picking up speed, shaking in disjointed rhythm, and soon someone was singing, a soft Yiddish melody, the syllables barely audible, but then again, Aron Hershkop already knew the words.

# *Acknowledgments*

I could not have written this book without the help of the residents of Crown Heights, who patiently answered my questions and, in many cases, invited me into their homes. I am especially grateful to Levi Huebner, Chaim Hershkop, Aron Hershkop, Schleimy Klein, and Ben Lifshitz for sharing their stories; thanks also to David Steingard and Joyce David, both of whom offered important insights into the workings of the criminal trial.

For their previous work on Crown Heights and Lubavitch Hasidism, I owe a great deal to a range of scholars and journalists, including Sue Fishkoff, Lis Harris, Edward Shapiro, Elie Wiesel, Jerome Mintz, Menachem Friedman, Samuel Heilman, and Henry Goldschmidt, on whose work I relied so heavily. To parrot a line from Sue Fishkoff, I am a journalist and not a scholar, and any errors in the body of the text are my own.

Thanks to my agent, Ted Weinstein, who supported this idea from the beginning, and to my exceptionally deft editor Eric Nelson, who steered the project from muddled first draft to bound book. For additional feedback on the manuscript, I'm indebted to Ari Mayteles, Kurt Pitzer, and Henry Goldschmidt. Thanks to Ted Ross, my editor at *Harper's* magazine; Anne Greene of the Wesleyan Writers Conference, where important work on this book was done; and Esther Kaplan at the Nation Institute Investigative Fund, which generously helped fund this project.

My appreciation to the talented Kate Vander Wiede, for carefully transcribing dozens of hours of tape, and to Nate Katz, for giving a tired journalist a couch on which to crash. Thanks to my family for their support, and thanks to my grandmother, who helped me learn my first—and only—words of Yiddish. Thanks to Oliver Henry Brown, that consummate detector of overly "dense" prose. And thanks above all to Katie Jentleson, who first introduced me to the borough of Brooklyn. This book belongs to you.

# *Index*